THE
NIGHT
AND THE
MUSIC

THE Night AND THE Music

ROSEMARY CLOONEY, BARBARA COOK, AND JULIE WILSON INSIDE THE WORLD OF CABARET

Deborah Grace Winer

Foreword by Rex Reed

SCHIRMER BOOKS
AN IMPRINT OF SIMON & SCHUSTER MACMILLAN
NEW YORK

PRENTICE HALL INTERNATIONAL
LONDON MEXICO CITY NEW DELHI SINGAPORE SYDNEY TORONTO

Schirmer Books
An Imprint of Simon & Schuster Macmillan
866 Third Avenue
New York, NY 10022

Library of Congress Catalog Card Number: 95-12901

Printed in the United States of America

Printing number
1 2 3 4 5 6 7 8 9 10

Library of Congress Cataloging-in Publication Data

Winer, Deborah Grace.
    The night and the music : Rosemary Clooney, Barbara Cook, and Julie Wilson, inside the world of cabaret / Deborah Grace Winer.
      p. cm.
    Includes index.
    ISBN 0-02-872954-4 (hard cover : alk. paper)
    1. Clooney, Rosemary. 2. Cook, Barbara. 3. Wilson, Julie
    4. Singers—United States—Biography. I. Title.
ML400.W56   1995
782.42164'092'2—dc20
[B]   95-12901
                                            CIP
                                          MN

This paper meets the requirements of ANSI/NISO Z39.48-1992
(Permanence of Paper).

To my family, always supportive,

and

To Rose, Barbara, and Julie,

for the stories they tell

p. 2. "Ac-cent-tchu-ate the Positive." Music by Harold Arlen, lyrics by Johnny Mercer. Harwin Music Corp., 1944.

p. 15. "It's Not Where You Start." Music by Cy Coleman, lyrics by Dorothy Fields. Notable Music Co., 1972/Aldi Music, 1972.

p. 25. "Civilization." Music by Carl Sigman, lyrics by Bob Hilliard. Edwin H. Morris Co., 1947/Better Half Music Co., 1947.

pp. 30–31. "Sentimental Journey." Music and lyrics by Bud Green, Les Brown, and Ben Homer. Morley Music Co., Inc ., 1944.

p. 48. "Let's Get Away from It All." Music by Matt Dennis, lyrics by Tom Adair. Music Sales Corp., 1941.

p. 86. "Lydia the Tattooed Lady." Music by Harold Arlen, lyrics by E. Y. Harburg. Leo Feist, Inc., 1939.

pp. 128–129. "Down in the Depths, On the Ninetieth Floor." Music and lyrics by Cole Porter. Chappell and Co., Inc., 1936.

p. 141. "Josephine." Music by Wayne King and Bruce Bivens, lyrics by Gus Kahn. Leo Feist, Inc., 1936, 1937.

p. 141. "Morning Glory." Music by Hoagy Carmichael, lyrics by Paul Francis Webster. Robbins Music Corp., 1942.

p. 167. "I'm Still Here." Music and lyrics by Stephen Sondheim. Valando Music, Inc. (Beautiful Music, Inc., Burthen Music Co., Inc.).

p. 185. "How Deep Is the Ocean." Music and lyrics by Irving Berlin. Irving Berlin Music Corp., 1932.

p. 189. "Ship in a Bottle." Music and lyrics by Amanda McBroom. © 1981 McBroom Music.

p 231. "Surabaya Johnny." Music by Kurt Weill, lyrics by Bertold Brecht, © 1929. Universal Edition, c. renewed and assigned to Weill-Brecht-Harms Co., Inc.

$\mathcal{F}$OREWORD

$\mathcal{G}$reat singing, like all great art, must come from the heart. Judy Garland and Edith Piaf knew that, and Billie Holiday, too. So do the three legendary ladies of music celebrated in this revealing, meticulous, and invaluable book. What makes them cherished blue-chip commodities in a market overcrowded with mediocrity is what James Mason, in *A Star Is Born*, called "that little something extra."

Their talent, timing, and technique can be studied but not taught. How else could three high-priestess practitioners of the fading art of the American popular song from three distinctly diverse geographical backgrounds—Barbara Cook from Atlanta, Georgia, Julie Wilson from Omaha, Nebraska, and Rosemary Clooney from the hills of Beverly by way of the hills of Kentucky—have so much in common? Because their art comes from within. They don't know how to fake it. And they communicate what they know with an honest directness that makes their listeners laugh, cry, and tremble from the truth. I know because I've spent countless hours of my adult life watching them do it.

Barbara Cook's dazzling Baccarat purity and awesome range, honed by years of experience in Broadway musicals and concert halls, allow her to "sing out, Louise" with the crystal clarity I expect to hear someday from the angels. Julie Wilson's smoky baritone, shaped by decades of toil in saloons and cabarets, gets directly to the emotional core of a lyric, like peeling an apple, with no baggage and no detours, imparting the spicy humor, "been around" sincerity, and stinging wisdom of a cobra with class. Rosie Clooney grew up with the demanding musical phrasing and savvy of a big-band vocalist before cutting her splendid chops on radio, television, movies, and hit records to develop the swinging, deceptively simple, no-nonsense, lyrical, honey-dripping style that has made her one of the most endearing and enduring popular singers of all time. Hip, sophisticated talismans to live by, these are not kids on their way to their first prom dance. These divas have polished their craft and earned their diplomas from the school of hard knocks. They've *lived*. And they *survived* to influence a whole new generation of wannabe singers who, so far, have mastered only the art of imitation. In a world of here today, gone tomorrow soundalikes, they are true originals, rare as unicorns—beacons in a musical world that often seems plunged into atonal darkness. Enriching our lives without any bull, they've got "that little something extra." They are simply, to be honest, the best we've got.

–Rex Reed

$\mathcal{P}$REFACE

$\mathcal{S}$omeone once shared the philosophy that all the people in the world can be divided into two categories: people you'd want to have dinner with and those you wouldn't. For me, Rosemary Clooney, Barbara Cook, and Julie Wilson all belong to the former group. During the 1993–94 New York season, I spent a great deal of time with them in one form or another: as they performed onstage, in planning their shows and in rehearsal, in dressing rooms before or after the show, on days off, in private life away from the clubs. Their cooperation was wholehearted and unswerving from the beginning. Each a different personality, all three share two main traits—uncommon candor and a great sense of humor, which simplifies much in life and work.

What has provided the climate for these women to come once again to the fore has been the resurgence of American standard pop, a repertory based in jazz and show music that predated rock and roll and is now again showing up everywhere in the mass consciousness. With the music, the cabaret scene has undergone a renaissance in cities across the country. The word "cabaret" is a catchall description often clouded by confusing connotations ("You're doing a book on cabaret?" people have said to me. "—oh, you mean the musical?"). I define it simply as live entertainment in an intimate setting—another word for the nightclubs, saloons, and other after-dark spots of years past. While cabaret's rebirth has enabled veteran performers to find new audiences, a great deal of the scene's activity and drive today emanates from young performers and songwriters.

This book represents a microcosm, in the sense that cabaret, in its basic, performer-to-audience presentation, is a microcosm of show business. But also, within the framework of this portrait, I concentrate on a relative few artists. This is in no way a reflection on the other personalities whom I do not include in depth (some are mentioned), but a necessity of focus. Similarly, there are a few places where assessments of subjects like the historical development of American music or the cabaret scene might appear oversimplified. Since this book is not meant to be a historical analysis, those thumbnail explanations are intended only to give general insight and context to the events of the book. It's also worth noting that because of the book's woven-together structure, narrative time over the course of the season has been somewhat telescoped. Barbara's, Julie's, and Rosemary's New York runs actually occurred consecutively, from September through February.

From the first stages of planning this project, I received enormous support from the cabaret community as a whole: whether moral support and enthusiasm from performers, encouraging words from my journalist colleagues, or the unending, courteous aid extended to me by the managers, publicists, and club owners and staffs. I am grateful to all the artists and shakers of the community who participated.

My thanks to the managements of the Cafe Carlyle, Rainbow and Stars, and the Russian Tea Room for their help and cooperation, especially Joe Baum and Faith Stewart-Gordon, and the clubs' representatives, David Lotz, Jackie Krull, and Tony Staffieri, for their consistant attention. Thanks, as well, to Bismark Irving of Rainbow, Gary Sullivan of the Russian Tea Room, and Ambrose of the Carlyle, and to Philip Caggiano and Andrew Freeman.

The artists' managers were always there to help with myriad things, from scheduling to information, and I'm grateful to Allen Sviridoff, Jerry Kravat, and their offices for all their help. Special thanks to Donald Smith, who, as the acknowledged kingpin of much of cabaret today, gave this project his encouragement from early on. Thanks also to Helene Greece and to the representatives of the other artists, venues, and events appearing in this book.

For their help along the way, I want to thank Ita Pasztor, Toba Brill Winer (my mother, who I think finds my sitting around nightclubs and calling it "work" a little suspect), and my sister, Jessica Daryl Winer, for her help with the manuscript and for providing the book's cover painting. Also, Fletcher Roberts of the *New York Times*, Diane Nichols of the Kathryn and Gilbert Miller Health Care Institute for Performing Artists for her valuable insights, Virginia Tulloch and Carol Sargent of the Barbara Cook International Appreciation Society, Louise Martzinek, Gabriel Ferrer, Tana Sibilio, June Havoc, Janet Stark, and my friend Dennis McGovern.

Special gratitude to Rex Reed for providing the book with a foreword.

Although I saw the book clearly in my head as I planned it, I came to realize that in the beginning, a lot of people had no idea what I was talking about. For appreciating my vision early on, I must thank my agent, Tom Wallace, for his advice and expertise; and for their early evaluation and support, Charles Maryan, David Black, and Amy Sperling. Especially, I thank Jonathan Wiener, my editor at Schirmer Books, and others at the publisher who have made this possible, including production editor Jane Andrassi.

Finally, there's Rosemary, Barbara, and Julie, who bestowed their confidence, generosity and consistent candor in areas that were always fascinating, sometimes painful. From its inception, this book took more than two years to complete. Would I do it all over again? As Rosemary likes to say—in a New York minute.

Deborah Grace Winer

THE
NIGHT
AND THE
MUSIC

Tucked amid the city streets, where crime is rampant and home-less people root through garbage cans, there is a mirage: a room blue with smoke, circled with intimate tables and hushed waiters; a gleam-ing piano; and poured into a red-sequin gown and elbow-length gloves, trailing a purple feather boa, Julie Wilson singing, her arms outstretched, her dark hair slicked back in a chignon, the trademark gardenia behind her ear. It could be the Algonquin, the Carlyle, the St. Regis; it could be 1950, but the street outside is a reminder that it's not. Then, as patrons linger in the afterglow of her closing number, she returns to her dressing room, strips off her gown (possibly an immacu-lately maintained relic from earlier decades), and transforms herself into a shapeless figure in raincoat, babushka, and running shoes. Hoisting a twenty-pound tote bag onto her bone-thin frame, she starts for the Port Authority and the 2:00 A.M. bus back to her house in Jersey City, in time to walk the dogs, fix herself something to eat, and face the domestic chaos wrought by performing two shows a night, five nights a week.

✳

Under iron-gray New York skies, they started to gather at eight o'clock in the morning. By lunchtime there are several thousand, a sea of silver hair blanketing the World Financial Center's Winter Garden. They are her people, people who ignored blizzard warnings and came by bus and subway and car from Queens and Staten Island and New Jersey to see an old friend. She finally appears, a grandmother in wire-rimmed glasses with a cold, singing love songs, and they cheer and shout "Rosie!" The young professionals by now cramming the stair-way and hanging from the galleries get caught up in the enveloping aura of this finger-snapping mama who sings and swings, and for an hour under the palm trees it's as if city life is suspended. There is only the music and Rosemary Clooney.

✳

As torrential rains pound Lincoln Center, the Juilliard Theatre is packed with people. They are watching, mesmerized, the succession of brave and petrified students being coached by the blond earth mother with the Tiffany earrings. She didn't come there today to be Barbara Cook. She trudged out onstage in gold-rimmed glasses, clutching a beige tote bag, ready for work. The students sang for her, and she told them what she knew. And when they demonstrated they'd caught on, her face lit up like a child's. Now she has hugged the last student for the last time. A yell goes up from the crowd. "You sing!" The students and faculty and fans who fill the house start to applaud, cheering, whistling, screaming out requests. The roar hushes as the piano begins a fire-and- brimstone introduction to "Ac-cent-tchu-ate the Positive." She stretches out her arm toward them. "Gather 'round me, everybody," she sings with the messianic fervor of a spellbinder, her black silk tunic flowing, "if you want to hear my story . . . ."

✱

This is the story of three women who, driven by their sheer, overwhelming need to sing, pulled themselves up from the ashes of devastated lives to find stardom for the second time at an age when most people retire. It is a story about the will to survive and the need to communicate. And about the fragile, nighttime world known as cabaret, the small clubs in which they have ultimately found their voice. Above all, in the force that drove them to start all over again from rock bottom, it is the story of what lies at the heart of a performer, indeed, of what lies at the heart of show business itself.

From opposite corners of entertainment, Rosemary Clooney, Barbara Cook, and Julie Wilson each found stardom in the 1950s: Rosemary with hit records like "Hey There" and in movie roles like the one opposite Bing Crosby in *White Christmas*; Barbara as Broadway's premier musical comedy ingenue, winning a Tony award as Marian the Librarian in *The Music Man*; Julie as the quintessential nightclub singer, steaming up posh rooms like the St. Regis Maisonette and the Plaza's Persian Room. It was only to be wiped away by mental and physical breakdown, family tragedy, and the arrival of rock and roll. At their lowest, Rosemary would find herself working Holiday Inns on weekends, Julie would sleep by day on the bus of musical-comedy bus-and-truck tours as it traveled to the next one-night stand, and Barbara, facing each month's rent with no work, would go through the motions of a daily life that reached barely beyond the confines of her apartment.

It is only in their second incarnations that they have become icons, linked by their converging viewpoint, representing show business boiled down to its most basic element. In the intimate quarters they share with their audience, one-on-one, person by person, they relate the truths of life, love, and loss that are a distillation of all their experience.

There is a reason why the small clubs of cabaret exert a pull, something in the candlelit setting, where the "entertainment" is only another human being close enough to touch, that feeds an instinct basic to our natures. It's the reason why people are drawn into the rooms where Rosemary, Barbara, and Julie spin out their visions, the reason why they are captivated. Because in an age dominated by high-tech mass communication and media hype, the women have returned a singer to a singer's most ancient function—telling a story, exposing part of their most private selves in exchange for the opportunity to create a hold over those willing to listen. Sitting in the dark, even the uninitiated feel the emotional pull, telling them this is how show business was invented.

*T*he Russian Tea Room mailed out the card in September. It said "Cabaret! At the Russian Tea Room. Back by popular demand! Julie Wilson—A Sentimental Journey. With William Roy." And in the painting on the front of the card, Julie Wilson and Billy Roy: he, the tuxedoed, silver-haired pixie at the piano; she, resplendent in red strapless dress and feather boa, in front of the standing mike.

The reason they would be back by popular demand is that last season was a bang-up year. Julie celebrated her fiftieth year in show business, and the town reveled in it. She is the undisputed Queen of Cabaret, the doyenne of nightclub chanteuses. Together almost twenty years, she and Roy have been the masters of all things intimately, deliciously sophisticated, the kind they supposedly don't make anymore, the two of them glittering like characters from a Nöel Coward play or a Cole Porter musical, complete with repartee and occasional duets like "You Fascinate Me So," recalling the ultra-"in" Julius Monk revues of the 1950s, of which Roy is an alumnus.

In the fiftieth-anniversary year, they had their own PBS special. Julie was honored with a tribute concert at Town Hall, where in front of a packed house, a long string of her colleagues turned out to sing and pay homage before Julie herself took stage in black sequins, and with emotion running high, drew ovations with a few numbers of her own.

In the *New York Times* feature "The New Season, Strictly By the Numbers," a listing read: "Feather boas the cabaret singer Julie Wilson will wear at the Russian Tea Room during her November engagement: 12."

It was the first extended engagement to be played at the Russian Tea Room since they'd opened a cabaret upstairs at the legendary restaurant a few years earlier. Celebrities and the general public squeezed in together in the candlelit green and gold room while over blinis and champagne they watched Julie and Billy deploy their magic over the four-week engagement. The critics raved, there was press galore and a Sunday *Times* profile.

Julie started thinking about this year's show early. There was going to be a live album recorded, and she knew she wanted to do a mix of material, not a show dedicated to one composer, as they had often done in the past. There had been a Stephen Sondheim show, a Rodgers and Hart show, a Harold Arlen show, Gershwin, Weill, and, of course, a Cole Porter show, which is something of a specialty. This time, she wanted to do something a little different, maybe swing a little more, like when she was starting out in the '40s as a band singer with Johnny Long's Orchestra.

At night, when she is luminous in beads and feathers, it's hard to imagine just how much an echo of her pioneer ancestors Julie really is. During the day, it's apparent. With the chignon replaced by one braid down her back, the opalescent gray-green eyes without their nighttime lashes, and her knocking-around uniform of running shoes cushioning the feet that bother her incessantly, it's easier to place her back on the plains around her native Omaha. Julie does everything deliberately. When she speaks in the smoky voice, it is slow, thoughtful, with long pauses. When she looks at you, it is right into you, as though she can see what is under your skin. She trudges around town with a purse, tote bags containing all the things she might need during her day in the city, maybe an umbrella and a raincoat over her arm, and a suit bag with a change of clothes if she's going out that evening.

By the summer, she had started preparing to work. One of life's frustrations for her is the number of songs she would like to sing that there will never be time for. She always wanted to do "Body and Soul." She went down to 46th Street to get the sheet music. Whenever Julie does anything new, she always begins by going back to the sheet music, to see the song as written by the composer. She played the piano as a child, and is a rarity among her colleagues, most of whom can't read music.

· One day during the summer, the phone rang. It was Billy Roy. He told her he had been asked to take a job working on a musical revue that the producer had ready to rehearse in Hawaii; the money was good. "Oh?" Julie said. "Well, that's great. When will you be back?" He said he'd be back a month before the Russian Tea Room opening. Only a month before the opening to put together a new show seemed like cutting it pretty tight, but they agreed that they'd really concentrate and work hard, and they'd pull it together. She wished him well in Hawaii.

The time he was to return arrived, and Julie prepared to go to work. Then the phone rang, and it was Billy Roy. He was back from Hawaii. But he had some news. He'd been asked to stay on with the show to rewrite it, and the money was good. What he had to tell her was that he was afraid he couldn't do the Russian Tea Room show. Julie didn't know what to say. "Well, Billy," she finally said to him, "you have to do what you have to do."

"I can't afford to keep Billy on retainer," she says ruefully. "I've kind of learned to roll with the punches. Nothing lasts forever. Billy has to make his way, and make his living, and do what's important to him. Because there's no security in this business."

There were four weeks until the opening. There was no pianist, and although she had certain ideas about songs she'd like to do, there was no show. Furthermore, if the thought of falling back on familiar repertory seemed comforting, it was shattered by the fact that there was no music for another accompanist to read. In all the years they'd worked together, Roy had never written anything down. He'd always done everything by ear. There were no arrangements, no notations of what her keys were. They were all in his head, in Hawaii.

She needed to find someone else to play for her. The give-and-take between a performer and an accompanist is like a marriage. And a lot of good pianists are rotten accompanists, never mind finding someone who is stylistically compatible. On such short notice, Julie surmised, the chances of finding just the right one were pretty grim. She picked up the phone and hoping for a recommendation, called Mark Hummel, a talented pianist and arranger she'd met when they were both working on Broadway in Peter Allen's musical, *Legs Diamond*. She had used Hummel before to play a couple of concerts when Roy had been unable to be there. She said, "Mark, do you know someone who's talented and plays like you, who might be available?" He said, "What about me?"

Julie couldn't believe her luck that Hummel was free. They found someone to do new charts by transcribing some of Roy's arrangements from her CDs, and they set to work putting the show together.

The show was called "A Sentimental Journey." "So I figured I could do whatever the hell I want," she says. She wanted to pull out some old torch songs she hadn't done in years, and do a few songs in tribute to Billie Holiday, her idol. She had fallen in love with some new songs by contemporary songwriters, like one by Steven Lutvak that she had heard him do at the Bistro Awards and then had got his phone number to tell him she would love to sing it and he'd sent her a copy. Also, there was still "Body and Soul," which she wanted to put together with "I'm a Fool to Want You."

The one catch was that Hummel was committed to doing a few benefits, including one where he was to do orchestrations for an eighty-eight piece orchestra. Julie also had benefits, and a date in Philadelphia, accompanied by Hummel. But they grabbed the odd hours to work on the show, and finally they got all the commitments out of the way, enabling them to focus intensely for the week remaining. Then something happened that nobody could have controlled. Mark Hummel's father died.

The day he died, Julie had agreed to sing at a private party after dinner at the 21 Club. Hummel, having just received the news, pulled himself together and played the show. Then, to be with his family, he went home to California for five days. He would not return until two days before the opening at the Russian Tea Room.

Julie stayed in New York, singing along with a tape recorder.

3

*R*osemary is up at 5 A.M. on the morning she is to go on *Live with Regis and Kathie Lee*, so she can wash her hair. She had arrived in New York a few days earlier with a bad cold. Dante Di Paolo, the man with whom she has lived for twenty years, has an even worse cold, and they have ensconced themselves in their apartment at the hotel in the East 70s with an assortment of prescriptions and home remedies in the quest to breathe again.

She arrives in the lobby at exactly 7:30. She hates being late, and as with all her early morning television appearances, she was up half the night to make sure she would be on time. She's going on *Regis and Kathie Lee* to plug her new album and the start of her monthlong engagement at Rainbow and Stars, the shiny club that sits sixty-five floors atop Rockefeller Center in what used to be the RCA building.

Outside it's just getting light, and the snow and sleet have begun to turn to rain. "This ice, or just wet?" she asks, squinting at the shiny pavement. She's got a bad knee that should be operated on, and in the delicate black pumps she'll wear on the air, she tries to avoid the slush puddles.

The weather people are already saying this is the worst winter in thirty years: five major snowstorms in the last month, and more on the way. The last one was two days ago, in the middle of which she drove to New Haven to do a benefit. Rosemary couldn't care less about the weather. Ten days earlier, she was in her home in Beverly Hills when the big earthquake hit, leaving her with a houseful of broken glass and the incessant, random aftershocks. New York was the first night's sleep she'd had since.

She settles into the car as it turns downtown onto Fifth Avenue on the way to the studio and opens up the brown purse that's always slung over her arm. They asked her to bring some family photos on the show with her, and she picks out some from the bunch she carries with her everywhere.

Five children, from her marriage to Jose Ferrer; eight grandchildren. Rosemary is a mother through and through: maternal of heart, maternal of figure, with honey-colored hair and deep blue eyes and an expressive mouth that mirrors either a look of compassion or her "Yeah, right" Irish deadpan, according to the situation. She talks in spurts in a hushed alto, ending sentences with "You know?," punctuating them with a rolling, asthma-touched laugh.

Sitting in the limousine, she tries singing a few notes. She's always a little nervous before she goes on TV. The show goes on at nine. That's early, even without a cold. Her younger daughter, Monsita, a blonde girl in her thirties, is sitting next to her. "How many pictures do they want, Mama?" They are still going through snapshots: the grandchildren, her oldest son, Miguel's, new baby, her youngest son, Rafael, the entire family at Thanksgiving. "That's a great picture," Rosemary says, holding it up. "Isn't that a great picture?"

Kathie Lee isn't in that day. Cristina Ferrari, who is subbing for her, stops by the dressing room where Rosemary sits in front of the mirror pinning a diamond pin on her charcoal pinstripe dress.

There's still forty-five minutes till showtime, and *Good Morning America* drones on from a television in the corner. Rosemary's manager, Allen Sviridoff, a fortyish man with a neat beard, comes back from seeing to details, and settles himself on the couch. On the TV, the number of promos for the upcoming Winter Olympics, set to start in a little over two weeks, is only exceeded by the number of promos for talk shows and evening tabloid shows featuring Tonya Harding explaining why she should be allowed to skate even though she was implicated in clubbing her chief competitor, Nancy Kerrigan, in the knee.

"Of course they're going to let her go," says Allen. "There's no way they're not going to let her skate." "I'm not so sure about that," Rosemary says. "She lied to the FBI. I think they're gonna draw the line." Allen offers to bet a hundred dollars, and Rosemary takes it.

John Oddo pokes his head in. A youngish man with a moustache and a slightly worried expression, he is her pianist, arranger, and musical director, and he's on his way in to see to the musicians, noted jazz players Jay Leonhart on bass and Joe Cocuzzo on drums, with Oddo, half of the sextet she will use for her Rainbow and Stars date. "We ought to be ready to rehearse in a few minutes. OK, Rose?" They'll do the Antonio Carlos Jobim/Gene Lees song "Corcovado (Quiet Nights)," which will also serve as the opening number at Rainbow and Stars.

The press agent for Rainbow, David Lotz, arrives with a briefcase full of cassettes of the new album, which is supposed to be delivered to the stores momentarily. It's called *Still on the Road*, and the cover painting shows a young girl waiting with a suitcase at the train station in Rosemary's home town of Maysville, Kentucky, looking east into the twilight on the Ohio River, toward New York.

She has a good feeling about this album. It employs a big band, which she loves because it takes her back to her roots. She learned a few weeks ago that last year's album, *Do You Miss New York?*, has been nominated for a Grammy. She doesn't feel as close to that one, and she is nominated in a category that includes Barbra Streisand and her old friend Tony Bennett, who beat her out the year before when her album *Girl Singer* had given her her first Grammy nomination in over thirty years (ironically, Bennett had supplied *Girl Singer*'s cover drawing).

The two recent Grammy nominations only highlight a year in which she's cemented her national stature with activities like opening the Newport Jazz Festival with the Count Basie Orchestra, an appearance at the White House, a concert at Carnegie Hall in tribute to her mentor, Bing Crosby, and a televised Boston Pops concert with Linda Ronstadt.

They come in to the dressing room to get her about the time Delta Burke, the previous guest, comes on the TV and perches herself on a stool near Regis. ("What is there, some kind of a theme here, or what?" Rosemary had said, referring to Burke's zaftig shape.) The show goes fine. Regis sings a few bars of "Come on-a My House." They show the new album cover. The song goes well, and Regis says he's coming to the opening. On the way out to the car Rosemary goes back to make sure they tell Kathie Lee she says "hi." On the way back to the hotel, the car inches along in traffic past the Dakota apartments, probably best known now as the place John Lennon was shot, but it's also where Rosemary lived for a short time when her children were small and she was still married to Ferrer. "What a really great place to live," she says to Monsita. "Isn't that just the best of everything? Huge apartments. Right next to the park. I remember in the winter, I was pregnant with Rafi, and I had the four of you, and getting you all dressed to go out to the park. And by the time I got the last one dressed, the first one had to go to the bathroom." She sighs. "New York is such a terrific town. Sometimes I really think I'd love to live here again."

Up in the hotel suite, Dante is waiting, in his dressing gown, and he helps Rosemary off with her camel hair coat and hangs it up for her in the closet. Tall and silver-haired, Dante is an ex-song-and-dance man who started as a seven-year-old hoofer in the movies. With a laid-back geniality and acute insight into human character, he and Rosemary are an affectionate, bickering Burns and Allen with the roles reversed. Her kids call it the Rosemary–Dante Show:

"You know, Rosemary, I took some of those little tangerines and squeezed them into my orange juice . . . "

"Whoa! What? You used those? I don't know where they're all disappearing to, you're makin' *juice*?"

"Naw, really . . . "

"Honey, just—just—never mind."

The apartment holds the things of a portable home: family photos in frames on the desk, a coffee maker and kitchen utensils, a humidifier. A large part of her year is spent on the road, and they've got it down to a science, with a knack for removing some of the rootlessness that a life on the road entails.

Rosemary travels constantly, with spells back home at her large house in Beverly Hills. Here's what some of her road schedule looks like from last summer until next summer:

6/3/93	Columbus, OH
6/5/93	Raleigh-Durham, NC–Crosby Golf Tournament
6/18/93	Washington, DC–performance at the White House
6/25–28/93	Pittsburgh, PA–Pittsburgh Symphony
7/1–4/93	Atlantic City, NJ (Resorts)
7/17/93	Atlanta, GA–Atlanta Symphony
7/23/93	Richmond, VA
7/26–31/93	Beverly, MA
8/13/93	Newport, RI–Newport Jazz Festival
9/93	Vacation
10/2/93	Greeley, CO
10/9/93	Orlando, FL
10/16/93	Jacksonville, FL
10/29/93	Boston, MA–Kennedy Library rededication
11/1/93	New York City, NY–Carnegie Hall
11/6/93	Springfield, OH
11/11–14/93	Baltimore, MD
11/22–23/93	Los Angeles, CA–record *Still on the Road* album
12/4/94	Schenectady, NY
12/10/93	Milwaukee, WI
12/13/93	Pittsburgh, PA
12/17–18/93	Costa Mesa, CA

1/13–15/94	Omaha, NE–Omaha Symphony
1/26/94	New Haven, CT
1/29/94	Toronto, Ontario, Canada
2/1–26/94	New York City, NY–Rainbow & Stars
3/25/94	Palm Beach, FL
4/16/94	San Francisco, CA
5/3–5/94	Burbank, CA
5/25/94	Los Angeles, CA–prerecord "Radioland Murders"
6/5/94	New Brunswick, NJ
6/18/94	Oyster Bay, Long Island
6/29/94	Merrillville, IN
6/30/94	Louisville, KY
7/1/94	Buffalo, NY
7/8–9/94	Cincinnati, OH
7/12–17/94	Orlando, FL–Disney College Program
7/20–25/94	Atlantic City, NJ
7/29/94	Boston, MA
8/10/94	Los Angeles, CA–Hollywood Bowl

Tomorrow morning, they're supposed to fly to Toronto for Rosemary to do one concert, and then come back the following day, Sunday. "I can't believe I have to go to Toronto," she keeps saying over and over. She's worried about shaking her cold by Tuesday night, when she opens at Rainbow. There's more snow in the forecast, and also Toronto isn't known for its balmy winter weather. But there's another reason. Rosemary hates to fly. It terrifies her. And she does it all the time, with tremendous anxiety days before each flight. "I know all the acts of faith, hope, and charity by heart," she likes to say.

Later this afternoon she'll check in with Wilbur Gould, the ear, nose, and throat doctor who looks after a lot of performers—not only to see about the cold, but to make sure that in spite of it, she'll be able to sing tomorrow night.

When she gets back to town on Sunday, she has just two days to focus on the opening of the Rainbow and Stars show, which is comprised of all new material, in which she's not yet secure. She's very nervous about this show, and she won't stop being nervous until she settles into the run. To do that she has to get through the opening, with the roomful of critics and elite who will be waiting for her on Tuesday.

*B*arbara has the underlying worry that at any moment her entire world is going to crumble. There is no good reason for her to think so. Along with Bobby Short, she is the jewel of the Cafe Carlyle, and traditionally opens this most elegant of New York's clubs for the season each September. She has sung at the White House twice in the last year, once at Bill Clinton's inauguration. Her new album of Dorothy Fields songs is winning gushy advance notices. And she is about to be inducted into the Broadway Hall of Fame. But around the edges, she's still uncertain.

It's Monday night, the day before her opening, and in a white silk caftan with streaks of color, she is sitting in her dressing-room suite near the top of the hotel, while downstairs in the Cafe, an invited group of friends and colleagues has begun to gather for a run-through.

She's nervous about the show, because there's so much new material, and she hopes she can remember it all. Last year, Stephen Holden in his *New York Times* review criticized her for clinging to the same material too long. Her fanatical following, however, who have been known to cross oceans to hear her, feel cheated when they don't hear the familiar numbers she is known for; this has also been reflected in print.

Barbara arrived at the suite at 3:30, and she's washed her hair and taken a nap. She has the use of it as a dressing room for the duration of her run: it's a setting in which most people would happily ensconce themselves for a lifetime, with a bedroom, tiny kitchenette, and living room with pale yellow walls, chintz covered sofa, and Steinway grand piano to the left as you walk in. This year, she'll be staying seven weeks, and with the necessities she's already started to bring over from her apartment on the West Side of Manhattan, it's already starting to take on the feel of home.

Barbara is a balance of contradictions. A cool blonde with a penchant for nifty gold and silver jewelry, she is petite—about 5'3", with the Rubenesque figure of a mother and the earnest, clear blue eyes of a child. Sunny by nature with a bawdy sense of humor, she can emit a reticence that is sometimes misperceived as aloofness. With the remnant of an Atlanta drawl, her speech is peppered with Yiddish expressions. Fully the show business veteran, take-charge and impatient with fools, she at times gets overwhelmed, and is nagged by fears and insecurities. She is a romantic, by turns an enthusiastic extrovert, then suddenly shy within the space of a sentence. She is a whiz at the *Times* crossword puzzle, is always well read, passionate about her opinions, and idealistic in her politics. "Well," she said evenly one night to a zealous young man who had begun to irritate her with his explanation of why he was going to produce his play in war-torn Bosnia, "I really don't know enough about this to discuss it." And then with perfect timing, "Not that it's ever stopped me before."

People come in and out of the suite. Wally Harper, her pianist, musical director, and alter ego for twenty years, has changed from street clothes into a tuxedo. Blond, with a narrow face and watery blue eyes, he sits on the side chair making wisecracks, and she clowns back. Her son, Adam LeGrant, a character actor and singer in his thirties, comes in. "Say—aren't you Barbara Cook?" he says when he sees his mother. He sits down at the piano and plays snatches of "Dancing in the Dark," then switches to Wagner, then chord progressions. "So, Ma. How are you doing?" "Well, I've got like 85,000 new things in the show I've never done before and I hope I can remember 'em all," she answers. "How'd your audition go?" she asks, and he tells her. John Beal, a bass player with a walrus mustache, comes in carrying a musicians' magazine and an apple, and sits down to read and eat.

She suddenly looks at her watch. "Oh, hell. Louise!" she calls for her secretary and girl Friday, a young woman with long, brown hair and a sense of irony. She appears from right behind her. "Yes, Barbara." "Oh, there you are. Come on, honey, it's time to see about that dress." They start toward the bedroom. "See you later, Ma . . ." She turns around. "OK, honey, I'll see you downstairs." "Remember," he says on the way out, mimicking Warner Baxter in *42nd Street*, "you're going out there a youngster—but you've *got* to come back a star!"

Barbara and Louise disappear into the bedroom to wrestle with the dress that Geoffrey Holder, the West Indian theatre director/actor/dancer and artist, has designed for her, which she'll be wearing in public for the first time.

Downstairs, people are filling the Cafe. Anybody who doesn't know what people are talking about when they talk about a "boite" should go take a look at the Cafe Carlyle. Madison Avenue, so crowded during the day you have to weave in and out just to walk down the street, at night looks like the deserted New York set for a 1950s MGM musical: in the absence of traffic, the blue-black sky silhouettes the skyline in the background, while the sidewalks and limestone shine white in the street lamps, the technicolor contents of the boutique windows luminous from within.

The Cafe Carlyle and its neighbor across the foyer, Bemelmans Bar, have their own entrance on Madison Avenue, separate from the main hotel entrance on 76th Street, under a white square canopy with gold lettering. In the foyer, with its black and white marble floor, there is a glass door on either side. You can turn either left or right and see New York the way it used to be. Bemelmans Bar, with its murals by *Madeline* author Ludwig Bemelmans, is on the left, and is usually presided over late at night by jazz pianist and singer Barbara Carroll.

To the right is the Cafe, presided over at all times with Latin formality by Ambrose, the dark-haired maitre d'. It is an intimate room, seating about ninety, close together, on banquettes and gold chairs covered in rose velvet. On pink tablecloths, candles flickering in frosted hurricanes light up the surrounding walls covered in blue-and-amber-hued murals of fanciful figures with musical instruments, by the Hungarian-born theatre designer Vertes.

It's almost 8:45. The room is full and the drink orders have been taken. It is one of the last places in New York to be staffed by career waiters. Tables come right up to the edge of the small platform at the front of the room, on which sits a grand piano, a microphone in a stand, a stool, and John Beal's bass leaning up on the right.

On a regular night, the first show is supposed to begin at 8:45, but it never does. And this is just a run-through, though it feels like the real thing. At 8:55 Wally Harper slips in through the door by the bar at the back, which connects to the lobby of the hotel. The bartender pours him a drink, which he takes a few sips of by the bar, checking his watch, then he puts the glass down, and goes to the piano. John Beal takes his position at the bass.

Barbara, by this time, is waiting just inside the back door, Louise beside her, having ridden down with the elevator operator and waited a few minutes in the hotel lobby before mounting the six marble steps that lead to the back of the Cafe.

The room is especially lively tonight because everyone there is an insider, and feels compelled to act accordingly. Gloria Vanderbilt is there in a white turban. Silver-haired men who look like lawyers stand up to kiss well-coiffed women. Small groups of gay men, a staple of Barbara's groupie following, cluster around tables.

When Wally sits down and begins to play entrance music, the place quiets. "Ladies and gentlemen," his deep voice booms into the microphone, "Miss Barbara Cook." He continues playing as Barbara wends her way through the applause to the front and picks up the mike in time to sing her opening number, Cy Coleman and Dorothy Fields's "It's Not Where You Start," from *Seesaw*.

The message a song puts across is important to Barbara. There have been songs, like Don McLean's "Starry Night," that she won't do despite her attraction to the melody, because the sentiment is jaded. Barbara's an optimist. Her opening number tonight suits her. "It's not where you start, it's where you finish," she sings slowly, elongating the first "where" and looking around from one person to another on all sides of the audience, making eye contact. Barbara moves a lot when she sings (she was a good dancer when she started on Broadway); she shifts her feet, swirls her upper body, waves her hands with and without the microphone. When she gets to the line about the hundred-to-one shot outrunning the favorite and sings "All he neeeeeeeds is the guts," she tilts her head back and closes her eyes, her black evening lashes standing out in profile.

She almost gets through the song, too, tonight, but comes to a point where she begins a line and comes to a dead blank, letting out an "ayyyyyy" accompanied by a glazed expression where the word should have been. Wally keeps vamping with his accompaniment. "I can't remember," she says to the audience. Wally makes an inaudible crack. "What's the word? Come on, Robert, help me out," she says to a man in the front. She finally gets it, and when she finishes, as she often ends her songs, it's with both arms raised exultantly in the air.

"Whew," she says to the audience when she's through, and then thanks them for coming. She's nervous. She does nothing to hide the fact she's nervous. She fixes the microphone in the stand. "Oy, gevalt," she sighs. "Why did I ever get into this business?"

She looks for a glass of water that should be on the piano, but isn't there. "I could use a glass of water," she says, looking for Ambrose, who's already on his way over to her, holding out a glass. "Thank you, Ambrose," she says. "How are you? It's nice to see you again," and as he gives her the glass, she leans over from the stage to kiss him on the cheek.

She picks up a white handkerchief from the piano and mops her face. "Gosh, it's hot in here," she says. "Or is it just me?" It is, and a few people in the audience tell her so.

She pulls a little at the dress. It is black, with a V at the neck edged with a thin string of rhinestones, and on top of it, a scarlet silk over-cape with the same rhinestone edging. "Gee, this new dress is hot," she says. "But pretty," a woman in the front answers. "You think so?" She stretches taller to see her reflection in a mirrored pillar. "Yeah, it is kind of nice," she muses. "Glitters a lot . . . Does a few tricks . . . I need those." She gets a laugh, and resumes the show.

This is the rundown for the rest of the show:

"Beauty and the Beast" (Alan Menken, music; Howard Ashman, lyrics; from *Beauty and the Beast*)

"Never Never Land" (Jule Styne, music; Betty Comden and Adolph Green, lyrics; from *Peter Pan*)

"On the Sunny Side of the Street" (Jimmy McHugh, music; Dorothy Fields, lyrics; from *Sugar Babies*)

"Make the Man Love Me" (Arthur Schwartz, music; Dorothy Fields, lyrics; from *A Tree Grows in Brooklyn*)

"I Must Have That Man" (Jimmy McHugh, music; Dorothy Fields, lyrics; from *Blackbirds of 1928*)

"I'm Beginning to See the Light" (Duke Ellington, Harry James, Johnny Hodges, Don George, music and lyrics)

"Soon" (Barry Manilow, music; Bruce Sussman, lyrics; from *Thumbelina*)

"Ship in a Bottle" (Amanda McBroom, music and lyrics)

"Ac-cent-tchu-ate the Positive" (Harold Arlen, music; Johnny Mercer, lyrics)

"Lullaby in Ragtime" (Sylvia Fine, music and lyrics)

"I Had Myself a True Love" (Harold Arlen, music; Johnny Mercer, lyrics; from *St. Louis Woman*)

"Carolina in the Morning" (Gus Kahn, music; Walter Donaldson, lyrics)

Barbara's voice is widely considered a phenomenon, like the Hanging Gardens of Babylon, or Halley's comet. In her Broadway days, it was remarkable because of the infallible purity and musicality of her soprano. Now it is because it is unheard of for anyone to possess a pristine lyric soprano into her middle sixties (or even into her middle fifties or late forties).

16

It is the world's most fragile voice type. With a lower, "chest" voice, pretty much anything, as long as it's on key, goes; it's not particularly strenuous to reach for notes, and there's virtually no such thing as hitting a clinker. Husky or hoarse is simply husky or hoarse. With a soprano, physical agility is the difference between right or wrong. Tired can mean cracked notes or pitch problems. Every weakness is glaring, even to the most unmusical listener.

At age sixty-six, time has overlaid Barbara's still-youthful vocal purity with a creamy, wistful mellowness. When she sings, there is a yearning, little-girl-lost quality that infuses everything she does.

With this show, however, partly because of the Dorothy Fields material, she has taken her biggest step toward becoming a blues mama, stretching away from the more lyrical and show-type tunes that were the bedrock of her early career. "That kind of takes me back to my Georgia roots," she says on finishing "Ac-cent-tchu-ate the Positive," wiping her brow with the handkerchief.

Her "Carolina in the Morning" is a rousing, revival meeting rendition with a big finish—cascading piano and Barbara holding a big note on "-nin'" (as in "mor-nin'") with her arms flung wide. It's a staple of her repertory, and always leaves the audience cheering, as it does tonight. She acknowledges the rampage as Wally reprises it as bow music, then she finally steps off the platform and wends her way back through the crowd, only to return a few moments later, to continued applause.

Then she does something that for those first-time audiences is unexpected. She does it at the end of every show. She leaves the microphone where it rests, and turns away slightly from the audience, quieting her breathing, as the applause hushes and Wally begins the alternating chords that introduce Irving Berlin's "What'll I Do?" He plays the chords again and again until she's ready. Then she turns around slowly, eyes closed at first, and purely and directly, without any amplification, she sings the simple waltz, with it's poignant lyrics about the spectre of being left alone. It is jarring, in this day and age, to hear the sound of a naked human voice singing, and the room gets deathly quiet.

The result is breathtaking. It's as if by rejecting the microphone, she has willfully removed the last barrier between herself as a performer and the people in the audience. The longing quality that always hangs about her is at its most intense. And you realize that what she longs for most is the connection with other human beings.

That's more than she could do in all her years in the theatre.

*I*t was on a midwinter day—February 1948—that Barbara first stepped off the train at Pennsylvania Station to start a new life in New York. Traveling with her from Atlanta were her mother and her mother's friend, who had a brother with an apartment where they'd all be staying. They were supposedly there for a two-week visit. Barbara kept explaining to her mother that she was planning to stay on, and had packed accordingly.

"I don't think my mother really believed me until the day came that she had to go back to her job, and we're standing in Penn Station and she's on the train, and I'm on the platform, and I'm waving good-bye."

She found a job as a clerk-typist at the Asiatic Petroleum Corp., a division of Shell Oil. Barbara was no stranger to office work. At home in Atlanta, she had gone to work after high school graduation at the nearby Navy Materiel Redistribution and Disposal Office, in the summer of '45, just as World War II was ending. She had to take a civil service exam to get it. There she was given a job as an assistant filing clerk, an unfortunate choice. "It's the worst possible job they could have given me," she says. "I'm terrible organizing things—awful, awful! I'm overwhelmed instantly." After a time her superior left, and she was moved up to head of the file room, with her own assistant. She daydreamed. She wrote in her diary a lot. Eventually, nobody could find anything and things got so out of hand that one day the entire outfit came to a complete standstill, and all the officers had to come in to straighten out the files.

At Asiatic Petroleum, she worked for forty-one dollars a week typing rows and rows of numbers in their Rockefeller Center offices. She hated it, but it paid for her singing lessons, which cost five dollars a week, and the sixty-dollars-a-month rent for the Eighth Avenue apartment that she shared with another girl and the girl's mother, who used to padlock the telephone when she went out of town, to save money.

She did anything she could to get away from her job. An inveterate museumgoer, she had discovered that the Museum of Modern Art showed old movies. She'd never seen Rudolph Valentino on film, and if they were showing something that would only be playing on a weekday afternoon, she'd think, "I've got to go. It's more important than doing this." So after lunch, she told them she didn't feel well, and she'd go off to the bathroom and take some of the mascara off her eyes and put it underneath, to give herself black circles. "Then I told them I threw up and I had to go home," she says, "and I went to the museum and saw Rudolph Valentino. Actually, I was right."

Continuing her voice lessons, and moving to a better apartment in the Murray Hill district with a roommate who worked for the house of Dior, she eventually landed a few club engagements: the Darbury in Boston, which was extended to nine months, the Blackhawk in Chicago, and later on, the Blue Angel in New York. Vernon Duke, after hearing her sing at a backers' audition for a revue he'd written with Ogden Nash, suggested she go to Tamiment, one of those summer mountain resorts where talents like Jerome Robbins, Danny Kaye, Sid Caesar and Imogene Coca, and scores of others tried their wings, putting together a new show every week. It was there that she was heard by Blue Angel co-owner Max Gordon, who gave her an audition and subsequently an engagement, where she sang songs like "Little Girl Blue," "My Funny Valentine," "It Ain't Necessarily So," and "Out of This World."

Through the Blue Angel date, she was brought to the attention of E. Y. "Yip" Harburg, the lyricist of *The Wizard of Oz*, *Finian's Rainbow*, and songs like "April in Paris." She auditioned for him, and in 1951 was cast in his new show, *Flahooley*, a political satire starring the exotic Yma Sumac and her touted four-octave range. The show closed after forty performances. Two years later Barbara won the role of Ado Annie in a new national tour of *Oklahoma!* (with Florence Henderson in the lead), and as a result was cast by William Hammerstein (Oscar's son) as Carrie in the City Center revival of *Carousel*.

A big break came in 1954, when she was cast in *Plain and Fancy*, a show about Amish life, which was a moderate hit; her notices were outstanding. William Hawkins of the *World-Telegram and Sun* observed how she "flings her own heart over the footlights with whatever she does, and sings and dances her way into the hearts of the audience," while Walter Kerr, for the *Herald Tribune*, wrote: "Barbara Cook, right off a blue and white Dutch plate, is delicious all the time, but especially when she perches on a trunk, savors her first worthwhile kiss and melts into the melody of 'This Is All Very New to Me.'"

She had become Broadway's perfect ingenue, everybody's sweetheart. Over the next decade and a half, she would average one new musical on Broadway every other year: *Candide*, *The Music Man*, *The Gay Life*, *She Loves Me*, *Something More!*; major revivals of *The King and I*, *Carousel* (this time as Julie), and *Show Boat*. For originating the role of Marian the Librarian in *The Music Man*, she was given the Tony award in 1957.

Public and colleagues alike stood in awe of her vocal abilities. Even today, confessions about complexes from actresses who had to follow her onstage, or in a voice lesson, are routine. She did the usual round of television appearances, like *The Ed Sullivan Show* and *The Bell Telephone Hour*. In her reigning years on Broadway, she racked up one of the most extraordinary collections of notices possessed by anybody in entertainment.

✴

Candide: "Miss Cook tears down the house . . . " (Tom Donnelly, *World-Telegram and Sun*).

✴

The Music Man: "If all our stack tenders looked, sang, danced and acted like Miss Barbara, this nation's book learning would be overwhelming" (Frank Aston, *World-Telegram and Sun*).

✴

The Gay Life: "As she lifts her sweet, precise voice and opens her earnest child's eyes, all of the atmosphere that has been lying in wait now wraps itself around her . . . " (Walter Kerr, *Herald Tribune*).

✴

She Loves Me: "Miss Cook is a constant joy" (Richard Watts Jr., *New York Post*).

✴

"The expression 'sings her heart out' certainly applies to Miss Cook, who has both the heart and the voice to do it. Her clear soprano is not only one of the finest vocal instruments in the contemporary musical theatre, but it conveys all the vitality, brightness and strength of her feminine young personality, which is plenty" (Norman Nadel, *World-Telegram and Sun*).

✴

Something More (which closed after fifteen performances): "How pleasant it would have been to have scrapped everything else and just made it a Cook's tour" (Kerr, *Herald Tribune*).

✳

In 1952, she married David LeGrant, an acting teacher and director, a dynamic man of strong opinions. They had met at Tamiment, a year earlier.

Pregnant during the last part of her run in *Music Man*, she gave birth to Adam shortly after leaving the show. Her life was all set up, with a husband, a new baby, a Tony award, and a comfortable home in Port Washington, Long Island. She cooked. She gardened. She cared for her son. She donned her white gloves and commuted to the city to rehearse or perform. Photographers came to do newspaper and magazine spreads showing how the pert young toast of Broadway, who had everything, also personified domestic bliss.

It did look picture perfect, except for one problem. She was told she was the toast of Broadway, but she didn't feel successful. She was told she had everything, but she felt a growing unease.

6

On Tuesday Mark Hummel returned from his father's funeral in California. Julie's opening at the Russian Tea Room was on Thursday.

Julie had been rehearsing as best she could with the accompaniments he had laid down for her on cassette before he left town; before he left, they'd only been able to grab a few hours of rehearsal time here and there. Virtually all the material, except for a few of her stalwart numbers like Cole Porter's "Down in the Depths, On the Ninetieth Floor," was new.

Any time a performer has new material to do it's nerve-racking, because if it's not something you've done before, it hasn't become part of you. It's right at the top of your memory, and can disappear in an instant. And that's with rehearsal.

Julie was not nervous. She was petrified.

It happened that that night she had been invited to a dinner party. A close friend of hers was having a gathering in his elegant apartment for some people who support the opera in Palm Beach. Julie picked up the phone and called him. She said, "Can I ask you a huge favor?" He said, "Yes, of course. Is there someone special you want to bring?" She said, "No, but would you mind terribly if Mark and I did a little show for you after dinner?" He said, "That would be wonderful."

Mark went with her to the dinner, and afterward, the guests assembled in the living room while Mark seated himself at the piano. Even with all the rehearsal in the world, it never really feels like you're doing a number until you do it in front of people.

This show was very different in feel from many of her shows in the past, beginning with the opening number. Julie is always concerned with finding just the right opening number. So is everybody. But Julie, especially, finds that certain things work better with her somewhat stylized image, and certain things just don't.

"It has to do with who you are," she says. "You walk out, and they're looking you over, and saying how much more you've aged, and you've gotten a pot belly, if your hair is thinner, or you've had a touch-up, or if you still look good in the gowns. You have to walk out there with confidence. It's saying, 'Well, here I am, and here we go again—let's do it.'"

Two of her favorite opening numbers, which she uses regularly, highlight the super-sophisticated, naughty chanteuse side of her image: Cole Porter's "Most Gentlemen Don't Like Love (They Just Like to Kick It Around)," a witty lament introduced by Sophie Tucker, and Cy Coleman and Carolyn Leigh's "Don't Ask a Lady," from the revival of *Little Me*. But she just couldn't use them as openers one more time; not in New York. Since the show was to be called "A Sentimental Journey," she decided "Sentimental Journey" would be the logical choice for an opening number. And as a twist on it, Mark gave it a sort of boogie-woogie rhythmic underpinning.

In front of the forty well-fed dinner guests, they commenced to stumble through the entire Russian Tea Room show, Julie fighting for the words all the way.

*

Last year Julie went to a reunion of Copacabana girls. She had a right to be there: she's an alumna. Every year the former chorus girls get together. They trade stories about their children and grandchildren, and reminisce about the old days in the line of the reigning nightclub of the forties and fifties. Julie had been looking all over her house for weeks to find the picture of herself with Frank Sinatra, singing "I Can't Get Started With You," but she couldn't dig it up in time.

The Copacabana wasn't her first job in a chorus line; Earl Carroll's Vanities was. At eighteen, in her native Omaha, when she was in her first semester at Omaha University (part of the University of Nebraska), she went to audition. She wanted to look sophisticated, so she took her hair and piled it on top of her head. Upswept hairdos were all the thing, anyway, when movie stars wanted to look glamorous in 1942: Ann Sheridan, Linda Darnell, Betty Grable, Mary Astor, Joan Crawford . . . .

She got the job, and the road eventually led to New York. She was making forty dollars a week in the chorus. She met Wally Wanger, who did the hiring for the Latin Quarter, and she was offered a job in the chorus of the Latin Quarter in Chicago, which led to another job in a Detroit gambling club. It was here she was introduced to the sleaze elements of the business and had her first bad experience, with a man who used to drive the chorus girls between the club and their hotel. "One night, he drove me home and said he'd buy me an ice cream soda and take me to a party he knew about," she says. "Well, there wasn't any party, and he finally gave me five dollars for a cab." Right afterward she packed up and went home to Omaha. Too embarrassed to go back to Omaha University, she enrolled instead in Duchesne University. But before long, she had a call offering her a job in the line at the Latin Quarter in New York. She took it, and remembers proprietor Lou Walters's young daughters, Barbara Walters and her little sister, Jackie, standing at the edge of the stage to watch rehearsals.

She was making fifty dollars a week. She needed an apartment. "I didn't know anything about New York," she says. "And I was down in the subway, and I said to some stranger standing there, 'If one were to look for an apartment in New York, could you tell me where one would go to look?' I didn't know anything. He said, 'There's going to be a train coming, an E train. Get on that train, it'll take you to Forest Hills. Get off at 71st Street and Continental Avenue. There are a lot of real estate offices there.'" She followed his directions. The war was on, and there was one apartment left, and she got it. The rent was a hundred dollars a month, which was not cheap.

But the subway cost a nickel, so it cost her five cents to get to work every day, and another five to get home, early in the morning. She ate, mostly, at the Automat, and had herself budgeted to about twenty cents a day. Her mother and younger brother came from Omaha to live with her for a while. There wasn't enough money for a phone, but they managed.

Still, when she had the chance to audition to be a Copa girl, she went, and was offered a job. She asked them how much they paid their girls. They said, "Seventy-five dollars a week." She said, "I'll take it." She was thrilled; the extra hundred a month was a godsend. She also felt bad, because the Latin Quarter had treated her well, and she's always had a strong sense of loyalty.

She went on to strike out on her own as a single, and got a job as the girl singer for Johnny Long's band. She was fired on Christmas Eve—in Chicago. With two weeks notice, the band's next stop was her hometown of Omaha. Long thought she was too dramatic. He told her, "Honey, I just wanted a band singer. You know, someone who could carry a tune and look happy and clap their hands along with the beat. You're doing all these funny gestures, and acting everything out. I think you're a little too sophisticated for our orchestra." "I don't know," Julie says now. "I guess that was kind of a backhanded compliment. But I was very hurt at the time."

She went off with a USO show that the Copa sent to Europe, and played France and Germany (today she serves on the board of the USO). In '46 she went back to the Copa, this time as a production singer. It was the time when nightclub shows, like the Copa's, were extravaganzas. There would be a brand-new show every four months. The shows ran a little over an hour. There would be a few featured spots for star singer, dance team, comedy act, and so on; they would be interspersed with lavish production numbers, in which Julie sang. In one of those, she would be the first to introduce "The Coffee Song" ("There's an Awful Lot of Coffee in Brazil"), before Frank Sinatra went on to have an enormous hit record with it.

It was an exciting time. Desi Arnaz, recently married to Lucille Ball and coming on the scene with his conga drum, had the featured spot, and did twenty minutes to a half-hour each show. Just before the show opened, Phil Silvers's sidekick Rags Raglan died suddenly, and Sinatra offered to fly in and do some comedy bits with Silvers. One bit revolved around Julie singing "I Can't Get Started With

You," and the three of them landed their picture in *Life* magazine. (That's the photo Julie was looking for before the reunion.)

Life at the Copa was fascinating for a girl from Omaha. She knew the girl who read fortunes. "She wore this kind of high frame on her head," Julie remembers, "and her hair was blonde, and she combed it over this thing, with a big French twist at the back. And she was very exotic. Her name was Anya. I think Anya had been from Brooklyn."

Julie was pals with a 250-pound bouncer, Nick Fiori, who used to take her home to his family in Brooklyn, where twenty-five people would sit around a table in the basement for five hours at a stretch, eating a never-ending procession of pastas and meat dishes. She'd never seen so much food in her life. (Then, as now, belying her rail-thin figure, Julie loves to eat.)

They did three shows a night. Once for a few weeks, they doubled at the Roxy, doing their slightly cut-down stage show between movie showings, starting at ten in the morning. They did four shows throughout the day at the Roxy, until eight in the evening, when they'd run back to do the first show at the Copa, then back to do the last show at the Roxy in between the Copa dinner show and the midnight show. Then there was the Copa 2:00 A.M. show. After which they'd go to breakfast at Reuben's on 58th Street. "Best apple pancakes in the world," she recalls. "And Virginia ham that was so delicious; ham and eggs, and that thin, wonderful rye toast." She'd get on her subway at six in the morning and ride back out to Forest Hills. Then it was back to the Roxy by ten.

"It was a good time," she says. "It was a time when people stayed out all night. They didn't think anything about it. It's just what they did. They'd leave the Copa show at three in the morning and then maybe go down to the Village to hear some jazz. And money was flying. People were drinking up a storm, and that was good for business."

Movie stars came in all the time, and sat ringside. One night she was introduced to Lana Turner, who'd loved a number she did called "Good for Nothing Millionaire." "I went out of there sailing," Julie says. "Lana Turner liked the little crack in my voice."

She went on to other jobs, at a couple of different rooms in New York. She auditioned for a Broadway revue singing "Civilization" ("Bongo, bongo, bongo, I don't want to leave the Congo") and lost the job to Elaine Stritch. She got a job at Mother Kelly's, a club in Miami, where for seven months she did five shows a night, the first at 9 P.M., the last at 4:30 A.M. She was really solo, now, and spent most of her salary on arrangements, subsisting on cornflakes and bananas at the local diner. In Florida she met agent Barron Polan, to whom she would briefly be married. Although it didn't work out, he continued to represent her, and they remained close friends.

But it was in the Mother Kelly's job that she began to find her look, taking her cue from the high-fashion models and ballerinas who slick their hair back into a chignon, and never worry about changing with the styles. For Julie, it was a decision based on economics: you didn't have to live at the hairdresser keeping up your bubble cut.

The first beaded gown came with her first big break. She was a winner for most outstanding performer on Mickey Rooney's radio show, *Hollywood Showcase*. First prize was a two-week engagement at the Mocambo, a favorite nightspot of the Hollywood crowd. For the occasion, designer George Karr made her a low-cut white jersey and lace gown sewn with tiny silver beads and seed pearls. Her agents borrowed a $28,000 necklace and earrings to go with it. The earrings kept falling off. She was so nervous she didn't want to worry about them, so she stuck a flower behind her ear instead. She started with a small orchid; the gardenias wouldn't come until later. There was something in the balance between the intense glamour of the gowns and settings she was working in and the earthiness of the flower that struck a chord with her. She virtually never performed wearing jewelry from that moment on.

Her Mocambo engagement was a hit. On opening night, Joan Crawford, whom she'd recently met at a party, sent her an enormous bouquet of flowers, wishing her luck for her career. (To this day, Julie refuses to read *Mommie Dearest*.)

A screen test, which revealed that she photographed remarkably like Gene Tierney, led to a couple of movies: Ben Gazzara's first film, *The Strange One*, and *This Could Be the Night*, with Jean Simmons and Paul Douglas, in which she played a blonde nightclub singer named Rosebud.

But her success really blossomed in the swank clubs of the period. A quintessential purveyor of the naughty and romantic, she quickly became a reigning star over rooms like the St. Regis Maisonette and the Plaza's Persian Room, where Ted Straeter and his fourteen-piece orchestra ruled the dance floor. Two things defined life in New York in the '50s: you met your date under the Biltmore clock; then you went to hear Julie Wilson.

"I went from dressing in toilets and crawling around backstage and living in basement rooms that cost seven dollars a week," she says, "to suddenly finding myself in the best. It was an eyeopener: that people really lived like this, and could afford to."

With her flair for the dramatic, she naturally gravitated toward the musical comedy stage, and in between nightclub work, she did Broadway and London stints such as replacing Mary Martin in the London company of *South Pacific*—the only time she cut her hair.

Choices, for Julie, are things you make with your heart and then go through the trial, right or wrong. It was around this time that she made a choice that she regards as one of the biggest mistakes of her career. After finishing up her *South Pacific* run, she enrolled at the Royal Academy of Dramatic Arts in London. In London, she received a cable from Barron Polan, telling her that the young producer Hal Prince was putting together a new show, and she was being offered the lead. It was called *The Pajama Game*. She said no. Polan pleaded with her to take it. She insisted she wanted to finish what she'd started at RADA, and continue with the voice coach who was trying to expand her vocal powers radically. The part went instead to Janis Paige, who starred opposite John Raitt. The show, of course, went on to become one of the longest running hits of the period, and it elevated Paige's star status when she returned to Hollywood. Ironically, Julie went on to play the role in the Broadway run after all, replacing Paige's replacement.

Nevertheless, there was plenty of work, and she was in demand. In sequin gown and feather boa, she continued to rule the night. As in her earlier Copa days, the money was flowing, and judging by the people out walking the streets from nightspot to nightspot, 1:00 A.M. was like the middle of the afternoon. In 1961 she married theatrical tour packager Michael McAloney (another early marriage, to a hotel owner, had lasted only very briefly), and gave birth to two sons, Holt and Mike.

But around the edges, the world she knew was about to crumble and with it, the music that was her life. The apocalypse was coming, and the four horsemen were named John, Paul, George, and Ringo.

*T*hursday morning comes, the morning of the Russian Tea Room opening. When Julie awakens, her anxiety is supplemented by something she hasn't seen coming. She has awakened with a bad cold.

On a good day, Julie's voice is husky. "A great voice, it isn't," she likes to say; and she works on it constantly, to keep up her ability to sing. Now, with a sore throat and laryngitis, it will take all her attention and energy just to get a decent sound and keep from croaking. It was attention and energy she had reserved for overcoming her panic about everything else, including the lack of rehearsal and insecurity with the new material.

She goes for her voice lesson with veteran coach Keith Davis as she has done almost every day for the last three decades. They try to loosen things up. It helps a little.

She is always nervous about a new show, just as every singer is, until the second night, when they can settle into the run. But it's been a very long time since she's been this stricken with fear. She isn't prepared, and she knows it, and she isn't used to not being prepared. And despite Mark Hummel's formidable musicianship, she doesn't have the old tried-and-true chemistry of her act with Billy Roy to fall back on.

At the last minute, she got a call from Roy. He said he was back in New York, on a break from his project, and would be able to play for her after all. But Julie was by this time committed to Mark, who had extended himself for her in good faith; and especially because there was a live album involved, she felt obligated to him. She also knew that if she were to dismiss Mark now, he would never work with her again.

The Russian Tea Room sits on West 57th Street, "slightly to the left of Carnegie Hall," as its owner, Faith Stewart-Gordon, likes to say in its radio commercials. With its red canopy, red, green, and polished brass facade, from the outside it looks like a Faberge egg. Inside, over red leather banquettes, the tinsel Christmas decorations are left up all year round, in keeping with the tradition set by Stewart-Gordon's late husband, Sidney Kaye, who bought the place in the late 1940s.

Everyone knows about the Russian Tea Room. Tourists want to go there (unless they're of a generation that prefers its neighbors Planet Hollywood and the Hard Rock Cafe, across the street). In the movies and on television, the Russian Tea Room is where entertainment people are always shown having power lunches. It used to be a hangout for musicians, in the old days when the Philharmonic played at Carnegie Hall, before there was a Lincoln Center, and when musicians could still afford to eat there.

The cabaret is up on the second floor, up a narrow stairway to the right of the main entrance, hung with paintings and costume sketches from the Tea Room's art collection. It is the smaller of two rooms the restaurant traditionally uses for private functions. The room at the top of the stairs overlooks 57th Street through a large picture window running almost the length of the restaurant. Down a short hall, a quick turn to the right and up two steps is the cabaret. The room, officially called the New York Room, is an intimate green and gold box, its dark green walls edged by brass molding hung with paintings and studded with polished brass sconces under shiny red shades, its perforated brass ceiling reflecting the pink tablecloths lit by tiny candles. Waiters dressed in red Russian peasant blouses belted with embroidered sashes carry hot borscht with perogi, and blinis with caviar.

On a platform the size of a postage stamp, a piano sits in front of the mirrored back wall. Most of the time the piano is sideways, with the pianist sitting on the audience's left, the singer standing at the microphone on the right. That's the way Billy Roy sat last year. This year the piano has been turned so that anyone able to see over it would find the pianist facing the audience, pushed over to the right. Julie's microphone this time is on the left.

Julie's is the only extended run the Russian Tea Room presents. Normally, the cabaret is mainly a Sunday night affair, with performers coming in for an early and a late show, a different performer every week. Perhaps more than any other room in town, it has the feel of an insider's room, its Sunday nights often packed with people in show business, come out to meet their friends and hear other friends perform. Partly, it's because everyone in show business has Sunday night off, which also means that it's one of the only places open on Sunday night. The Tea Room is able to attract a variety of the town's leading performers because as a one-shot event, their appearance there doesn't violate any contractual or loyalty obligations to whatever other venues they might work in the rest of the time.

It's almost 8:30, and Julie sits waiting in her dressing room upstairs, actually a conference room that has been converted for the purpose. Her son Holt, an actor, comes up to wish her luck, then returns to the people downstairs, where the room has filled and the waiters squeeze in between the cramped tables to finish serving dinner before the show begins. Faith Stewart-Gordon is a small, blonde former actress whose soft-spoken manner belies the hard business head that built the Russian Tea Room from hangout to high-profile icon. She is seated at a table with Julie's manager, the publicist and cabaret promoter Donald Smith, a big man with wavy silver hair and a cherubic face, who buzzes from table to table greeting press and VIPs.

It's 8:35. Julie starts down the steep, narrow stairway leading from her dressing room to the cabaret. Downstairs, the room has quieted when Stewart-Gordon steps up to the microphone on the platform, welcoming everybody to the Russian Tea Room. She says how thrilled they are to have Julie back again, following her momentous fiftieth-anniversary engagement last year. She gives special thanks to their sponsors, including WQEW-AM radio, one of the major stations in the country devoted entirely to American popular standards. Then she reminds everyone that for every glass of Mumm's champagne they buy, Mumm's will make a donation to AIDS research. "And now," she concludes, "the Russian Tea Room is pleased to present Julie Wilson in 'A Sentimental Journey.'" She goes back to her table to a round of applause, and Mark Hummel comes in through the back of the room, squeezing past the row of tables that line the side walls. He seats himself at the piano.

He begins the slow, eighth-note beat of his arrangement of "Sentimental Journey." Julie suddenly appears through the hidden door in the mirrors at the front of the room, surprising everyone, who expected her to come in from the back of the house as usual. She steps up to the platform, regal and elegant in a black Pauline Trigere gown that hugs her figure, which Trigere has loaned her for the occasion.

The room and Julie are a good match. Both of them have a luminosity that comes out in the dark. Julie's genius is the sheer magnetism with which she can hold a roomful of people spellbound, the palpable electricity she generates when her gut-level rawness combines with her polished sensuality, communicating with the audience intravenously. The effect is searing: unnerving when too close to the bone, elating in its expertly wrought brilliance.

Now, onstage, with Mark to her left, she begins to sing, her voice showing the brittle hoarseness of her cold. "Se-ven, se-ven, se-ven, se-ven/that's the time we leave at seven" she sings through her laryngitis, fighting for every note. Afterward, Julie would remember very little of the entire evening, so terrified was she and focused on getting through one number at a time as best she could.

The content of the show had gelled into an interesting collection of material:

"Sentimental Journey" (Bud Green, Les Brown, Ben Homer, music and lyrics)

"Mean to Me" (Roy Turk, Fred E. Ahlert, music and lyrics)/"The One I Love Belongs to Somebody Else" (Isham Jones, music; Gus Kahn, lyrics)/"I Guess I'll Have to Change My Plan" (Arthur Schwartz, music; Howard Dietz, lyrics)

"Down in the Depths, On the Ninetieth Floor" (Cole Porter, music and lyrics)

"Louisville Lou, the Vampin' Lady" (Milton Ager, music; Jack Yellen, lyrics)

"That Old Feeling" (Lew Brown, Sammy Fain, music and lyrics)/"Good Morning Heartache" (Irene Higginbotham, Ervin Drake, Dan Fisher, music and lyrics)

"The Tale of the Oyster" (Cole Porter, music and lyrics)

"Inside My Body Is a Dancer" (Steven Lutvak, music and lyrics)

"Somebody Else Is Taking My Place" (Richard Howard, Bob Ellsworth, Russ Morgan, music and lyrics)/"I Ain't Got Nobody" (Spencer Williams, Dave Peyton, music; Roger Graham, lyrics)/"You're Nobody 'Til Somebody Loves You" (Russ Morgan, Larry Stock, James Cavanaugh, music and lyrics)

"He's the Kind of Man . . ." (Charles De Forest, music and lyrics)

"From This Moment On" (Cole Porter, music and lyrics)

"Hey, Look Me Over" (Cy Coleman, music; Carolyn Leigh, lyrics)

"All the Lives of Me" (Peter Allen, music and lyrics)

"Don't Ask a Lady" (Cy Coleman, music; Carolyn Leigh, lyrics)

Julie works admirably, and the audience understands her nervous missteps on some of the lyrics, and that her health is undermined. They are supportive and enthusiastic. Still, there is an undercurrent of unease. Billy Roy's absence is noticed. Not that Mark Hummel isn't a topflight pianist and arranger. He is, and is much sought after in the music and theatre communities for his musicianship and professionalism. He's just different, with a distinct personality. He is a generation younger than Julie, and his thinning hair is in a ponytail. Rather than a traditional tuxedo, over striped pants he performs in a dark brocade vest and a black silk floppy bow tie. The look is hip. The audience is caught by surprise. The dynamic is suddenly different from what they're used to. Roy had the role of an elfin, dinner-clothed partner, a silver-haired contemporary trading the shared experience of their generation in a sophisticated give-and-take. Mark is supporting her strongly. But there is an aloneness about Julie up there that people did not expect to see.

In the middle of the show, something unsettling happens. A well-known designer is there, sitting down front. He is an old friend and fan of Julie's, and has brought along a woman client, who has proceeded to get very drunk. And she doesn't want to shut up during the show. The people around their table get irritated by the disruption, and the sounds of "sshhh!" increase. The designer tries desperately to get her to be quiet, only to receive full-voiced responses along the lines of "I'm not talking loud—and don't tell me to be quiet, you little shit!" Finally one man from the next table, who's had enough, turns around and says, "I am trying to listen to the performer, if you don't mind, and I'd appreciate it if you could just stop talking. . . ." The man is Wayman Wong, the critic for the *Daily News*. He is of Asian extraction, which wouldn't be worth mentioning except that the woman flings a racial epithet at him. He will not take it lightly. The designer, mortified, will call Julie the next day to apologize. Julie, in her anxiety and concentration, hasn't even noticed. She is just worried about finishing the show.

She does finish. Despite her cold, despite stumbling on the lyrics, she gets through it as befitting someone who has done thousands of shows in hundreds of places for the last fifty years. But unmistakably, over everything, the air has hung with the perfume of uncertainty, that indefinable whiff that audiences can't identify, but that instinctively puts them on guard, the scent that, in the wild, prompts predators to attack.

For a performer, it is a chilling reminder of the fragility of it all. That in this business, no matter how glossy things look in a magazine layout—security, fame, voice, health, professional support, the ability to draw a crowd—it is only a house of cards, ready to collapse for any reason, teetering all the time.

*R*osemary is asleep with the radio droning in the background when she hears the announcer say it. Rosemary is a light sleeper, going back to the days when she was hooked on barbiturates, and she always sleeps with talk radio making a soothing hum around her. She has returned from Toronto the day before. The concert went well; the weather was freezing. She still has her cold, and she is trying to rest. It is the middle of the night, and the noise is droning on. That's when she hears the announcer say her son's name. He says Rafael Ferrer has been killed in an automobile accident.

There's no more information. They have gone on to something else. In a panic, she picks up the phone and tries to call Rafael's apartment. His answering machine picks up. "Rafi, this is Mama," she says into the machine. "You call me right away." She hangs up. Then she tries to call the radio station, but she can't get through. The minutes go by, and she keeps dialing the station. Finally she gets through, and then finds that it was not her loss, but the loss of another singer, Mary Wilson of the Supremes, whose son, also Rafael Ferrer, has been killed in his Jeep Cherokee.

A little while later, her phone rings. It's Rafael, telling her that he's fine, he was just out, and that from the number of calls on his and his wife's machine, he hadn't realized he'd been so well thought of. He is an actor and her baby, the fifth and youngest of her children.

Relieved but still badly shaken, she tries to go back to sleep. She needs the rest. It is less than forty-eight hours until she has to open. She lies there, the radio still droning on.

＊

Radio was where Rosemary got her first job. Or rather, Betty got it. Betty and Rosemary were the inseparable sister act, on and off the air: the Clooney Sisters. They were together all the time; Rosemary, the shy, responsible older sister, Betty, the laughing, nervy younger sister, who in high school had the idea they should audition at Cincinnati's WLW radio—and who then, when they were offered a job on the spot, asked for an advance on their salaries, because they had no money to take the streetcar home.

The audition was one of the open auditions WLW had every Thursday. Rosemary was seventeen, Betty, fourteen. They auditioned with the three songs they could sing well together, "Hawaiian War Chant," "Patty Cake Man," and "Dream," Rosemary on lead, Betty on harmony. They were offered twenty dollars a week apiece, a veritable fortune for two teenagers in 1945. "I think I saved more money then than I do now," Rosemary likes to say.

They worked on the radio after school and during summer vacation, and soon they were doing outside jobs, playing high school dances and other functions with local bands. They were band singers; that's what was important. It was the thing to be. The Clooney Sisters began to make a name for themselves in the Cincinnati area, and after a while, with extra work, their radio paychecks would sometimes come to as much as $130 a week each.

They sang on WLW for two years, and joined a big band in the area led by Barney Rapp, with whom Doris Day had started. They began to play their first big club dates, and by this time, had become local celebrities.

Tony Pastor, a bandleader who got his start with Artie Shaw before going out on his own, was looking for a new girl singer. He was coming to Cincinnati to play a date, and his road manager was a friend of Rapp, who suggested that Rosemary and Betty audition. They did, and again, they were hired on the spot, this time at $250 a week each.

In 1946, the Clooney Sisters went on the road with the Tony Pastor band, chaperoned by their young uncle George Guilfoyle, recently home from the war. He kept a sharp eye on his teenaged little ladies, who'd been suddenly thrust into a den of male musicians, and he made sure everyone knew it.

There is a special connection between a performer and the Road. It can be a love-hate connection. Sometimes the excitement and adventure outweigh the loneliness and rootlessness; sometimes vice versa. But it fulfills a part of what being a performer is all about—bringing what they have to say to all kinds of people, wherever they are, much as traveling players did centuries ago. It was here, going out with the Pastor band, that Rosemary developed a feeling for the road that is still with her today, when she continues to tour so much of her year. It's not that she loves or hates the road; it's simply what she does. She enjoys recording, she likes being at home. But usually after about a month or so, she gets restless to get back out again.

Touring with the band also expanded her world. She had never been out of the tristate area of Ohio, Indiana, and her native Kentucky. Now she traveled all over the country, and if they stayed in one place a week, it was like settling in, because most of the dates were one-night ballroom jobs. She took her first plane trip when the band played the Hollywood Palladium, and she fell in love with California. It was where she would live most of her life.

The late forties were the tail end of the big-band era. Until then, most singers were affiliated with one band or another, and hit records would reflect that: Doris Day with Les Brown; June Christy with Stan Kenton. Bing Crosby was an exception and, later, Frank Sinatra, who'd gone out on his own after leaving the Tommy Dorsey Orchestra. Now, as the whole system was breaking apart, more and more singers were doing the same.

The time came for Rosemary to do it. Betty got tired of life on the road and decided to leave the band and go home to a normal existence. (She would later go on to her own radio show at WLW, and a solo career.) They had already done some recording with the Pastor band. The Clooney Sisters' first record with them was an album of music from Walt Disney's *Song of the South*. They sang "Zippity Do Dah," and, alone, Rosemary sang "Sooner or Later," about which *Down Beat* magazine wrote, "Rosemary Clooney has an extraordinarily good voice, perhaps the nearest thing to Ella Fitzgerald we've ever heard."

She began to win serious attention with a song called "I'm Sorry I Didn't Say I'm Sorry When I Made You Cry Last Night," which the band had recorded for Columbia. Her fear during the recording session caused her to sing it just above a whisper, which the critics immediately identified as a revolutionary new singing style. Columbia began to promote the record with disc jockeys like Martin Block, of *Make Believe Ballroom*, one of the most popular record shows on radio in the country. The record did well. She made her first record under her own name with the Pastor band, shortly before she left. It was called "Bargain Day," and it was written by Billy Roy.

When Betty left the band in 1949, Rosemary honored the two weeks' notice in her agreement with Pastor, and then went out on her own. She was twenty-one. She went to New York and signed with Columbia, where Tony Bennett was also starting out, and where Doris Day and Dinah Shore had come before her. She bunked on a friend's couch and hunted the Seventh Avenue wholesale places for clothing bargains, and she found work on radio shows like *The*

Camel Caravan. Frank Sinatra had been looking for a girl singer to record a couple of things with, and she was recommended, and did the job. She had a record that was a regional hit in Philadelphia, called "The Kid's a Dreamer," which meant she could play clubs there and get good money.

Her first hit record for Columbia was "Beautiful Brown Eyes," an old country standard, and it would sell over half a million copies. By this time, Mitch Miller, the bearded, former oboe player, was heading up A&R (artists and repertoire) for Columbia. One day he played her a demo record of a novelty song called "Come on-a My House," written as an imitation Armenian folk song by playwright William Saroyan and his cousin Ross Bagdasarian, who would later become David Seville and create "The Chipmunks." Miller wanted her to record it. Rosemary hated the song immediately on hearing it. She thought it was a cheap way to get people's attention. Miller threatened to fire her if she didn't make the record. She showed up for the session the next day and recorded it. It would become an astronomical hit, and make her a star.

It was 1951. By this time she was living in an apartment at the Hampshire House on Central Park South, with a roommate, Jackie Sherman, whose mother owned the apartment. A swanky address, but often not enough money to buy food. Now she went to Florida for a job with Buddy Rich, and when she came back to New York, driving up Broadway in a cab, every one of the dozens of record stores on the street was blaring "Come on-a My House" on loud-speakers. The song was everywhere. Suddenly, everybody knew her name. Every newspaper in the country was doing a feature story about her. She had a big layout in *Life* magazine, and was on the cover of *Time*. The publicity machine was rolling. The money was rolling in.

She was in demand at cocktail parties. She dated people like Dave Garroway, who hosted the *Today* show, and was close friends with Marlene Dietrich, whom she had met on Tallulah Bankhead's radio show before "Come on-a My House" and with whom she made a number of recordings at Columbia. Touted as "the next Betty Hutton," she tested at Paramount, and began what was to be a series of movies for them. The first picture, *The Stars Are Singing*, was released in March 1953 with a big premiere in her hometown of Maysville, Kentucky.

She went on to film *Here Come the Girls*, with Bob Hope, and her third picture, *Red Garters*. It was at Paramount that she met Bing

Crosby, with whom she would make the one movie for which she is most remembered, *White Christmas*. They were friends from the beginning, though having idolized him as a youngster, she was at first intimidated. Crosby would continue to be her friend, mentor, colleague, and champion until his death in 1977.

There were more hit records—"Mambo Italiano," "Botcha Me," "Hey There," and her favorite of the early records, "Tenderly," which she had insisted on recording although it had been recorded twenty-two times previously by other people. She made a series of records for children called "Clooney Tunes," and her rendition of "Teddy Bears' Picnic" was reputed to be the favorite of the young Prince Charles; Columbia sent him a gold record.

She had met Jose Ferrer when they were both living in New York, and in the summer of 1953 they were married in Durant, Oklahoma, outside Dallas, where he was appearing at the Texas State Fair in *Kiss Me, Kate*. They moved into the house in Beverly Hills where Rosemary still lives, the house where crooner Russ Columbo had accidently shot and killed himself, and which subsequently belonged to George Gershwin. He and Ira had written "A Foggy Day in London Town" and Rosemary's favorite song, "Our Love Is Here to Stay," in what was now her living room. (Rosemary and Ferrer bought the house from the singer Ginny Simms and her husband.)

Her five children came about a year apart beginning in 1955, and they were all named for members of Ferrer's family, wealthy owners of a sugar plantation in Puerto Rico. First Miguel, then Maria, Gabriel, Monsita, and Rafael. She continued to work all during her pregnancies and probably had the most extensive and glamorous maternity wardrobe of any performer who ever lived. She recorded "Hey There" and "This Ole House" a week before she went into labor with Miguel, when Mitch Miller was so insistent that he told her he would send an ambulance and that she could record in a wheelchair if necessary (it wasn't).

When the children were young, she and Ferrer used to pack them up with two nannies and take them wherever they went. As they got older and started school, she had to leave them behind whenever she went off to work. She was working all the time. She had her own television show. She was recording. She was doing other television and radio work and personal appearances. She was making an enormous amount of money and was the primary support of the entire household, her husband, children, mother, and a staff that included a cook, butler, upstairs maid, laundress, gardener, and secretary. Everywhere she went, the press and the fans were right there.

She was trying to please everybody, as she always had. But the treadmill had been accelerating since "Come on-a My House" had hit number one. Her marriage to Ferrer was disintegrating. The pop music scene as she knew it was commencing its dying convulsions. But those things were external. Within Rosemary, something more ominous was taking root.

The run-through was scheduled for 2:00 at Rainbow and Stars, the afternoon of the opening. At noon, in the hall outside Rosemary and Dante's hotel suite, you could hear her new album blasting, while inside, she was in the bedroom singing along with it over and over again, trying to remember all the words to songs like "Let's Get Away from It All," with the umpteen lost choruses she had asked co-writer Matt Dennis to send her.

She had been to see Dr. Gould about her cold, and he'd given her something to alleviate the congestion and loosen her voice so she'd be in shape to sing by tonight. She's tense. She gets quiet when she's tense. Dante, on the other hand, is talking a mile a minute, and helping her gather together the things that she would need to settle into her dressing room at Rainbow and Stars. "Look at him," she says. "He's more nervous than I am." She turns to him. "Listen to you. What are you saying?"

The suite has been filling with flowers all day, friends wishing her luck. From Bob and Dolores Hope. From Liza Minnelli, with a card that says "Take no prisoners."

At 1:30 Dante calls for the bellman, who comes to take the bags down to the car, which is waiting outside the hotel. Allen Sviridoff meets them by the car, and rides up front with the driver. Outside it's snowing, and driving down Fifth Avenue toward Rockefeller Center, you can't see six inches in front of your face. Rosemary looks out the car window. "Well," she says, "all those people are going to be screwed out of their view."

She's holding the stack of pale blue card-stock sheets she's had in her hand since the hotel room. They have her lyrics printed on them. She keeps flipping through them.

"I talked to the woman from Tower Records," Allen says, as the car inches along. "The album is in." Rosemary laughs. "Yeah— try and buy it outside New York," she says. "Try and buy it in Vermont."

In Rockefeller Center, Rainbow and Stars is at the top of what was for decades the RCA building, now the GE building, a massive hunk of art deco stone opposite the skating rink. When the driver opens the trunk, everybody takes a bag, Dante carrying the garment bag containing the Bob Mackie beaded gown she'll perform in. "Just feel how heavy this is," Dante likes to say. "It'll break your arm."

Coming across the lobby, she meets two of her musicians, saxophone player Scott Hamilton and horn player Warren Vaché. "Hi, Rose," they say. "We're just going to get a hamburger," Hamilton says. "We'll be right up." It's five of two. "When are they going to get a hamburger?" she says on her way to the elevator.

The gray-haired guard at the elevator recognizes her. She smiles at him. "Hello, how are you?" she says, and he holds the door open for her. "Nice to see you again, Miss Clooney," and he presses the button for the 65th floor. As the doors close, the sounds of the wind-tunnel effect of the elevator shaft wail like a cross between restless spooks and a Hoover vacuum.

Upstairs, they dump the bags in the dressing room, a small closet of a room in the pay phone alcove outside the cabaret. It used to be a plushy washroom before it was converted for the purpose. There are more lavish accommodations on the 67th floor, which performers who play there have the option of using. But most of them use this one because it's just a few steps away from where the show is. Except Lainie Kazan. She wanted to use the other one, and one night after the late show she was in her comfortable dressing quarters on 67, and people forgot she was there and everybody went home, and she couldn't get out because they shut down the elevators, and it took until around four o'clock in the morning and many calls to the authorities before someone came to let her out of the building. And then it was in the *New York Times*.

Dante stays behind to unpack a few things, while Rosemary and Allen head inside to rehearsal. Inside, the room is undergoing preparations for the opening later, and metallic mesh tablecloths lie crumpled, tables and chairs askew, somebody's pack of cigarettes, pieces of lighting gel. The musicians are already there, except for Hamilton and Vaché, who arrive momentarily with their lunch in paper bags. They sit around alongside the platform and spread out their foil-wrapped burgers and french fries on the same tables where in a few hours, people will pay exorbitant prices to have waiters bring them oysters by candlelight.

Musicians don't care about things like that. "Anybody want a bite?" Hamilton says, holding up his burger. There are six of them, each a star player in his own field. They are wearing sweatshirts and turtlenecks and jeans, mostly. Three are of Rosemary's generation: Joe Cocuzzo, the drummer, a thin man with curly gray hair and a moustache, who's wearing a white Celtics sweatshirt; Jay Leonhart, the bass player, a tall, lanky man with wire-rimmed glasses, who takes Hamilton up on the offer of some of his burger, and talks about how he and his grown children are starting to do club dates as a family; Bucky Pizzarelli, silver-haired with glasses, wearing a tie and a pale blue shirt and sitting in the middle of the platform noodling on his guitar. The other three are younger: John Oddo, her musical director, who is at the piano sorting through music for the rehearsal; Hamilton, who has just come back with his saxophone from a job in Amsterdam; and Vaché.

Rosemary sits down at the tables with them and flips through her cue cards again, and Tim, the lighting man, comes over to say hello before going back to hanging lights. There is a time pressure because Hamilton has to go out to the airport to pick up his wife. He puts down his burger. "No, no, it's OK," Rosemary tells him, "we have time. Finish your lunch."

One of the guys is saying how he hasn't been feeling that well, he thinks he may be getting an ulcer. Rosemary is concerned. "Have you been to the doctor?" she asks him, but he hasn't had time. "Gaviscon," Leonhart says. "Go out and get some Gaviscon. It's an antacid. It's the best stuff. It'll fix you." He'd been using something else. "No," insists Leonhart. "Gaviscon." He writes it down. Dante has come in, and Rosemary sees him and asks him to go down to the drugstore and get some. He leaves, and returns a little while later with the bottle in a paper bag, and gives it to the guy. "Thanks, Dante," he says. "Thanks, Rose." "Sure, honey," she says. "You should try to get to a doctor."

They finish eating and pick up their instruments, and Oddo begins to lead them through rehearsal, starting with the opening number, "Corcovado," which they did on *Regis and Kathie Lee*. She sings a couple of choruses, and then gives the musicians a chance to play. "Where do I get back into that?" she asks John Oddo. "OK," he says to the band, "let's take it from letter A." They start to play again, Rosemary singing to herself on "Ba, da da da da da da." "OK," she says. "I've got it."

Next to her on the platform is a black music stand, and she's put the lyric cards on it. "Oh, honey," she says to Tim, who's still hanging lights, "you'll get the light on that stand, right?" "Sure, Rosemary." "Don't forget that one. I mean, never mind the one on me, just hit that stand."

They go through the rundown, Rosemary pausing to say, "OK, there'll be some talk here . . . ." Allen and Dante sit watching from the opposite banquette. She was right about the view. There, in the floor to ceiling glass panels behind the musicians, poised at the very top of New York City, is panoramic white.

They do a Johnny Burke/Jimmy Van Heusen medley of three songs that Bing Crosby used to sing, "But Beautiful," "Moonlight Becomes You," and "Like Someone in Love." "Hey! I can read great!" she exclaims suddenly, the light having come on the music stand. Her relief is visible. They go on to start the new Dave Frishberg song she is putting in this year, a bossa nova called "Let's Eat Home." "Wait, wait," she says, stopping them in their introduction. "I won't be able to get all the words in. You have to start slower." "OK." John starts them again, with a slower beat.

Rosemary likes to tell people she inherited John from Woody Herman, which is sort of true. John is one of a handful of young musical director/arrangers who are chronologically of one generation, but have the training and professional sensibilities of another. He is forty-one, a native of Brooklyn, and of Italian extraction, like a lot of the big-band musicians Rosemary used to pal around with in her Tony Pastor days.

It's more complicated than just having a feel for standard jazz and pop. A good litmus test for which generational sensibilities a musican has is how he or she makes a record. Jazz musicians and singers who got their start before the '60s go into the studio and record "live"—

they get together and play and sing. That's it. They may do more than one take, but it's more or less like a performance. Contemporary pop and rock musicians go into the studio and lay down one track at a time, overdubbing the layers of each component until they have just the effect they want; one musician may not ever physically be in the same place at the same time as another doing the same song. Most contemporary music albums take months. Rosemary's latest, *Still on the Road*, was two days in the studio. That's the way they recorded before there was the technical capability of doing anything else; they just went in and did it. Anyone without that training, which is pretty much anyone under the age of fifty-five, would have a heart attack at the idea.

After graduating from the Eastman School of Music, John went to work for the Woody Herman band as an arranger, and touring the country as his big-band predecessors had done, he learned by necessity. He met Rosemary in the mid-1980s when she and Herman collaborated on an album for Concord Jazz, their mutual record label, and John provided some of the arrangements. He left Herman shortly afterward, and has worked with Rosemary ever since. He has a feel for swing and for style that she's comfortable with. Oddo is in charge of seeing through all the music-related details of Rosemary's performances, from arrangements to deciding with Rosemary which musicians to hire in any given place. "When we work in New York with this kind of a small jazz group, there's a lot more freedom and improvisation," Oddo says, "and Rose really likes that, she really likes the guys to play. There's also more freedom in the kind of material we do in New York; we'll do more 'in' stuff, like the Dave Frishberg songs. Rose really loves this job. And she'll put together the whole rundown. She called me up and said, 'I want to do this, this, and this—and I don't know about right here—but then I want to do this.' And we kind of talked it through and figured it out. She really puts thought into it."

Rosemary starts thinking about next February's Rainbow and Stars show sometime around May, when she also starts worrying about what to put on the album she will record around October to be released with her New York opening. She tries to feel for a theme, a balance, songs she's loved but has never done, or used to do when she sang with Betty but hasn't done lately. During the summer she'll hear a cocktail pianist in a restaurant play a tune she hasn't thought of in years, and she'll whip out a pen and a little book and write it down, so she can consider putting it in.

At rehearsal, they are running through another of Bing Crosby's stalwarts, a hyperactive up-tempo rendition of "Ol' Man River." "How are we doing on time?" Rosemary asks Allen when they finish, thinking about Hamilton having to get to the airport. "Fine," he says, "we've got lots of time." "OK, what's next?" she says, flipping her cards, "'Hey There'—we don't need to do 'Hey There.' Everybody know 'Hey There'?" There is a general positive mumbling from the guys.

This New York engagement is the most important thing she does all year. She's only been doing it for the last five years, and it has spearheaded her arrival back on the map nationally as a serious musical power. It's important to her for a number of reasons. Mostly, because it's New York. Although she lives in L.A. and spends most of her time giving concerts in towns across the country, she readily acknowledges that effectively, New York is the center of the universe. The run here and its concurrent publicity are what gives her national clout. The reviews she gets for this show are what sells her everywhere else in the country for the rest of the year. The show she does here sets the tone for what material she'll do for the rest of the year.

Oddly, there are two professional Rosemary Clooneys, and they are always struggling with each other. One is the Rosemary Clooney who has become the serious pop–jazz icon, with definitive interpretations of the standard repertory that she has built mostly in the last decade or two. That's the Rosemary Clooney of Rainbow and Stars and the yearly albums and the critical following. The other Rosemary Clooney has a lot of the fans. That's the Nostalgia Rosemary: the Rosemary of "Hey There" grown older with all the people who used to listen to her in the '50s, the people who fill her concerts in middle America, and who come for their anniversaries to Rainbow and Stars from Larchmont and want to hear "Come on-a My House." She always sings it for them, because she has a great respect and affection for them. They're her audience, and they made her, and without them, she wouldn't be where she is today. On the other hand, if that side of her were to dominate, she would be relegated to the realm of the nostalgic, like others of her era who may give nice concerts to nice people and rekindle memories, but are not viable artistic forces in the music world.

It's a constant balancing act: one has the musical stature, and— New York and major cities notwithstanding—the other draws the crowds. Added to her dilemma is that a lot of the early material that made her so popular, with a few notable exceptions like "Tenderly," was lesser-quality novelty material that she was forced to record and that she had very little affinity for.

As a concession, she usually throws in "Hey There" as a nostalgic favorite, and will always do a *Reader's Digest* version of "Come on-a My House." Everything else is strictly for her own musical fulfillment. And inevitably, in concerts around the country and on Friday and Saturday nights at Rainbow, those are the two songs that unfailingly draw a sigh of recognition and burst of applause after the first bar.

At the run-through, the band is finishing up Duke Ellington's "Nothin' But the Blues," and Warren Vaché, who has the big solo in this number and has been chewing gum while he plays, hits a high G on his cornet before Rosemary comes in with her last phrase.

Tim the lighting man has brought her a glass of water. Bismark Irving, an African-American man in gold-rimmed glasses, who presides over the room as its maitre d', comes in to say hello and sit in on the rest of the rehearsal, which is almost over. They run through the last couple of numbers. Scott Hamilton has packed up his saxophone in a flash and is off to the airport with a "See you later."

Outside the windows, it has stopped snowing, and the view has cleared. Rosemary only dawdles a moment, and is back in the dressing room to get her coat. A girl dressed in the Rainbow Room's traditional gray elevator-operator uniform with the round hat at a jaunty angle shows her that flowers have been arriving there, too, and they're sitting on the counter where they sell vintage jewelry and stuffed animals. "How do you think the rundown is?" she asks Allen on the way out. By the elevator, she runs into Charlie Baum, a youngish man with dark hair and glasses, whose father is Joe Baum, who owns the Rainbow Room complex. Charlie also works for the firm.

"I like Charlie," she says in the car on the way back to the hotel. She's looking forward to a nap before she has to start getting ready around 4:00 or 4:30. "Great," she says. "I can get an hour." She looks at her watch. "I can get an hour and a half."

10

There are certain places in New York, like the Carlyle, that people love to go to because they make every tourist feel like a New Yorker. The Rainbow Room has the distinction of making every New Yorker feel like a tourist. It's the view. You can't help it; it catches you by surprise. It's not that Rainbow and Stars, the cabaret arm of the famed nightclub, isn't as inside, or happening, or hip as the next place. In fact, Rainbow and Stars is closer to the Broadway community than most other places, and the trendy and show biz suck up their champagne and seafood bisque regularly, especially during the week, when the out-of-towners are safe in suburbia.

It's only that just when New Yorkers are there on the 65th floor, feeling quintessentially sophisticated because living in New York they see it all, they make the mistake of looking out the window. And it's breathtaking. Hundreds of thousands of yellow and blue and green lights. Actually flickering. Stretching out for miles in every direction, silhouetting a dwarfed skyline. They boast that you can see ten bridges. Who's going to argue? You probably can. And expanses of blackness where Central Park should be, and the Hudson River snaking a path through the glitter to meet the blue-black sky. You can have lived in New York every day of your life, doing whatever New Yorkers do, and then go up there and look out the window and say, "So this is what it feels like to be in New York." You see why the tourists come.

When you step off the elevator on 65, there are two coat checks on either side of the elevator banks, manned by young men and women in those gray-and-orange '30s-style uniforms. They all look like aspiring actors or singers. They greet you and ask you where you're going so they can direct you. Down the hall to the left, for dining and dancing, is the celebrated Rainbow Room, with its polished-wood sunken dance floor that rotates slowly, and two alternating bands playing, Latin and swing, surrounded by enormous high-ceilinged walls of glass showing off The View.

In the other direction is a short hall and on the left-hand side, the Rainbow Promenade—the bar. On the right is the circular lobby for

Rainbow and Stars, with a glass counter selling jewelry and stuffed animals that are also taken around on trays, cigarette-girl style, by uniformed young women. On one wall there is a bank of nine television screens, silently flickering with different stations or with scrolling information about upcoming events, around which there are always people standing zombie-like, having become mesmerized on their way to or from the rest room. Other walls are hung with a photo history of Benny Goodman and his orchestra. Off to the right, the area narrows and there is the entrance to the cabaret room. It's a narrow room from side to side, very long, with a low, drop-panel ceiling. The right edge is lined with semicircular banquettes and tables, and near the entrance are two carpeted steps down to the "pit," where tables ring the performer's platform; the two levels are separated by a brass rail. The View runs along the back wall, behind the platform.

Everything about it is shiny and deco, from the brass inlay on the paneled walls to the metallic mesh tablecloths with the souvenir plastic-faceted "diamonds" and "rubies" and metallic stars strewn around. The room seats about ninety, but it's more spread out than a place like the Carlyle, so it looks much bigger.

Regis Philbin shows up for Rosemary's opening as he said he would, with his wife, Joy, and Bismark puts them at a table in the pit directly in front of where Rosemary will be singing. Julie Wilson is also among the crowd, as is jazz pianist Barbara Carroll and opera singer Eileen Farrell. Rosemary's two youngest children, Rafael and Monsita, are there with their spouses, sitting up by the rail where their mother can turn her head slightly to her right and see them there. Monsita keeps jumping up from her dinner to check back in the dressing room and offer moral support. Rosemary is there, nervously taking the rollers out of her hair and combing it through, fixing her makeup, and wishing she could just skip the opening entirely and go right to the second night.

They've decided to hold the start of the show tonight ten minutes, until 8:40. A young woman "cigarette girl" moves about the lobby and bar selling stuffed animals from a tray hung around her neck. Her name is Rhonda, and she wants to be an actress. At 8:20, John Oddo knocks on the dressing-room door and disappears inside for a confab, emerging a few minutes later. At 8:35, Rosemary appears, ready to go onstage, in the dark blue, scoop-neck, beaded Mackie gown, with its long sleeved beaded over-cape of the same blue. Waiting outside the door to the room, she greets the musicians, who have been loitering in the adjoining windowed lounge just beyond. At 8:38, it's time for them to go in ahead of her. "OK, guys, let's do it," she says to them, and they file into the room, taking their places with their instruments. Bismark closes the doors to the room, but not before he's let her in, and she stands waiting in the dark just inside the doors, unseen by the audience.

A voice over the loudspeaker reminds people to refrain from talking or smoking during the show and then announces, "Ladies and gentlemen, Rosemary Clooney." John gives a nod, and Warren Vaché plays a seven-note intro on his muted cornet, and the band joins in with the Brazilian rhythms of the opening number, as Rosemary enters to applause, escorted by Dante down the two dark steps to the pit. Up on the platform, she picks up the microphone in time to come in with the words about quiet nights of quiet stars.

Behind her, all the lights of the panorama below have come out on cue, making any previous worry that the room would be fogged in seem paranoid. The familiar husky-smooth voice with the catch in it sounds fine, the cold and the nervousness only showing themselves in a shortness of breath when she talks. "I'm glad you're here," she tells the audience. "God, I wish I could just start on the second night. You know?"

The reason this job is so important to her is not limited to reviews or stature. It's because in a room this small, where people have faces, she can follow to its conclusion her natural affinity for just standing up there and saying what she has to say. Watching Rosemary perform is almost like not watching a performance at all. It's more like being there while one of your talented relatives stands up at a family birthday party and does a few songs and talks to you in between. She comments on the day, or cracks wise with the musicians, and varies her remarks about the material a little every night, in search of the perfect laugh. There is nothing remotely casual about what she does. She just does it with the appearance of ease and comfort, and the only giveaway is when she mops her face with the white handkerchief that sits beside her glass of water on the piano.

She tells the audience that her last album, *Do You Miss New York?*, has just been nominated for a Grammy. She interrupts the applause with, "And I was on this stage last year when I'd been nominated for an album called *Girl Singer*, and I learned that Tony Bennett won. And this year—I mean—listen to who's in this category: Nancy Wilson; the wonderful Diane Schuur; Tony Bennett; and Barbra

47

Streisand." She gets a laugh. "I mean—how do I get out of this category? I think they should have a category for Women Over 65 Who Were Born in the Ohio Valley.

"I called up Matt Dennis, and I told him to send me every lyric Tom Adair ever wrote for 'Let's Get Away from It All,'" she tells the audience, "and he did; he sent me like thirty-five choruses of it. So I figure I'll do thirty-five choruses of that, and then I'll do a couple of choruses of 'Come on-a My House,' and we'll all go home early." She gets a big laugh, and the band starts up an introduction. "'Let's take a boat to Bermuda,'" she sings, shifting her weight from side to side, turning her head to look at every part of the room with a gentle smile, snapping the fingers of her left hand, bobbing her head to the beat. "'Let's take a kayak to Quincy or Nyack'"—each line is a simple declaration; she slightly lowers the mike from her face between phrases (as is her habit) and then raises it again in time to continue, as though she's just thought of what to say next. When she reaches for a note, her eyes scrunch up behind the blue-tinted glasses. (She always performs in glasses. She tried contact lenses years ago, but after one folded up on her when she was driving on the freeway in California, that was it.) "'Let's get away from it all!'" she insists, and then, giving over the floor to the musicians for a few bars, she propels the guys on with a shouted "Ho!" as she turns away from the audience, adding a "Go, Scotty" as Hamilton wails away on his saxophone solo.

Her visions of the pop repertory, swing or ballad, are colored with a husky-smooth, introspective warmth. If the sound of a singing voice could be measured in degrees Fahrenheit, Rosemary's would be exactly 98.6—body temperature. The effect on the listener, as the sound washes over, is to understand the argument for birthing babies in water.

Rosemary is the Walter Cronkite of music. Both of them, in their work, say what they have to say plainly and directly, and you accept it without the slightest doubt that what you're hearing is the absolute, honest truth. And if the truth should be difficult or painful, somehow the fact that they're the ones telling you makes it easier to bear.

Here's the rundown for Rosemary's Rainbow and Stars show:

"Corcovado (Quiet Nights)" (Antonio Carlos Jobim, music; Gene Lees, lyrics)
"Let's Get Away from It All" (Matt Dennis, music; Tom Adair, lyrics)

"But Beautiful"/"Moonlight Becomes You"/"Like Someone in
   Love" (medley; Jimmy Van Heusen, music; Johnny Burke,
   lyrics)
"Ol' Man River" (Jerome Kern, music; Oscar Hammerstein II,
   lyrics)
"Hey There" (Richard Adler and Jerry Ross, music and lyrics)
"Nothin' But the Blues" (Duke Ellington, music; Don George,
   lyrics)
"We'll Be Together Again" (Frankie Laine, music; Carl Fischer,
   lyrics)
"Let's Eat Home" (Dave Frishberg, music and lyrics)
"Still Crazy After All These Years" (Paul Simon, music and lyrics)
"How Deep Is the Ocean" (Irving Berlin, music and lyrics)
"Come on-a My House" (William Saroyan, Ross Bagdasarian,
   music and lyrics)
"Will You Still Be Mine?" (Matt Dennis, music; Tom Adair, lyrics)
"Take Me Back to Manhattan" (Cole Porter, music and lyrics)

At the end of every New York show, she's made it a tradition to
sing "Will You Still Be Mine?" It's her own nostalgia, and she tells the
audience how it reminds her of her first glimpse of the city in the late
'40s when she and her sister, Betty, came in through the Lincoln
Tunnel with the Tony Pastor band, and how the next night Pastor
took them to the clubs on 52nd Street and she heard Ella Fitzgerald
sing live for the first time. "It was the most exciting city in the world
then," she says, and turns to look out the windows. "And it ain't too
bad tonight."

But it's not really the end of the show, and everyone knows that.
They know, through the cheers and applause, that there's going to be
an encore, and Rosemary knows it too. When it quiets down she says,
"Well, I could pretend to go off and come back on again to do one
more. But why don't I just save you and me both a little time, and I'll
just do it." At which point she launches into "Take Me Back to
Manhattan."

The comfort factor is so high in a Clooney show because she's
learned to trust the audience. That if you make a mistake you just
start over again ("although Margaret Whiting really has the gift of
making up words if she's forgotten them," she says. "One time in
'Moonlight in Vermont' she said, 'Treetops on a carousel . . . '
Nobody blinked. Another time, 'Footsteps on a sunny shore . . . ' In

Vermont?!") Trust is why the music stand with the crib sheets can stay next to her, when earlier in her career it would never have been there. Trusting the audience is one of the things she learned from Bing Crosby when they were touring together in the years before his death. "I remember I was doing Paul Simon's '50 Ways to Leave Your Lover,' and I was in the wings beforehand working on it because I was having trouble with the words, and he saw me standing there, and I was really worried about it. And he said, 'So take a piece of paper out there with you with the words. They're not going to form a posse and come up and get you. That's not their job.' It gave me such insight. He trusted them totally; and they trust you as long as you aren't trying to put anything over on them."

People respond to her in part because of her sense of maternal hip—intuitive, intelligent, without pretense, projecting an acceptance of the universe. The heart of Rosemary's artistry is not rooted in style or passion. Rather, coupled with her rhythmic and vocal talents, what pervades her work is a compassionate wisdom in which life's bumpy and joyous passages are simply part of an organic design. She didn't always feel that way.

* 11 *

*I*n 1968, Rosemary was on another stage, this one at a club in Reno. This time she was having a breakdown. She looked out at the people in the audience who'd come to see her that night. "Why are you here?" she said to them. "This is so unimportant, what I'm doing. You don't care about me. I'm not a monkey in a cage. I'm a person." Then somebody made the mistake of shouting out for "Come on-a My House," which she had grown to despise. She hurled abuse. The audience was stunned. Then she said, "You want to hear how 'Come on-a My House' really sounds without my voice on it?" and she turned to the band and said, "Play it, gentlemen." And she walked off the stage. Within days she would awake in the psychiatric ward, held down by restraining straps.

"The whole country had a nervous breakdown in 1968," she says. Robert Kennedy's assassination. Martin Luther King's assassination. Vietnam was raging. A generation was in revolt. It was a year the country came close to blowing apart at the seams. For Rosemary, the problems went deeper, and had begun much earlier.

The treadmill of recording, movies, television, concerts, and club dates had been accelerating since she'd hit stardom. Added to that were the pressures of home life. Raising five children, she was separated from them much more than she wanted to be. "For many years Joe and I schlepped them all over the world," she says. "But then they were going to school, and I couldn't anymore. So it was always a choice. And there were some times I couldn't be there."

Her marriage to Ferrer had grown more and more difficult. As with many couples in show business, they were constantly working in opposite places, crisscrossing each other, then flying to another city, or back home to spend brief time together before flying out again for the next job. Apart from that, the marriage was plagued by his repeated infidelities, the first of which she learned about by overhearing it in a conversation on her honeymoon. "You know, I wasn't prepared for that," she says now. "I really was not prepared for that. Joe used to have one kind of book that he kept hidden. So I'd, you know, look at it and see who was in it. You know, it's silly to think that somebody's going to change totally. But when you're very young and you really fall in love, and want to get married and have children and raise a family, you think everything's going to be perfect and wonderful, and he's never going to meet anybody else. And there's no experience that can tell you any different."

The marriage foundered. They got back together and tried again, but it didn't work out any better than it had before, and by the end of the marriage, Rosemary, as well, found herself in an affair with someone else. In 1966, they were finally divorced. While Ferrer went back to New York, where most of his work was in the theatre, Rosemary and the children continued to live in the house in Beverly Hills where she still makes her home today.

"I think women always find fault with themselves if things aren't working perfectly," she says. "You find a way to blame yourself."

That had been programmed into her from a very early age. Growing up as the oldest child in an unstable household, she had always believed that it was her responsibility to fix everything for everyone, to take care of everything. "Rosemary's the strong one," she had heard her whole life. "She can handle it." But nobody was taking care of Rosemary.

She had begun to feel more and more that she had become a commodity, valued only for the tones that came out of her throat and the material rewards they brought, from which everyone was taking their cut. She'd begun to feel that the audience was only interested in her for her glossily packaged entertainment value, with no insight or caring into who she was as a human being. As a woman and artist of increasing sophistication, she inwardly raged at the cute novelty material, like "Come on-a My House," that had made her fortune, and that, no matter what she did, audiences kept clamoring for. She was rapidly losing not only the will to perform, but all the joy she'd ever had in singing, and the void was being filled by anger.

But it was the addiction to prescription drugs—downers—that pushed her to the edge, and finally outside reality, and propelled the descent into madness that would find her institutionalized, restrained, and from which she would emerge without a career.

She had been taking barbiturates for years. Everyone did. In the '50s, they were popped like jelly beans, freely prescribed by doctors for sleeping or smoothing the edges off, just as amphetamines were freely distributed for weight loss or lethargy. Though she would use amphetamines to lose weight after her children were born, or for an occasional antidote to exhaustion, she prefered the smooth time that downers gave her, and her dependence on drugs like Percodan and Seconal increased with time. "Any kind of downer was wonderful," she says, "and I went spinning off."

The crisis began in the months before she would turn forty. She was taking so many pills that they began to have the opposite effect on her. She was up to six Seconal capsules a night, an amount that would have overdosed anybody who had not built up a tolerance. Yet she was unable to sleep at all, wired all the time, and compulsively on the go, never coming to rest.

She became manic-depressive, flying high and partying one minute, and the next on a crying jag, consumed by despair. She began to exhibit a Jekyll-and-Hyde personality, her native decent nature turning on a dime to spells of berating everyone around her, screeching orders, complaining about working conditions (which she had never done in her life), and generally throwing herself around, demanding to be treated like a "star."

The obsession with the pills ran her life, and she was constantly in fear of running out. She would be invited to a dinner party, and at the first opportunity would be in her hostess's medicine cabinet, pilfering whatever she could find. She worked out a system of hiding small caches of pills in different parts of her luggage, so she could travel with a significant supply and not be stopped at customs. "I found out that to get drugs was the easiest thing in the world when I traveled," she says, "because I'd call the house doctor and say I left my prescription at home. I'd take Seconal, and they'd say, 'What do you need?' and I'd say, 'Well, I just need two.' You ask for two, they give you a hundred."

From time to time her jaw would lock from the dosage, and she would have to call the doctor, who would give her a shot of Demerol, which would knock her out enough to unlock it. That she is not dead because of all this she attributes only to the fact that she was not a big drinker, and never washed down the drugs with alcohol, a combination that has killed many of her colleagues.

Rail-thin and not eating, she was becoming more and more a woman possessed, her bouts of irrationality and conversational non sequiturs increasingly noticed by the people around her. They knew something was very wrong, but for the most part, they didn't know what. "Rosemary, you need some rest," they'd tell her, looking concerned. "You've been working too hard." She didn't know what they were talking about. Her reactions and the things she was saying made perfect sense to her.

She was booked into a tour of the Far East a few months before her fortieth birthday. She had been having an affair with a twenty-five-year-old musician, who broke things off just before she was to leave, though she had implored him not to.

The lines between reality and what was beyond were beginning to blur for her. Starting in Japan, she cut a swath across the Far East, blowing up at people for imagined slights, making unreasonable demands and going on exorbitant spending sprees. Yet the more she threw herself around, the more invisible she felt. The only time people could see her, she felt, was when she was singing. And then what they were seeing wasn't really her at all.

She had long been outspoken against the war in Vietnam, and had been scheduled at one time to make a stop to entertain the troops. When the Tet offensive rendered that impossible, her disappointment at not going fed her growing paranoia that somehow she was being persecuted. Instead, while in Manila, she made a visit to the veterans' hospital at Clark Air Force Base. As she visited the rows and rows of maimed young boys, where in each succeeding ward their injuries were more horrific, she was momentarily brought back out of herself to touch reality again. Numbed by what she saw, but never acceding to the nurse's instruction to stop when she'd had enough, all she could think to do as she sat helplessly by their bedsides was to fill little books full of names and telephone numbers of their loved ones back home. On returning to California, she made every call.

Back home for her fortieth birthday, she was off to work again, and her erratic behavior and the autocratic power plays she now reveled in were joined by memory lapses in which whole chunks of her activities represented complete blanks. It was her involvement in Robert Kennedy's presidential campaign and the way it ended that sent her over the edge.

She had worked ardently in his brother JFK's 1960 campaign, and being a fellow Irish-American, she had been friendly with the Kennedy family, especially with Robert and Ethel. When they asked her to appear at a few rallies while he was making the campaign push in California, she was delighted to do whatever she could to help. She was quickly caught up in the fervor of the campaign, and in the wave of hope for what this man, in the presidency, would do to heal the country. She walked around in a Kelly-green suit flashing a coat lining studded with Kennedy buttons. She flew down with his party to campaign in the Republican stronghold of San Diego, and then back to Los Angeles to appear with him at the Ambassador Hotel. She was among those at the Ambassador, that night, who heard the shots ring out from the pantry, as in a recurring nightmare, Robert Kennedy was gunned down just as his brother had been less than five years before.

She instinctively grabbed for her two oldest children, who had come to the rally with her, and in the bedlam in which a gunman was still loose, hid with them under a television set, saying the Rosary until they were dragged out of the hotel by her musical director just as the police and ambulance arrived in a wail of sirens.

In the days that followed, the country watched the television coverage of the funeral as though it were a rerun of JFK's assassination in 1963, and Rosemary just snickered at the irony of it all. She had been seized by the paranoid delusion that it was all a hoax. That Robert was not really dead. It was just a strategic ploy, and he would emerge any minute and the nation would recognize the necessity of having him lead it. She couldn't understand how other people couldn't see that, how she was the only one. She wanted to tell people, but when her assertions were not met with the appreciation she expected, she surmised, with a shrewdness mental illness often brings, that they were either in on it or just didn't see.

The reactions of her family and friends to her behavior ranged from disbelief to alarm. Her mother lived with her, looking after the children. When she told her her views, her mother called the doctor, who admitted her to St. John's Hospital in Santa Monica for forced rest. She still never missed her six Seconals a night. And although doctors tried to sedate her with shots of Demerol, her system was so saturated that she could not be sedated. Within a few days, she was out of the hospital and back on the go. (Betty, who had been with her constantly when they were growing up, was now separated by miles and the constraints of raising her own family.)

She went off to her club date in Reno. When Jerry Vale, who was working nearby, came to see her and showed her a copy of a magazine with Robert Kennedy's face on it, she just snickered and said, "Isn't that the most foolish thing you've ever heard in your life?" leaving him staring in total bewilderment.

Through the engagement she was manic, spending money, gambling (she'd never been a gambler), and making a daily list of complaints about everything and everybody to her manager. On the night before she blew up onstage at the audience, she called him at three in the morning and demanded that he call a press conference for 6:00 A.M. sharp, and that she wanted Frank Sinatra there. The more he told her to get some sleep, the more infuriated she became, and she threatened to fire him.

By the morning he'd forgotten all about it and was on his way home, so she set up a press conference with the help of the hotel. The pretext was to announce that she was going to retire. But what she really hoped was that somehow she would be given the opportunity of bringing the whole Robert Kennedy hoax to light. It wouldn't turn out that way. After a few polite questions from reporters about her retirement announcement, and as the conference was breaking up, a *Time* magazine stringer said she looked unhappy, and was everything okay, at which point she said she was upset about Robert Kennedy, and she started to cry. For just a moment, she'd had a grasp of reality.

When she stormed off the stage that night as the band played "Come on-a My House" without her, she slipped past the doctor who was brought to her dressing room to see her between shows, and barefoot, dressed only in a light shift, she ran out and got back to her hotel room, and tore the place apart in a rage. Then she got into her car and in what she now remembers only through a hallucinatory haze, she defied God. She hurtled up the wrong side of the narrow, twisting mountain road to Lake Tahoe, and as the headlights from the oncoming cars came straight toward her then swerved to miss, she decided that if God wanted her to live, she would.

She arrived at the house she'd rented, and one of the next things she remembered was being strapped down to a stretcher with restraints and taken by ambulance to the local hospital. She was then flown by air ambulance back to St. John's Hospital in Santa Monica, the same place where she'd given birth to her five babies. This time, she yelled herself hoarse for them to take off the straps.

She soon convinced the doctors to send her home, albeit with a round-the-clock nurse. At home she was visited by her cousin's husband, a doctor, who was alarmed by what he saw. He immediately called the psychiatrist Dr. J. Victor Monke, who insisted that she sign herself into the psychiatric unit of what is now Cedars-Sinai Hospital in Los Angeles. It was only her priest who convinced her to go.

As soon as she got there, she changed her mind, but it was too late. She'd been committed. She was searched for contraband and they took away her purse. Behind the locked doors of the psychiatric ward, she was taken to her room. And there, the first thing she saw when she looked through the industrial wire barring her window was a large billboard advertising her arch-rival Patti Page, in Las Vegas. It set off such a wave of hostile behavior that they locked her in isolation.

Thus began Rosemary's recovery. During her summer in the hospital, they would take her through withdrawal from the drugs and begin treatment that would turn out to be eight years of analysis and group therapy. It would be difficult, infuriating, discouraging at times. But when they had restored her system to chemical balance, and she slowly returned to herself, she would find something again that signaled the first bud of spring. It was something she had lost a long time ago, something it's difficult to imagine her without. She got back her sense of humor.

*R*osemary waited for the reviews to come out on her Rainbow and Stars opening. The opening was on a Tuesday. Cabaret is not like Broadway theatre; the reviews are not out late that night, when you can sit around eating and drinking with your friends and wait for them. Or the next morning, when you can get it over with. You have to wait. Maybe Thursday, maybe even Friday, or the next week, if the *Times* is busy. You never really know.

She worries about what kind of reviews she's going to get, because of the New York critics' importance in determining, for the rest of the year, her standing as an artist outside New York.

People say to her all the time, "What do you care? You've been in the business a long time, you have fans that love you—what difference does it make?"

It makes a big difference to her. "I don't understand when people say they're not going to read the critics," she says. "I don't know how you can be that insular. It could be bad, but you have to get some outside input. Aside from your friends, who think you're wonderful, and your relatives, who think you're wonderful, and the people who work for you, who'd damn well better think you're wonderful, you've got to have some objective person."

She remembers once doing a show at the Fairmont Hotel in San Francisco, just after having closed in Las Vegas. "I opened at the Fairmont with the same show, really. And because I'd been doing it seven days a week, two shows a night, it was slick. And I wasn't thinking about what I was doing. It had gotten to be a habit. The man who was reviewing for the *Chronicle* was Wasserman. And he nailed me. He said 'Vegas,' too. He said, 'It's a Vegas, slick, glitzy show.' And he was right. He was right on the money. And I wrote him a letter and told him so."

There's another reason that Rosemary—and Barbara, and Julie, and everyone else who does a show—is so concerned about what the critics have to say. They know how important good reviews are for business. And these three women, especially, have been around long enough to know that drawing an audience is the bottom line, and that no one is immune to the bottom line. Julie says it best: "If you don't get the bods in the seats, they don't ask you back."

The *New York Times* is the one that everybody worries about, for obvious reasons. It's like the old TV commercial about some guy in a crowded room that falls silent when he tells someone else that his broker is E. F. Hutton: when the *New York Times* says something, people listen. Which means everybody's worried about what Stephen Holden, who at this time is the critic who covers cabaret, has to say.

Rosemary's review comes out on Thursday. It's a good review, and she's very happy.

Holden writes, for example (referring to "Still Crazy After All These Years"): "Its composer treated the song as a wistful 4 a.m. reflection and Ray Charles has done it as a joyous declaration of eccentricity, but Ms. Clooney interpreted it as a blues-flavored waltz with a common-sense message. Ms. Clooney has always projected the down-to-earth solidity of an unshockable mother confessor, and the years have only deepened her aura of humanity.

"Although her singing today is blunter than it once was, the softer edges of her voice haven't entirely disappeared. Everything she performed on Tuesday was stamped with wisdom, humor and secure rhythmic command." He goes on to talk about the exceptional jazz players backing her up, and runs down some highlights of the program.

She's thinking of dropping Holden a note to thank him.

Rainbow and Stars is also happy the review is favorable. They're a little disturbed, though, at the dearth of superlatives in the review. There's nothing that literally says, "She's the absolute greatest and you have to go out this very minute and make a reservation." There's really no reason that it should be spelled out that way. Holden clearly thinks she's a master artist with definitive readings of her material backed up by six star jazz musicians. And he reviews her show every year, and he always likes it. What more is there to say? Except Rainbow and Stars needs those superlatives to pull out from the review and use in advertising. They've already got an ad running in the *Times* with the slogan "Rosie's Back and Rainbow's Got Her!" There was a little space beside her smiling face where they were planning to put a nice quote from Holden. They're glad that Rosemary's happy. But they're a little leery of the review. They spend the next couple of days trying to figure out what they can pull out and use in the ad. They will end up using a quote from Liz Smith.

"Well," said one of the Rainbow team the day the review came out, "we'll see if the phone rings."

*B*arbara had to wait over a week for her review to come out in the *Times*. It was a tedious, edgy week—again, because of the implications it held for good business. The reason it took so long was that though theoretically she had opened on Tuesday, there was a problem. It was called The Divine Miss M, and she was opening at Radio City Music Hall on the same Tuesday night. It was Bette Midler's much-heralded New York opening of her first national tour in umpteen years, and anybody else in Gotham City who had officially opened on Tuesday night could have jumped off the Brooklyn Bridge singing "Ramona" and nobody would have paid attention.

So Barbara sang, all right, on Tuesday, and the Carlyle advertised and people came. But wisely, everyone had decided that the press opening would be on Friday.

She had some cause to be nervous. In his review of her show last year, Holden had written: "Her new show lacks a firm sense of direction, and includes only minimal patter," mentioning a "great reluctance over the years to change her repertory," and going on to suggest that "the time has come for her to consider lowering the keys of her songs."

This year's show is significantly different, not only in terms of additional material, but in feel, with a bluesy quality. The show is a strong reflection of the new Dorothy Fields album, and with Harold Arlen songs like "Ac-cent-tchu-ate the Positive" and "I Had Myself a True Love," it pushes her into exploring a style heretofore unfamiliar, with lower keys employing a gutsier register.

On Wednesday of the second week, eight days after she's started her Carlyle run, Barbara's press agent, Tony Staffieri, tells her he's heard the *Times* review probably will be in tomorrow's edition, coming out later that night.

When she finishes her first show, she goes up to her suite to wait around in her silk caftan and eat the baked potato that room service has sent up. Tony is there. Wally is there. Her secretary, Louise, is there, and her son. A couple of old friends come up to say hello, and the suite momentarily takes on the carnival atmosphere that it is wont to. "Tony says he hears the review might be in tomorrow's paper," Barbara says. She's nervous.

She shows everybody the orchid bloom that stands in water on the table beside the couch. She cut it herself from one of the legions of orchids she raises in the window of her Riverside Drive apartment. It bloomed for her this morning: two white flowers with magenta and yellow splashes. She had awakened and gone into the living room, and there it was. She wanted it with her in the dressing room. "Isn't it beautiful?" she says as she shows it off proudly. "I mean, it's just so amazing."

It finally comes time to get ready for the 10:45 show, which never starts before eleven. Downstairs, the diners left over from the first show are clearing out, and by the time they're finished, the house is about half empty, not uncommon for a late show on a rainy night early in the week, early in an extended run.

Barbara commences the show. As she moves, the jewels in her dress catch the lights and project swirling constellations onto the ceiling. Ambrose and his staff have seated people in clusters in front of the platform, with any empty tables left for the edges. An already intimate room becomes an even more intimate group. Barbara shines at moments like these, because it's a special chance for her to bond with people on an even more individual level, rather than "put on a show." The sparsity of the crowd, the lateness of the hour, the rain outside—all give the show a "we're just a bunch of people huddled here together" quality. "We're few, but we're mighty," she tells the audience.

"I like to feel connected to people," Barbara says, "not apart from them, or different from them. That's what I try to do in my work. I love to feel that I have moved people, because when I see a performer, I want to be moved. It doesn't have to be sad, I just want to be touched in some way. So that we see we're all together in this boat, somehow. Because we are so alone in this world. Ultimately. We're born alone. We die alone. So if for one moment we can make a human connection, and if for one instant because of it, we can forget how alone we are—why not?"

It would be a long time from her early stardom on Broadway before she would find the spiritual satisfaction of people gathered around her, as they are gathered late on this rainy Wednesday night.

$*$ *14* $*$

$\mathcal{I}$n 1966, Barbara was cast as the spunky ingenue, Magnolia, in the Lincoln Center revival of *Show Boat*. She wasn't feeling particularly like a spunky ingenue. She was about to turn forty. Her marriage of thirteen years to David LeGrant had ended the year before, and with it the perceived vision of idyllic life in suburban Long Island. She had moved with her young son into an apartment in the city and continued to work. She was looking down the road, and spunky ingenues were not what she saw in the eternal landscape.

Nevertheless, she went on to play the innocent nightingale of the "Cotton Blossom," steaming up and down the Mississippi while singing "You Are Love" and "Make Believe" to characteristically enthusiastic reviews. She found playing the part thankless and irritating.

"Even before, when I was thirty-five or thirty-six," she says, "I began to think, 'Where am I headed? What do I do now? I can't keep playing these parts. What do I do now?' I even gave it a name, 'middlescence,' instead of adolescence. I think a lot of people go through middlescence. We realize, 'I'm not this young anymore. How do I shift gears?' You have to get your ducks in a whole different row."

As a child and a young woman she had always been tremendously insecure, going back to an unstable childhood in Atlanta. Even when she was an adult, at the top of her profession, married with a new son, she never felt like she had it all. Closing night of every show she thought, "Will I ever be hired again?" and when the new script would come, she'd think, "Will I ever be able to do it again?" "It's amazing that I should be in this business," she likes to say. The paradox of Barbara's personality is that the performing side of her nature, what she likes to call "the showoff" side, was always immune. When she was working—onstage, singing—she was sure of what she was doing. In life, it was different. "I never felt like, 'I'm safe, I'm married, I'm working,'" she says. "I was always scared. I couldn't take it in; I couldn't appreciate what was happening."

From a southern background that celebrated the helpless female, and coming to stardom in the age of 1950s womanhood, she had married a man to whom she looked for authority. "David had very strong ideas about things," she says. "And it was like, 'Oh, well then, I don't have to think about it, he'll sort of do all my thinking for me.'"

Early in her marriage, she had been tremendously dependent on her husband, terrified that something was going to happen to him—even though she was earning a considerable independent living. The divorce had been coming on for a long time. When it finally happened, she took it with mixed feelings—a sense of relief, mingled with terror at the thought of being on her own. It contributed heavily to her crisis of confidence. "I had married this man who I thought had all the answers," she says.

She also was never fully able to appreciate the professional status she had earned, though the press and public were all over her as she kept racking up the shows and albums. "I didn't have any idea whatsoever of any impact I may have had on the theatre," she says. "The first time somebody said to me, 'Somebody's asking for a Barbara Cook type,' it was, 'What? I've come to be a type? What is this?'"

She turned forty, and *Show Boat* was over, and she began a gradual downward spiral that would mire her deeper and deeper in emotional, physical, and financial disarray.

"Middlescence" was upon her, and it began with her questioning her life. Suddenly, she was struck by the belief that what she had been doing up until now—musical comedy—was a valueless exercise, especially in light of what was going on in the world: things like Vietnam and political upheaval. She saw her professional achievements as having been pointless.

She may not have known what she wanted to do with herself from then on, but she knew that she wasn't going to play another ingenue. At the same time, the American musical theatre, as everyone had known it, was disintegrating rapidly in the wake of a show called *Hair*, which would go on to run 1,705 performances. (*The Sound of Music* ran fewer than 1,500.) *Hair* and its followers, *Jesus Christ, Superstar, Godspell,* and a slew of other rock musicals, sounded the death knell not only for the traditional Broadway musical theatre of *The King and I* and *Bells Are Ringing,* they also signaled the death of traditional show music, which, bent into pop or jazz renditions, had always provided the foundation for the music of American mass culture. No more. Rock and roll had changed all that, as it had the Broadway stage. And if Barbara thought she was getting too old to play another ingenue, she sure wasn't going to play a nude one with a guitar.

She began to use food to sedate herself. Her addiction to it became increasingly stronger. She would be offered a job, and scripts would come in; she turned them down because she felt she had to lose weight first. Then she couldn't lose weight, so she didn't work. "I kept thinking, 'I can't let people see me like this,'" she says.

Actually, she was using her weight as an excuse not to work because she needed not to work, needed to regroup, but couldn't acknowledge it as such. She didn't know what to do with herself. She was sinking into a depression that was growing deeper and deeper. The only structure she had to her day was to get her son off to school in the morning.

Then there were the crippling panic attacks, which had come on suddenly one day during the run in *Show Boat*, while she was across the street at the Ginger Man. She had never heard of panic attacks, and she thought she was having a heart attack. Terrified, she wound up in the emergency room of Roosevelt Hospital—where the moment the doctor looked at her he said, "You're having an anxiety attack," and gave her an intramuscular shot of a tranquilizer. It was the beginning of a period in which, on and off, she would be plagued by the terrifying episodes. From that day on, she would never know when they were going to come. They wouldn't necessarily be that severe, but she slid into the vicious cycle that rules those who suffer from panic disorder. The fear of getting one and not knowing where you'll be when it hits breeds its own panic attacks. In the late '60s and early '70s, panic disorder was not yet recognized for the illness that it is. Not knowing what was wrong with her (and she never talked about it) was frightening in itself, and only added to her general feeling of somehow being defective. Though she was seeing a therapist for her depression, there was not much he was doing for the anxiety. Instead, she learned to talk herself through the attacks, and by breaking down the overwhelming feeling into recognizable symptoms, she was able to recognize the same symptoms the next time and reason with herself that she was going to be okay.

Before she knew it, her drinking had gotten out of control. Even then, instead of recognizing that excessive drinking was a problem, she viewed it as more calories, which only further prevented her from losing weight (and thereby accepting work). "Like with so many people who drink too much," she says, "it's there before you know it. It becomes a habit, and then you don't know how you can live your life without it. It's the way you get through life."

She was immobilized, and daily she put off dealing with her problems. Until finally the day came when the money ran out. Finally, she had to take a job.

She wasn't ready for it. It was 1973, and the job was in summer stock, touring in a revue called *The Gershwin Years*. Along with Barbara, it was to star other veterans from Broadway's heyday, Helen Gallagher, Harold Lang, and Nancy Dussault, who would later be replaced on the road by Julie Wilson.

"It was the first time I'd appeared at that weight," she says. "It was so hard to go onstage for the first time weighing that much. Particularly the way our society views overweight. It was so hard—it was really painful."

Audiences, who remembered the fresh-faced young girl with whom they had fallen in love, weren't ready for who she had become. She wasn't Marian the Librarian anymore. And they sometimes told her so. "The world does not help," she says. "At one point early in the run of this thing, I was standing in the lobby of the theatre with Helen. And this lady came up to me and said, 'Oh, you're Barbara Cook!' And I said, 'Yes.' She said, 'Are you pregnant?' I said, 'No.' She said, 'You shouldn't be so good to yourself,' meaning I shouldn't feed myself so well. But I didn't get it. So in my embarrassment, I kept trying to make polite conversation with the lady until Helen dragged me away."

That was only the beginning. Though there were stirrings in her career that would point her in a new direction, at that time they also served to put her before the public in an emotional and physical condition that was not improving, but worsening. (When she was to appear at Carnegie Hall a couple of years later, the *New York Times* ran an article in the Sunday Arts and Leisure section with "before" and "after" pictures.)

She had become an object of ridicule for some, and felt like she was on display. She tried not to pay attention, and learned to react with more than stunned silence. She was on a talk show when a man called in and said to her, "You used to be so beautiful." "I still am," she answered. "It's like you're not a real person," she says, "like you don't have feelings. If I hadn't had to make money, I wouldn't have been out there. Because I wouldn't have had the courage."

Even so, she was forced to give up her apartment when she could no longer keep up with the rent. She consigned her furniture and possessions to storage, and for over a year, she lived with friends and in hotels, until she eventually found a sublet.

Amid her personal turmoil, the only level on which she was able to function was her singing. By this time, she had begun to shape a solo career in cabaret, and had been accepting engagements. But the bind continued to be that she had to be out there to make money at a time when her physical and emotional condition was compromised by the overeating and drinking and continued inability to stop her behavior. Every day was a constant battle to gain control. And despite the success she began to experience again in her work, she lived with a constant sense of failure.

Something had to give. The moment came in 1976 when, while playing a small club in California, her body gave out altogether. She was able to play only fifteen out of twenty-one performances of the engagement. And every evening, by the time she was ready to start the show, she was already exhausted. Finally, her body just wouldn't do it anymore.

It was lucky for her that it wouldn't. She was diagnosed with hypoglycemia, and back in New York, a physician friend took her in hand. She was put on a high protein, low-carbohydrate diet, the prescribed treatment for hypoglycemia at the time. She was forced to stop drinking, and somehow found the willpower to do it. She had been so frightened by her physical collapse in California that, for the first time, it was clear to her what she had to do.

Barbara had hit rock bottom, and fright was what had finally turned her around. As the months progressed, her health began to improve, both physically and psychologically. Some of the weight began to come off. As she stopped drinking, the depression began to lift. The panic attacks would still come, but she found herself better able to handle them.

For the first time in years, she saw a future for herself. But to meet it, she would first have to learn to be comfortable with the person she had become.

Barbara finishes her second show at the Carlyle. The waiters bring the tabs to their tables, and the people pay them and begin to leave. "Goodnight," says Ambrose the maitre d' as they go through the glass door to the coat check outside in the foyer, where the coat-check lady has been doing a rush business selling the Dorothy Fields album, displayed on the counter. Outside, the rain has stopped, and they push through the revolving door out onto midnight Madison Avenue, where a couple of yellow cabs have pulled up to the hotel, waiting for people to come out.

In the Cafe, Barbara has gone over to talk with a table of friends sitting with Adam. She stands behind the banquette where they sit, leaning on the back of it. "You know, Tony says the *Times* review is probably in tomorrow's edition," she says. She's still waiting to hear. It's five after twelve, and if it is going to be in tomorrow's edition, it's out by now.

Tony Staffieri does come in. He's a tall, balding, loquacious man who smiles a lot because he has his own PR agency. He's smiling now, and he goes right over to Barbara. He's called someone at the *Times*, and he's heard Stephen Holden's review. He's smiling for a reason. "It's a money review," he tells her. "It's a money review. It's fabulous. He loved it." "Oh, good," she says, pleasantly. "Isn't that nice?" But the look of relief on her face is considerable.

Holden has turned himself around on last year's review.

"Sometimes all it takes for an artist to reach a deeper level of expression is a seemingly small adjustment in technique. That is what Barbara Cook, one of Broadway's greatest lyric sopranos, has accomplished in her new cabaret act. . . ."

"The material in Ms. Cook's program is also unusually strong," he writes, and goes on to talk about the Dorothy Fields album. "The most sweeping change wrought by Ms. Cook has been the release of her southern roots. In her performances on Friday of 'I Must Have That Man,' 'I'm Beginning to See the Light,' 'Ac-cent-tchu-ate the Positive,' 'Lullaby in Ragtime,' and 'Carolina in the Morning,' the

Atlanta-born singer showed that underneath the decorous Broadway soprano a sultry blues belter has been lurking.

"Friday's show ended with a stunning encore: an unmiked rendition of 'What'll I Do?' with a flowing line from which Ms. Cook extracted equal measures of yearning and reassurance."

Tony is right. It should be what's known as a money review.

After Julie's opening at the Russian Tea Room, her reviews trickle in on schedule. Wayman Wong, the critic from the *Daily News* who had been slurred by the drunken woman who wouldn't shut up, writes in his review: "When the chic chanteuse was singing Cole Porter, she was mesmerizing . . . Her 'Down in the Depths (on the 90th Floor)' was a poignant portrait of a lonely socialite. As her eyes watered and her eyelashes fluttered, you could feel a flood of despair welling within her. And her stirring 'From This Moment On' was out of this world.

"Wilson also shimmied and shook the room as she sang, 'You're Nobody Till Somebody Loves You,' with her gravelly growl.

"But she seemed ill at ease with her new songs," he notes, and goes on to tell how, "looking strangely distracted, she fumbled with the lyrics" to the new material. "Maybe it was just a case of opening night jitters," he writes, and mentions that she's unused to working with Mark Hummel—and without Billy Roy.

He then spends a paragraph on what he calls the "boorish old woman," and relates how "I told her she'd been unconscionably rude to Wilson and the rest of the audience; ironically, she turned and told her friends that *I* was rude to her and was lucky to be living in this country!"

But Stephen Holden's review in the *New York Times* wasn't there. And it wasn't there. And it wasn't there.

Here's what Holden had to say about Julie before. "Right now no other cabaret singer brings to the long view of life the searing honesty and depth that Miss Wilson offers."

And before that. "If Miss Wilson's grandeur recalls a bygone era, she is far more than a symbol of times past. A great theatrical interpreter, she infuses songs, both familiar and obscure, with a thunderous dramatic intensity. Pushing a husky contralto to its physical limits, she becomes a kind of emotional lightning rod who at moments seems to be buffeted about by the very lyrics she is interpreting."

And before that. "Miss Wilson's expressive power in a cabaret setting remains unequaled among her peers. At her best, she does more than simply interpret a song. There are moments when a lyric seems to erupt from within her slender, elegantly clothed body like a small, dramatic epiphany."

On the day of Julie's opening, after she had awakened with the cold and was spending her day trying to steady her nerves and her memory for the lyrics to prepare for the impending evening, she was on the phone with Donald Smith, her manager. Smith picked up on the unusual severity of her anxiety. He asked her if she would like him to call off Stephen Holden for the opening, to ask him to wait a few days and come back on a different night. Julie was relieved at the suggestion, because being more secure in her new show before she was reviewed would be a blessing.

So Smith called Holden, and told him the situation, and asked if he could arrange to skip the opening and come back another night. Holden obliged, and to his word, he left her to an opening night free of the looming shadow of the *New York Times*.

There was one problem. He never did come back. The days and then weeks of the engagement would tick by—one, two, three, four—and there was no Stephen Holden. And there was no review in the *New York Times*. And because there was no review, there was also no mention of her show in the "Sounds Around Town" column in Friday's Weekend section, which is fed by current reviews.

Last year, *Times* readers had seen a review and a Sunday feature at the time of the Tea Room run. This year, the only ink Julie would get in the paper would be the small, square ads placed by the Russian Tea Room among the other club ads in Friday's and Sunday's editions.

*T*he epicenter of everyone's anxiety does not fit the popular fantasy of what a critic is supposed to be like. In the movies, they're all like George Sanders in *All About Eve*. They have names like Addison DeWitt, and they're suave men-about-town who oil their way through smart cocktail parties in black tie, stunning everyone with the polished brilliance of their acid tongues. They smoke cigarettes in holders. They begin sentences with "My dear." And if somebody they don't like makes the mistake of addressing them, they say something really, really cutting. You may not understand it, but it's really cutting, and it makes the other person go away looking kind of dumb.

Stephen Holden is a thoughtful man of fifty-two, of medium height, with thinning sandy hair and deep-set blue eyes. Soft-spoken, his manner is, in fact, so shy that when he talks he will frequently look down or over your shoulder.

When there are opening night parties after a show, he seldom stays, usually slipping out shortly after the end of the performance, leaving everyone running around with drinks in their hand asking each other, "Have you seen Stephen Holden? I know he was *here*. Is he gone *already*?" And they try to read what they can into the timing of his departure. It does make people nervous, what he does. After Rosemary's opening, for some reason he left before saying hello to her, as he usually does. She wondered about it for two days, until his review came out.

He lives on the upper floors of an apartment building on the West Side, near Lincoln Center. When he's not out reviewing at a club, or a theatre or screening room, it's where he spends most of his time. Unlike the critics of yore, who'd go into the office after a show to hack out their reviews on the old Remington, Holden rarely sets foot in the *New York Times* building at all. Home is where he does all his work, in a tee shirt and khakis.

The apartment is bright, with a wall unit holding a stereo system and books on music and the performing arts. And CDs. Every record company and publicist in the world who has a CD remotely sounding like any kind of popular music sends one to Holden. Or two.

They're stacked up everywhere, mostly rising like a plastic Tower of Babel from the length and breadth of his glass coffee table.

In the firmament of the *Times*'s cultural coverage, Holden refers to himself as "the utility infielder." He's third-string movie critic, third-string theatre critic, and second-string pop critic, which is where most of his work is concentrated. The main reason he's The Man in cabaret circles is that with his affinity for standard pop and jazz, he's the only critic at the paper with an interest in cabaret, today's repository for most of that music. And as the de facto "cabaret critic," he sees his majority of oneness as a responsibility.

At the *New York Times*, with its mass circulation and national scope, he finds himself in the position of being the champion for an art form and a brand of music that, while resurging in popularity, at the same time is ecologically fragile and needs protection.

It's a lot like the rain forest. Everybody is aware of the complex functions the rain forest performs that have environmental repercussions all over the world. But a lot of people don't grasp that it's actually all about a bunch of trees in Brazil. Cabaret and jazz-based pop music are the same. The standard pop sound track to *Sleepless in Seattle* becomes the number-one selling sound track of the summer, and all over the country people tap their feet to big-band TV commercials for chocolate chip cookies. But the ecological breeding ground for all of it is a group of clubs, mostly in New York, where the music is disseminated by veterans and cultivated by young performers, where new writers write, and where audiences gain new familiarity.

The problem is that any press coverage necessarily fights for precious space with the rockers and rappers, who generally win the mass-appeal sweepstakes. Newspapers, in their quest for more and younger readers, are prone to favor the trend of the moment.

"Cabaret is such a fragile world," Holden says, "and it gets so little publicity, that simply by writing about it as much as I do, I feel I'm sort of helping it to continue. And the *New York Times* is the *New York Times*. So it validates its existence in a way that's important to keep the vocal tradition, and the song tradition that goes with it, alive."

Last year Holden reviewed about 150 performances. That's about three a week. He didn't like everything he saw. But on the whole, even his negative reviews had a constructive tilt to them. He is widely considered one of the more compassionate critics around. It's not always easy, in review after review, day after day, often of the same people over again from year to year. There is always the risk that readers might perceive it as boring.

"I want to write about music," he says. "I see it as analyzing the form, analyzing singers, looking at the historical aspect of it, putting it all into a larger musical context."

Holden concedes that his first allegiance is to the public, whom he's been hired to inform. But for him, as with many critics, work is an ongoing balancing act between "protecting" the public, serving the art form in question, and fulfilling his career potential as a writer.

Readers like witty critics. They like zingers, and quotable quotes that will make them amusing when they repeat them at dinner. Like when George S. Kaufman wrote, "I saw the play at a disadvantage. The curtain was up." Or when Dorothy Parker wrote, "This book should not be tossed aside lightly. It should be thrown with great force." Unless it's your play or book, that's witty.

They don't make critics like Parker and Kaufman anymore, but there are a lot of critics who really, really try. Some of them write well, and are respected. Some of them can't write at all, but their earlier career plans didn't work out, and they drifted into criticism out of a craving to be part of the perceived glamour of show business, enjoying the power that enables them to manipulate at will the lives of the people whose attention they crave. The power to play God is inherent in the job, and the temptation to take advantage of it—especially late at night in solitary communion with a typewriter—is very heady.

The acid-wit trap is also easy to fall into. After all, the critic, too, is a performer with a desire to entertain the reading audience. So if a show is being reviewed, whose performance takes precedence? Purely as a writer, it's more satisfying to be represented by a statement like "Her top notes went through the listener's head like a nail," rather than "Occasional vocal strain suggested that some keys should be lowered."

The difference lies only in the momentary predilection of the reviewer. For the performer, it can mean the difference between finding work, or not.

"I do have an instinct to be cruel, you know," Holden says. "When I was younger, and as a rock critic, I did some very vicious things for pleasure. And the karma of those things was so bad to me, I felt so lousy about it, and so irresponsible for having been so gratuitously cruel and nasty, that I decided I wouldn't do it anymore." He admits that at times even now, if he's in a bad mood, things sometimes creep in that he tries to keep out.

Holden grew up in New Vernon, New Jersey. As a teenager, he played the piano and wrote songs, and was always a popular-music fanatic; classical music, as well. He attended Yale, graduating with a degree in English in 1963. After college he went to work in publishing for nine years. He started writing for *Rolling Stone* magazine as a pop and rock critic, and his first assignment was reviewing Streisand's *Barbra Joan Streisand* album. Two years later, he went to work for RCA records, first as a photo editor and bio writer, for a year and a half, and then as an A&R man, in which capacity he discovered and signed Michael Bolton. "He made two albums for RCA," Holden says. "Nothing happened with him." After Holden left RCA, he wrote a novel about the music business, called *Triple Platinum*, published by Dell. Within the next few years he was freelancing for the *New York Times*, becoming an official freelancer in 1981 and formally joining the staff in '87.

"The downside of what I do is that it's hard to write about the same people over and over again and try to find new things to say. If it's somebody that's new, that you haven't written about before, it's easier. But when you don't want to write about the same people because you're going to repeat yourself, and at the same time you feel a responsibility to let the world know that they're still out there . . . it's tough to make those decisions. But I'm always going to make the decisions to write about them, no matter what."

The critics who cover jazz and cabaret for all the top New York papers tend to be individuals with a genuine affection for what they're writing about. Also, it's a very small community, everybody turns up for the same events all the time. And it's harder to be vicious when, unlike movie, literary, or theatre criticism, the object of your ridicule is right in front of you, and is also likely to run into you by the rest room at somebody else's opening next month.

In terms of judging people, it's a subjective medium. An opera critic can listen to a singer and, if he has ears, can hear whether it's sharp or flat, whether the singer's in good voice or not, or whether the big aria was lackluster, or a difficult tessitura badly negotiated. But if the music is Ellington or Berlin, and the singer is a smoky-voiced veteran backed by a small combo, there is no absolute right or wrong. Judging it is much more nebulous. Pitch shouldn't really be a problem, because unless the singer has special handicaps, the vocal range in this repertory seldom necessitates acrobatics. There are countless different ways to vary a song, any one of them satisfying. So who's to say what's right or wrong?

That, and the fact that a critic's personal likes or dislikes lie in the murky unknown, are the main reasons people like Rosemary or Julie or Barbara, who between them have 150 years' experience in the business, can sweat bullets every time they are waiting for an important review to come out.

Holden has his own methods of scoring a performance, basing his judgments somewhere between his personal taste and what it is that the performer is trying to accomplish with what degree of success. "There are different kinds of cabaret artists," he says. "You know very quickly what kind of cabaret artist you're dealing with, whether it's someone who's really basically a voice, or someone who's really basically an interpreter. Those are the two poles, I guess, by which you can judge things. Usually, if you have a beautiful voice, you want to show off the voice, no matter what. Like Ann Hampton Callaway. She's an interpreter of sad love songs—she's great at that, because there's something in her that relates to it. But it's always in terms of the voice. Someone like Barbara Cook is like that. She's a voice, first. She lets the voice do the work. Then you have more personality voices. Like Julie Wilson, obviously, at this point in her career."

It's the medium's lack of absolutes, and its technically forgiving nature, that celebrates a performer's getting older by putting a premium on the life experience that person can bring to the work. The mass media, however, are traditionally driven by a very different set of values, where the ink, or the air time, goes to capturing whatever is considered "cutting edge." That's why Holden works so hard to get cabaret coverage in the *Times*.

"We live in a culture in which, you know, you're over at thirty-five," he says. "No matter what you do. Because you're just not so sexy anymore, or whatever it is. And it's heartbreaking to me. The idea that you're only interesting if you're the new kid in town. And that if you've slowly polished your art, and you do something year after year after year and really care about it—nobody's going to give a damn because you're just old, and a known quantity.

"The fact that you're a known quantity, that's the worst thing against you, because you've already been codified by everybody else. And there you are, you know. So why write about that anymore? On to the new thing. And I really object to that. Julie's a great example of somebody who doesn't really have a voice now. But a whole lifetime of feeling goes into everything she sings."

The reason Holden never did review Julie at the Tea Room, by the way, was that having forfeited his opening night attendance, his reviewing schedule was so solidly booked for the remainder of her run that he simply couldn't make it back (actually his schedule let up in Julie's last week—but by that time it was too late). With his added movie and theatre reviewing responsibilities, November, right before the holidays, is the height of his season. It was just one of those things.

All their lives, Julie had always promised her two sons that when they got to high school, she would stop working and be with them full-time.

Next to show business, having children had always been the strongest drive in Julie's life. The designer who made her first gown for her debut at the Mocambo had told her never to have children, because it would ruin her figure. "I said, 'Sorry, George; it's have kids or die.' I was so excited with the birth of both kids. I didn't go to sleep for three days—both times. It was like I was charged with electricity; I was on the high of my life."

When the boys, Holt and Mike, were very little, in the early 1960s, she could take them with her when she went out of town for a club date, or on the road with a show. But when they got old enough to go to school, it was no longer possible. And Julie had to earn a living.

As the '60s wore into the early '70s, less and less of her work was in the New York nightclubs that were her stamping ground, anyway. For a good reason. There were no nightclubs anymore. The age of the great, glamorous nightspot was over. In the wake of the social turmoil that spawned Woodstock, the music everyone listened to now was different. A new generation of audiences had barely heard of Gershwin. Berlin was a city with a wall through it. Witty lyrics were hardly in demand, and romance was replaced by free love.

The era would see the death of rooms like the St. Regis Maisonette and the Plaza's Persian Room, and clubs like El Morocco. The Copacabana would eventually convert to a disco and inspire Barry Manilow to write a song about it. Other spaces would meet the same fate (without the song).

People didn't go out anymore, the way they used to; suddenly, 1 A.M. was the middle of the night. Or if they did, it was to the discos or little folk or rock clubs with psychedelic posters and black lights.

Julie had ruled as the height of supper-club chic, and starred on Broadway. Now she took the few club offers that came along, and joined bus-and-truck companies of shows like Stephen Sondheim's *Company* for six-month tours, where a contractual coup was getting two seats on the bus instead of one so that when she slept by day on the bus traveling to the next one-night stand she'd be able to stretch out.

Her marriage to Michael McAloney had not been successful, and had been in trouble almost from the beginning. "The most difficult problem," she says, "is that Michael enjoyed drinking more than anything else. That doesn't work for families, and little children, and when you're working hard."

One of the hardest blows to her early on was that he forced her to separate from her agent, ex-husband, and friend Barron Polan, who had been with her since her early career. McAloney wanted to call the shots instead. "If I were to say I ever regretted anything in my life, it would be leaving Barron Polan," she says. "But I couldn't stand the tension, because my husband was so insanely jealous of him. It was like a choice: 'Choose Barron Polan or me.' I cried for a week writing a letter to Barron, telling him how I had to leave because of Michael and the babies. It was the hardest thing I ever did. And I felt I had sold my soul."

Thinking it would help save the marriage and be good for the children, Julie took the advice of a friend and decided they should rent a house in Ireland, from where her husband and his family had come. All that happened was that McAloney went off to try and produce a show, and Julie had to go off to work to support the family and pay for everything. The boys, who were just starting school, stayed with a couple who were good friends, with a son the same age.

It had always been up to Julie to support the whole family and keep things together. "Michael had no respect for money," she says. "He was like sixteen Peck's Bad Boys. He was a great storyteller, a great raconteur, and had a fabulous sense of humor. But no real sense of responsibility for family life. He was like the gay bachelor, and I was trying to be everything: housekeeper, mother, wife, mistress—cleaning, shopping, taking care of everything—and working."

Although Julie thought the move would be a starting over, the marriage only got worse.

"Just recently, I was up at Rainbow and Stars to see Mary Cleere Haran. And I ran into this playwright who stopped me and said, 'You're Julie Wilson, aren't you?' I said, 'That's right.' And he told me how Michael had produced a play of his. And he said, 'And boy, could he drink.' I said, 'Yes, I know.' He said how he'd never forget, they'd gone out to spend an evening in one of the pubs. Michael loved to go to the pubs, and drink and tell stories. And he said, 'I counted the drinks, and I couldn't believe it. He was drinking Scotch.' And I said, 'Yeah, I bet I know what kind. He was drinking Johnny Black.' He said, 'He had thirty-eight Scotches. And he was still standing up, and still talking.' That's a lot of Scotch."

They were divorced when she took her sons, aged six and four and a half, back to the States. They stayed with her parents in Omaha while Julie went out to earn a living. When they were high school age and her work had grown scarce, Julie kept her promise to her sons. She disappeared from public view and went back to Omaha.

She set up housekeeping in a house near her parents. Her father was a coal broker, who now, in his late seventies, still got up at six in the morning every day and went to work. Her mother, with whom she'd always been very close, had once been a hairdresser.

Back in Omaha, Julie suddenly had the opportunity for some kind of orderliness in her domestic life, something she could never find in all her years of turned-around days and nights and running from job to job. Now she was a housewife. She cooked, she cleaned, she drove the boys to school in the morning so they'd be on time. She held Sunday dinners at her house for the whole family, including her parents and her older brother, Russell, whom she adored, who lived six blocks away with his wife. "That's the only time I ever kept my house clean," she says. "It was just pride. Because I didn't want my mother and dad to come down and find out I was a total slob."

Russell was eighteen months older and an animal nut like Julie. They had been close since they were children. One Sunday, he said he couldn't come to dinner. He had a backache, and he said he felt lousy. This went on. The doctors kept giving him arthritis pills. Then one day he had a scan, and it found him to be riddled with cancer. For the few months more that he would live, Julie would go over to his house every night and care for him on the late shift, arriving at 11:00 P.M. and staying with him until six in the morning. "I would make him milkshakes, and we'd sit and talk through the night. I was so grateful I'd stuck to my plan to be with the boys when they were in high school. The night he died, I'll never forget it. He'd fallen down, and his wife had called me to help her get him off the floor. We got him back into bed, and I then went back again at eleven o'clock. And we talked, and Russ said, 'Sis, thanks for the good time.' And I said, 'Well—sure. I've been having a great time with you.' That was the last thing he said.

"He'd wanted a nude lady to hang over his bed. Do you know how hard it was in Omaha to find a painting of a nude lady? I finally wound up ordering 'September Morn' from the Museum of Modern Art. They shipped it out to Omaha. It cost me like seventeen dollars. Then I had the best framers in Omaha frame it. It cost me ninety dollars to get it framed. And it hung over his bed.

"And the day after he died, his bitchy wife, who I couldn't stand, called me up and said, 'Julie, I don't want any nude woman in my bedroom. So you can just come and get this old thing if you want it.'"

Two years went by. Then, ironically, her father was diagnosed with the same cancer, at age seventy-nine. "It was also ironic because my dad was not very nice to my brother," she says, "or very sympathetic."

A difficult man who had quit drinking and smoking the same day fifteen years earlier, he too would be gone in a matter of a few months. Still, until three weeks before he died, he got up to go to work every day. Six days before he died, he got himself to the school-yard that was adjacent to his house, and voted.

But the biggest blow would come during her father's illness. In the stress of the situation, her mother, Emily, an easygoing woman whom she had always worshiped, suffered a severe stroke a few days before her eightieth birthday. It left her totally paralyzed except for one hand.

In the Omaha hospital where her mother was taken, Julie was appalled at the negligence with which her mother was being treated. She stood up to the doctors, and fought with the nurses. "I couldn't fathom that a stroke specialist could be so inhumane. He would not order a catheter. So within like five days of being in intensive care, she had three-inch, third-degree burns in the inside of her legs, from the acid in the urine. She was like one big, open sore."

She demanded to know from the nurses how they could allow this to happen and was told, "We only take our orders from the doctor. If it was not ordered, it is not done." Julie nursed the wounds herself, changing the dressings twice a day, and finally called in her old family specialist to help.

When her mother was moved to a rehabilitation hospital, the care did not get better. Julie would stop in twice or three times a day, and would witness five people holding down her mother, who could not swallow, and force-feeding her. She couldn't stand to see it. She went and told her father, who was ill at home, that she was going to take care of her mother herself. "We had a big fight," she says. "He said, 'No you're not, goddammit, she's going to stay in the nursing home and get proper care.'"

Her mother was moved from the rehab hospital to a nursing home, after six weeks, when they said they couldn't do any more for her there. The family had looked all over for a reputable home, and placed her in one that was considered good. Julie found the conditions to be as gruesome as in the places her mother had been before, the medical negligence only exceeded by the number of cockroaches crawling out from the drawers. "I said, 'Oh my God, I can't stand it.'" Her father had died during this period. Julie enrolled in a six-week program in nurse's aide training, and she took her mother home.

At home, she cared for her mother around the clock for three years. She turned her every four hours. "She never had a bed sore. I'm very proud of that." She fed her through a feeding tube. Twice a day, she'd get her up, to watch three soap operas, and then she'd get her back to bed. Once a week a nurse's aide would come over and help her, and they'd wash her mother's hair.

In between everything, she was also cooking for her sons. When she had taken her mother home, she'd sat down with Holt and Mike and tried to explain the situation. "I just said to them, 'Look—my mom comes first,' and they'd have to understand that."

During those three years, the only time she had for herself was the odd hour when her mother would be upstairs resting, leaving her free. These were the times when Julie would take on the occasional student, a local young person who needed some coaching in singing.

In fact, working with the students was practically the only link to music, and her past life, that she maintained during her exile in Omaha. Once, earlier on, she'd come back to New York briefly to open a new room at the Edison Hotel called the Savannah Room. Then she was gone, back home again to Omaha. "Had my mother lived," she says, "I'd still be in Omaha."

But her mother died at home, finally, in the winter of 1983. Julie looked around at what her life in Omaha held. Suddenly, her family was all gone. The boys had grown up and left. By the time of her mother's death, Holt was in school in Paris, and Mike had gone to California.

She walked around the empty house and tried to figure out what to do next. New York and show business seemed another world. As far as her former life was concerned, she had for the last years been living in a vacuum. But at least she had been busy. With crisis after crisis, each moment of her everyday life had held such purpose that she never had time to think.

Ironically, while Julie's mind had been on anything but the New York scene, the desolation in which she had left it had been recently undergoing some stirrings of regeneration. Linda Ronstadt had begun recording albums of standards arranged by Nelson Riddle, and they were selling en masse to a new generation. The music, long since squelched by Aerosmith and the Bee Gees, was coming back. Clubs for jazz and vocalists were beginning to do business. All of a sudden there was a little world of these clubs, thriving, although no longer in the mass musical mainstream, and the little world was starting to be called "cabaret"—as in, "the cabaret scene."

All these things had been happening, without Julie. Then while she was sitting in Omaha after her mother's death, trying to decide what the next step would be, her answer would come in the form of a phone call from Michael's Pub. She would reenter the club scene, but the landscape would be entirely changed from the nightclub world she had grown up in. She had been away seven years. She would come back to it a different performer, playing a different role.

19

*L*inda Ronstadt doesn't like to take credit for things. It embarrasses her. With her round, brown eyes peering from beneath the trademark dark bangs, she would much rather deflect the issue with a wry comment or a giggle, seizing any opening to wax enthusiastic about somebody—anybody—else; how Emmy Lou Harris sings to her over the phone and moves her to tears; or the brilliance of songwriter Jimmy Webb; or how the first time she shared a concert with Rosemary, she left rehearsal to spend the afternoon in the bathtub frantically practicing her diction, having suddenly felt how comparatively inadequate it was.

But the fact is that this intensely shy ex-rocker, who just this year turned forty-eight, deserves a lot of the credit for bringing standard, jazz-based popular music back into the mainstream. When she recorded a trilogy of albums with the venerable arranger Nelson Riddle in the early 1980s, she revolutionized the way a generation thought about music. For baby boomers beginning to mature out of their Grateful Dead tee shirts, suddenly there was life beyond rock and roll.

The 1970s, with its various nostalgia crazes for everything from the '50s to movie musicals, had produced nostalgia-paved attractions like Manhattan Transfer and Bette Midler's renditions of such vintage hits as the Andrews Sisters' "Boogie Woogie Bugle Boy," which had caught on in cultish audience pockets. In a much wider sense, Ronstadt's albums, with Riddle's lush big-band arrangements, introduced the Woodstock generation and beyond to a world of music they barely knew existed. The albums, for the Elektra label, sold phenomenally well, presenting the music not as campy nostalgia for an "in" crowd, but reintroducing it as valid and viable for a wide, contemporary audience.

For Ronstadt, the move into classic pop mirrored the same maturing artistic values that her public was undergoing, and she embraced the music's sophistication and "adult" quality that she had increasingly begun to miss in the repertory that had made her the number-one female rock and roll star of the '70s. Celebrated for hits like "When Will I Be Loved," "Desperado," and "You're No Good,"

Ronstadt had been brought up on standards when she was growing up in Tucson, Arizona (standards, and the Mexican mariachi songs of her father's heritage). From a musical family in which her father played guitar and her mother the piano, when the Ronstadts gathered together, they sang. Having chafed her way through Catholic school ("I'm not cut out for religion," she says, prefering the spirituality she finds in music), she began as a folk singer, and with the Stone Poneys, she had the hit "Different Drum." As the 1970s progressed into the early '80s, having brought her rock stardom and all the public scrutiny that accompanies it (which Ronstadt despises, being shy and private, and terrified of performing live), she began to feel a general dissatisfaction with where she was headed. She wanted to grow as an artist, but she felt the world in which she was immersed was stunting her, symbolized by the limitations imposed on her work by the sports arenas that traditionally served as rock venues. "The only thing you can hear over the rumble is screaming guitars," she says. "Singing just becomes this comping thing that you do while you're waiting for the next high, arching guitar solo. It was too limiting to me, musically; I could do much more."

Mostly, it was the material that had begun to pall. "I just wasn't finding songs that were as good as George Gershwin—surprise, surprise," she says. "Whatever those songs were I did on those rock albums—they just weren't as good as a Rodgers and Hart song. They just weren't. I'm sure they were well intended; I'm sure those guys stayed up late, and did all those things you're supposed to do. But it's the craftsmanship—those songs weren't written for singers the way these earlier songs were."

Ronstadt could never be called an artistically stagnant performer, even in her rock and roll days, when she was constantly evolving from the country end of the spectrum through the new-wave-flavored work that preceded her jump into standards. Since then, she has baffled many by embarking on divergent musical *affaires de coeur* with everything from Mexican mariachi albums and Afro-Cuban love songs to Gilbert and Sullivan and Philip Glass to contemporary pop. The album trilogy with Riddle had begun as an exercise to improve her phrasing for her rock and roll singing. In London doing a movie of Gilbert and Sullivan's *The Pirates of Penzance*, which she had played on Broadway, she spent all her off-time reading Henry James and listening to Frank Sinatra records. "Once I started singing the standards," she says, "there was no turning back. It was, 'I have to sing this, it's so beautiful.' I couldn't get it out of my head."

The albums *What's New* (the cover shows Ronstadt stretched out on satin dressed in miles of chiffon and elbow-length gloves, with a personal stereo and headphones resting beside her), *Lush Life*, and *For Sentimental Reasons* followed. With songs like "Straighten Up and Fly Right" (with background vocals by James Taylor), "Lover Man (Oh Where Can You Be)," and "You Go to My Head," Ronstadt acclimated the ears of her listening public to a new set of musical values. Rock and roll, driven largely by beat and sound, was supplanted by a music that was more about things like melody and emotional/intellectual subtleties of the lyrics. It made different demands on the listener. But the sophistication of the material that Ronstadt found herself growing into was to fill the same need in the record-buying public.

Many other folk-rock stalwarts—Melissa Manchester, Paul Simon, Willie Nelson, Carly Simon, Maureen McGovern, Toni Tennille, among them—furthered the trend with their own albums of standards, bringing the music even farther out into the mainstream. Eventually, Natalie Cole would win top Grammys with her *Unforgettable* album of songs made famous by her father, Nat "King" Cole, and she'd follow it up with a second album, going platinum twice, as had its predecessor.

In turn, it all made first Michael Feinstein, then Harry Connick Jr. possible. Connick came out of the clubs that began to reemerge in the '70s and '80s; and backed by CBS Records, he launched his national career from an engagement at the Algonquin—to which he has never returned. Connick, with his big-band and early-Sinatra image designed to make young girls swoon, is considered in some quarters to be more a phenomenon of media hype than substantial musical accomplishment. But his sold-out arena concerts and enormous record sales have served to introduce the music to a mass of young people who may or may not credit him with having invented it, but who nevertheless have since developed an appetite for it.

The wake of a climate in which musicians like Rosemary, Barbara, and Julie (along with veterans like Tony Bennett) are embraced by rejuvenated audiences is one in which television commercials use Benny Goodman recordings to sell everything from banking to furniture, and in which more and more, movie sound tracks, like that for *Sleepless in Seattle*, employ classic and current renditions of standard pop, which then become bestselling albums in their own right.

"Standard" or "classic" pop is closely related to both traditional jazz and show music. It forms a family where often the differences are measured by freedoms taken with melody, rhythm, or the quality of the arrangement. Distinctions among the three become blurred. Until the advent of rock and roll, the mass music of America often appeared first in a Broadway show or movie musical (supplemented by Tin Pan Alley and the big bands), and was then translated into various pop and jazz versions. Jazz singers are usually defined as those who take license with melody and rhythm, while traditional pop singers may do less improvising but are usually backed by a jazz or jazz-flavored arrangement.

Rosemary, if you ask her, says she's not a jazz singer, and points out that she doesn't have the improvisational inventiveness of someone like Carmen McRae. In the 1950s, when she was at the top of the charts, she was definitely not considered a jazz singer, but a "sweet" singer, with a big-band sensibility. However, ask anyone in the business today, and most will categorize her as a jazz singer, by nature of her rhythmic sense—her ability to swing. (And of course she is always backed by first-rate jazz players.)

Julie is not a jazz singer, especially with her penchant for going back to sheet music to apprise herself of the composer's intentions regarding melody and note values. Barbara, with her background in the lyric—rather than jazzy—Broadway repertory, is certainly not a jazz singer. And yet, there are numbers she does, like "Ac-cent-tchu-ate the Positive," where she can and does swing, and increasingly, her repertory is becoming blues flavored.

Critics and music mavens love to argue hotly about whether this or that person (like Rosemary) is a jazz singer or is not a jazz singer. Mostly, it's because it gives them something to talk about. It always brings to mind the old *Saturday Night Live* debate "It's a floor wax/No, it's a dessert topping" (the answer, of course, is "It's a floor wax *and* a dessert topping"). In an age where most mass-market music doesn't relate remotely to jazz, definitions within the category of jazz-based music blur between who is singing jazz in a technical sense and who is singing pop with jazz underpinnings; hair splitting runs rampant. Ella Fitzgerald is a jazz singer, but also a major pillar of the recorded standard pop repertory. Sarah Vaughan is a jazz singer who had pop hits; Peggy Lee is a pop singer who sings jazz. And Billie Holiday, perhaps the most legendary jazz singer of all time, doesn't habitually depart radically from the melody at all, or do a lot of those vocally dramatic "jazz" things.

The small clubs that now house most live performance of jazz-based music began to spring up as the music reasserted itself with the public.

There was a renaissance in the mid-1970s, when such singers as Karen Akers started at clubs like Reno Sweeney, or Bette Midler at the Continental Baths. The clubs, most of which were on Manhattan's West Side, operated with a (largely gay) underground "in" feel, and they have since virtually disappeared. The mainstream renaissance, establishing tonier spots like the Algonquin's Oak Room, Rainbow and Stars, and a slew of supper-club-style restaurants frequented by people outside show business, took flight during the 1980s, as young professionals began to discover that an intimate setting with food, drink, and music made a nice evening out. "Cabaret" is actually a catchall word that can generally be defined simply as live performance in an intimate setting. But not everybody knows that, and the term "cabaret" occasionally puts people off because it conjures up either a movie with Liza Minnelli, degenerate cavorting in Weimar Germany, or over-precious Noël-and-Gertie-being-oh-so-amusing-at-the-piano entertainment. Overall, however, "the cabaret scene" as applied in America today merely picks up from the nightclubs, saloons, and boites of the pre-rock era.

Acknowledging that the small clubs are the breeding ground for young singers and songwriters in the field, Stan Martin tries to support them as much as he can by putting them on the radio. Martin is the program director of WQEW-AM, 1560 on the dial (in New York), perhaps the nation's foremost radio station devoted to standard pop. It is, as their slogan goes, "the home of American popular standards." The station has a peculiar history. Martin, a large, middle-aged man with brown eyes and graying hair, built the station from scratch less than two years ago. But actually the station's soul is much older. In fact, WQEW is a carefully reconstructed reincarnation of WNEW radio, the station that was legendary for some fifty years, the station where Martin Block reputedly coined the phrase "disc jockey," where he presided over the influential hit-making show *Make Believe Ballroom*, later taken over by the equally legendary William B. Williams. It was where a young secretary in the office, Frances Rose Shore, got her first singing break, and was told she should call herself "Dinah," like the song.

After decades as a focal point of American music, WNEW fell victim to changing times, becoming dilapidated with turnovers in management, converting to a rock and roll format in the 1970s, during which time its prodigious record archive was disposed of, and after which it returned to its original format, which became increasingly dissipated as programmers infused additional styles of music to try and be all things to all listeners. Losing audiences and advertising dollars, it faltered, and in 1992, it was announced that WNEW would cease to exist, and its slot on the AM dial, long fixed by its jingle in the collective mind as "e-leven-three-oh-in-New-Yoooork," would become a business-news station. When a search was begun by concerned parties for a new station to be a home for the classic pop format, a deal was struck with the New York Times Company, whose AM half of the classical music icon WQXR-FM and -AM had become a millstone they didn't know what to do with. Martin was hired to build the new station. He hired a number of WNEW veterans, and developing a no-frills presentation (rather than an expensive jingle, for instance, he employs voiceover I.D. spots by a vast array of personalities from Liza Minnelli to Tony Bennett), the station went on the air the morning of December 2, 1992, flaunting its new call letters, WQEW.

Martin, a native New Yorker, grew up listening to WNEW, and built a career over several decades as both a program director and on-air talent at stations around New York City and the East Coast. At one point he was called in to help save the floundering WNEW, but the station was sold before he could come on board. Like many who are basically creatures of radio, Martin glows when he talks about his love for the medium. "Radio's an emotional experience," he says, "and you don't want anything to get in the way of the emotion. You just want people to feel, 'Boy, that's a great song.'"

Where the 300 or 400 radio stations across the country that play the same type of music generally draw from a list of past hits numbering about 700, the list at WQEW numbers 3,000 songs, not including additional collections brought in by on-air personalities like Sinatra aficionado Jonathan Schwartz (the son of "Dancing in the Dark" composer Arthur Schwartz). Within its first year, the station had multiplied its market share of listeners fivefold from WNEW's share. According to Martin, it holds the longest listener time per week of any nonethnic station in New York City.

Every Monday afternoon, Martin brings musicians and singers into the station's five-million-dollar, state-of-the-art studio to perform live on his weekly show. Almost everybody has passed through here at one point or another; often, it's whoever's currently appearing at the clubs around the city. If you're a performer doing a run, it's fairly standard publicity procedure to go by the studio on lower Fifth Avenue and sing a couple of songs on Martin's show.

Martin feels a responsibility to have the station support the cabaret community and he rarely ignores valid performers appearing in a

leading club or concert venue who want to come on the show to promote their engagement. WQEW is also heavily into sponsorship and
promotions of a good deal of the classic pop, jazz, and big-band
activities in the city, like Friday night broadcasts from the Rainbow
Room, or summertime dancing to live bands under the stars in
Lincoln Center Plaza and South Street Seaport. Although demo-
graphically most of the station's listening public is over forty-five,
aided by events like the open-air dances, which are heavily attended
by the young professional crowd, the station is increasingly attracting
younger listeners.

A major player in the resurgence of standard pop has been Michael
Feinstein. Unlike Linda Ronstadt and the colleagues that followed
her, Feinstein began with classic pop in the cabaret field and from
there broke through into the mass arena, with his national-scale concerts, TV appearances, and record sales. He's a beacon for cabaret
artists, who are reassured that even though their music may not be
the music of today's mainstream top-40 radio, mass success can happen. Feinstein, who's thirty-seven, also comes in a different package
from the macho-hip image of the more recently arrived Connick.
While speaking to audiences his own age, Feinstein is particularly
adored by their mothers, to whom he's "that nice boy."

It is a clean-cut package. Youthful, with wavy dark hair and
translucent gray-green eyes, Feinstein has always been able to present
himself in performance or interviews and articulate his passion for
the nation's musical heritage. Enthralled with exploring the American
popular song to initiate and educate, Feinstein is a singing archivist as
much as anything else, never happier than when lost in dusty troves
of vintage records or sheet music, unearthing some long-ignored trea-
sure. His approach is reverential, his joy in performing enhanced
when he sees his audience, especially young people, respond to the
material—the lyrics of Cole Porter, or Ira Gershwin, or Yip Harburg,
for instance, in an age where clever lyric writing is a rarely practiced
art. "People want to hear songs like 'Rhode Island Is Famous for
You,' or songs like 'Can Can,' things with such brilliant wordplay,"
Feinstein says. "Or 'Lydia the Tattooed Lady.' Everybody loves
'Lydia the Tattooed Lady.' I put it on my kids' album, because it's so
clever: 'When her muscles start relaxin''/Up the hill comes Andrew
Jackson'—I mean, it's just great."

Feinstein grew up in Columbus, Ohio, and though he listened to
the records his older brother and sister bought, like the Rolling
Stones, Joni Mitchell, and Carole King's *Tapestry* album, he responded

much more to the show tunes that came to him over the TV in old movies and shows like *Sing Along with Mitch* and through family functions (his father belonged to a barbershop quartet society, his mother had been a tap dancer). "It's in my genetic code," he says. "There're always the kids that are the weird ones in the family because they love show tunes. Somewhere there's the little boy or girl who's five years old, hearing Ethel Merman for the first time, making a connection. It's like discovering someone who speaks your language."

His tastes isolated him at school, where one year, when he was in charge of his high school public address system, he created a contest for the school paper, broadcasting a quiz featuring the voices of Bing Crosby, Fanny Brice, and Al Jolson. "I mean, in retrospect, I realize how ridiculous it was for me to think that anybody would know who Fanny Brice was," he says. "But at the time, it was not something that crossed my mind."

He eventually landed in Los Angeles and went to work for Ira Gershwin (Mrs. Oscar Levant referred him) to catalog his extensive phonograph collection. (It was there he got to know Rosemary and her family, who were the Gershwins' next-door neighbors for some thirty-five years.) After Ira's death and philosophical differences with his wife, Leonore, Feinstein went out to work in piano bars, mostly in L.A., until the time when Liza Minnelli hosted a party for him that included guests like Elizabeth Taylor, Gregory Peck, and Melissa Manchester. (Minnelli has remained his loyal champion. Ira Gershwin was her godfather, which is how they met.) Donald Smith, who manages Julie's career and masterminded Andrea Marcovicci's, was at the L.A. party and offered to book Feinstein in New York at the Algonquin's Oak Room. To do so, Smith had to convince then Algonquin owner Andrew Ansbach to take him. Feinstein had already been writing Ansbach letters requesting employment, but had been told that frankly, there wasn't even enough work for the people in New York—why should he be booked? Arriving under Smith's tutelage, with an opening night party again hosted by Liza Minnelli, Feinstein created a sensation.

Speculation about Feinstein's enormous success is usually tempered by ranges of amazement, jealousy, or most accurately, the realization that it seemed to be exactly the right time for him to burst on a scene that had been primed for what he had to offer—the likable young presenter with the historical view. (The jealousy is often directed toward the celebrity friends, particularly Minnelli, who were willing to rally for him early on. Minnelli, it's worth noting, is known for her consistent support of young talent.) From the success of his Algonquin engagement, his contract with the small record label Parnassus was bought out by Elektra, and from that time, his career took on national proportions. Right away, the *New York Times Magazine* had run a feature written by Stephen Holden, and with a barrage of media attention, Feinstein went on to appear at the Smithsonian, in major concerts (he toured with Rosemary), television appearances, including a PBS special with Jule Styne, and an offer to take his show to Broadway, which he did in 1988.

Feinstein still makes his home in Los Angeles, though he just bought an apartment in New York, near City Center. Currently, he's writing a book about the songwriters he's known (he also worked for Harry Warren for two years), which he's been trying to get finished in between his stints on the road, where he spends most of his time. He's happy that finally, over the last few years, he's seeing real growth in the size of his younger audiences (he rode to success on a generation that had grown up with this music). It's something he tries to cultivate. "Since this is not mainstream music," he says, "I feel sometimes the weight of responsibility to perform the songs in a way that will show them off to their best advantage, because I know there may be somebody out there who's never heard 'They Can't Take That Away from Me.'"

He was recently stopped in the recording studio by a young techie, who also had a heavy metal band, who said to him, "Hey, man, I like your stuff. I've never heard this stuff before, but it's really great." "When somebody like that pays me a compliment," Feinstein says, "that's the highest compliment. Because it's somebody who just heard it and liked it. Now, that's not going to change his taste in metal music. But I get very excited about that. Annie Lennox, on her *Diva* album, included a 1933 Harry Warren song called 'Keep Young and Beautiful.' A number of pop stars include one or two standards on their albums. And people who buy the albums don't know the vintage of these songs; they just know they like the songs. I've just always loved this music ever since I was a kid. I'm passionate about these songs because they express feelings of emotion that resonate within my heart. It is the perpetuation of that expression that brings me joy. Because I feel that people will garner the same enthusiasm once they are exposed to the material."

*R*osemary has been told that Michael Feinstein is coming up for the second show that evening. It's early in the second week, and there is a snowstorm going on outside. Her car slip-slided all the way down Fifth Avenue toward Rockefeller Center. Now, on the 65th floor, the snow can be seen coming down past the windows, but through it all, the view is still relatively intact.

It's early—only about 6:30. Normally, she and Dante don't arrive until around 7:30, which gives her an hour to get ready before her first show. But tonight, David Lotz, Rainbow's press agent, has lined up a photo call and two interviews. Lotz is a tall, outgoing man with glasses. He was once an actor. He leads the camera crew for the television interview into the glassed-in conference room off the side lounge where the musicians usually hang out between shows. It's the same room that serves as the bar during the opening-night parties held in the lounge.

On the way to her dressing room, Rosemary has stopped at the counter where they sell the vintage art deco jewelry. "Hi, honey," she says to Mary Jane, the girl who sits behind the counter. "I forgot my earrings. I just want to see if you have anything I could wear." Mary Jane shows her a few pairs. Rosemary admires a rhinestone bracelet. She looks at the earrings again. "I guess I'll take these." She gives Mary Jane a credit card, which they have to call in to verify just like everybody else's credit card. Mary Jane has dark hair and wants to be a writer. She tells Rosemary to go on into her dressing room, she'll bring the slip by to sign when it's ready.

When the camera has been set up by the Fox News people, Lotz comes over and knocks on the dressing room door. "Just wanted to let you know they're ready to go when you are," he says through the door. "It's OK, Rosemary, don't rush," he adds. "Take your time."

The interview is being conducted by Marian Etoile Watson, a Fox News reporter who's been on the air in New York for a good many years. She's interviewed Rosemary several times in the past. "How are you, Marian," Rosemary says when she comes in, wearing a beige dress and silk scarf and escorted by Lotz, and embraces her. The interview is routine, except during the preliminaries, when Dante makes a remark and she starts to laugh, throwing herself into a coughing jag, and she steps out of the room into the lounge outside to compose herself before going back in. They talk mostly about her new album. And at the end, Watson asks Rosemary to autograph her copy of the CD, as well as the promotional poster she's been given.

Watson and her cameraman will be fed dinner in the cabaret before the first show, which the cameraman will partially shoot. While they're eating, Rosemary holes up in her dressing room to get dressed and ready for the show early so she can do the photo shoot that the club has lined up to advertise Valentine's Day. She will come out briefly to do another interview, and be photographed by a newspaper photographer, before returning again to her dressing room.

In the tiny room, the dressing table is crammed with necessities like makeup and Kleenex and a bottle of water and rollers to set her hair between shows and pictures drawn by her grandchildren stuck in the mirror. She spends a lot of time in that little room during February. If she's not actually involved in getting ready, mostly she reads. That's her way of relaxing. Right now she's started Pete Hamill's autobiography, which has recently come out. "It really puts you right inside the mind of an Irishman," she's been saying about it.

Outside, threading their way through the usual clump of people standing transfixed by the bank of television screens, is a group of people in costume, eight of them altogether, four boys, four girls, trailed by David Lotz and a woman who keeps pulling at hemlines—obviously, the designer. They are the Great Lovers of History, and they're there for the photo shoot. Rainbow and Stars has talked Rosemary into working on Valentine's Day, though this year it falls on a Monday, her usual night off. She'll take Tuesday off instead. Meanwhile, the club is gearing up for one of the biggest commercial nights of its year, when both shows will be crammed with tables full of people who want to spend a romantic evening holding hands with their Valentine, high atop the glittering city, while Rosemary Clooney sings love songs.

Thus the Great Lovers of History, who will be roaming the club in costume on the big night, distributing little gifts and generally reminding everyone that it's Valentine's Day. They all look like aspiring actors, and when Rosemary comes out of her dressing room dressed for the show, they all seem excited to be having their picture taken with her. There's Romeo and Juliet; Scarlett and Rhett (on their way in, Rhett had said, "Man, I don't know where we're going," and

Scarlett had asked to use the phone); Antony and Cleopatra; and twin cupids. Rosemary comments on how beautifully the costumes are made, and congratulates the designer, who's still fussing with doublets and bodices. The photographer poses them in the lounge against the wall, with Romeo kneeling and presenting Rosemary with a red rose. He starts to shoot. "OK, now let's do this," he says, and he moves them around, with Rosemary still in the middle, still smiling. He shoots some more. "OK, how are we doin' here?" Rosemary says, still smiling for the camera. She's getting a little antsy. The photographer takes a few more. "OK, guys, got a show to do," she says smiling, and the photographer finishes, and the group breaks up.

Doing press is important in order to get people to come in and see the show, and everybody knows it. That's why Rosemary comes into New York a week before the opening, to do it in advance. But it doesn't always necessarily line up that way. She'd spent Saturday afternoon before getting ready to go to work with a reporter from the *Wall Street Journal*. One of the magazines wants to do a feature, and a reporter has been hanging around, trying to get some time in between shows. There's more television on the schedule, too, for later in the week, which involves a lot more preparation than print interviews. The problem is that the energy and concentration it takes to keep up a routine of two shows a night, five nights a week for a month, are tiring enough. The extra effort and talk to do press, especially on a performing day, quickly become exhausting. And although Dante's cold is just starting to sound better, she hasn't shaken hers, and is still on antibiotics.

The trouper side of Rosemary is always inclined to go along, hesitant to say no to the practicalities she knows are part of her business. She isn't talking about it, but the schedule is beginning to wear on her.

Michael Feinstein does come up to see the second show. It's still snowing heavily outside, and he comes in just before eleven o'clock with a couple of friends. She's already waiting with her musicians outside the room. "There he is!" she says when she sees him coming down the hall, and embraces him. The musicians go onstage, and he follows Rosemary inside the cabaret, where she'll wait by the doors in the dark for them to start playing. "I'd better sit down," Feinstein says. The musicians are about to play her cue to come out onstage. She looks out the windows at the snow coming down. "Drive ya home?" she calls after him. "Sure!" Feinstein answers, knowing that she knows there won't be a taxi to be found in the whole city by the time the show lets out.

As the oldest child in her family, Rosemary spent her life worrying about everybody. "It's an oldest-child syndrome," she says. "You've got to take care of everything, sort it out, straighten it out."

Growing up in Maysville, Kentucky, she had always felt like she had to perform; she had always wanted to please. "I knew what the coin of the realm was," she says. "In most instances it didn't take me long to find out 'What works here?' And I'd adjust accordingly." Childhood held such constant uncertainty for her, it was the only way she had learned to get by.

She was born on May 23, 1928, to a family that was devoutly Catholic in a Protestant town, located just across the Ohio River from Cincinnati. Her father, Andrew Clooney, was a sometime housepainter, when he worked. He was also an alcoholic. His family never knew when he would be on or off the wagon, and there would be times when he would simply disappear, only to return later and apologize to the people he had disappointed. But he was kind, and fun, with a keen sense of humor. When he was sober, Rosemary adored him.

Her mother, Frances, was secretive, manipulative and self-involved, and though she would later live with Rosemary and her family for almost twenty years in California, mother and daughter never really got on. As children, Rosemary and her sister, Betty, who was three years younger, were shuttled between both sets of grandparents while their parents continually disbanded and reassembled their marriage. They would live together as a family only for brief periods. Then when her parents would split up, either the girls would be deposited to live with Grandfather and Grandmother Clooney in Maysville, or their mother would flee to the house of her own mother, Grandmother Guilfoyle, taking Rosemary and Betty with her.

Early on, they lived mostly with Grandfather and Grandmother Clooney. Rosemary's grandfather was probably the most stable influence in her life. His parents had emigrated from Ireland, and he had educated himself and studied law, and passed the state bar at age twenty-two. He was a watchmaker and jeweler, fascinated with politics, and served for a long time as the mayor of Maysville. He would make up bedtime stories and talk to the girls about politics. He was a Roosevelt Democrat, which, during the Depression in the poor state of Kentucky, was a natural thing to be. Roosevelt was worshiped in the household. Grandfather Clooney's liberal political views would color Rosemary's own political leanings for the rest of her life. "He talked to Betty and me as though we were adults," she says, "which was wonderful. I mean, we didn't understand half of it, but it was wonderful being consulted and informed by somebody we admired so much as our grandfather, telling us why Alben Barkley was a good man for vice president. And of course, the president was President Roosevelt—there just wasn't even a consideration of anything else."

Her grandparents lived in an apartment above the jewelry store, and a lot of Rosemary's early childhood was spent playing in the street in front of the store while her grandfather watched from inside. Betty was the spunky, outgoing one. Rosemary was a quiet child, shy and worried, who loved to read, and didn't have many friends: only her sister and her best girl friend, a black girl named Blanchie Mae Chambers, whose mother worked in the hotel across the street. When they were very young, they would sometimes put on shows inside the store window, while the window was being changed.

On Saturdays the sisters went to see James Cagney and the Buck Rogers serials at the three movie theatres in town. On the radio, they'd listen to *Amos 'n' Andy, Jack Armstrong*, and Bing Crosby's show. Crosby had always been her father's favorite singer. The rest of the time was spent in Catholic school or church. If things were going well between her father and mother and they were living together, the family would go to the Russell Theater on Sunday nights, where they had movie musicals.

On the occasions that they were taken to Grandmother Guilfoyle's house, they shared the house with those of her nine children who were left at home. The youngest of them, Rosemary's Aunt Chris, was only three years older than Rosemary. Grandmother Guilfoyle, a widow, was from the country, and had been a schoolteacher before her marriage. Now she did practical nursing at night to support her family and make ends meet. She was a big woman, earthy, a great cook and seamstress, and a gardener.

The Depression was still on, and no one in the family had much money. Clothes for the girls were mostly hand-me-downs from their cousins. "I had so many problems that were life and death," Rosemary says, "like where and who was I going to live with, and where was the next meal coming from, and where was I going to go to school and could I get a new pair of shoes for the beginning of school—all these really very basic needs. The thing that was always constant was the fact that my sister and I were together. We could figure out anything if we were together. And we always were."

By now, Rosemary and Betty had a younger brother, Nicky. Their mother was always away, gone off to work. When Rosemary was ten, her Grandmother Clooney died, and her grandfather would never really recover. She and Betty and Nicky were sent to live with Grandmother Guilfoyle. By the time Rosemary graduated from elementary school and moved on to junior high, the family had picked up and moved to Ironton, Ohio, where two of her uncles were going to open a service station.

Rosemary and Betty sang from an early age; all anybody had to do was ask. When they were little they'd sing for their grandfather and his friends in the shop. Music was on both sides of the family. One of their father's sisters played the piano. Their father played the ukulele and sang. Their mother, on the other hand, who had always wanted to be a performer, had no sense of rhythm. Rosemary remembers singing as a tiny child, and having her mother criticize her for taking the pauses that came naturally to her even then.

But their mother's sister Ann was a nightclub singer. A dramatic and tempestuous young woman, Aunt Ann would come home to lick her wounds whenever she had a brawl with one of her boyfriends. She fascinated her two young nieces, who had come to live in the house, with her glamorous gowns, swanky luggage, and temper tantrums.

"We were close," Rosemary says. "She was younger than my mother, the fifth child of nine. She encouraged me to be a singer. She had a terrible temper. She would leave her boyfriends, and arrive at my grandmother's house, always with this dumb set of golf clubs."

One Saturday night Ann took an overdose of pills, and was taken to the emergency room. They never got to her, and she died there, left outside on a gurney. She was twenty-five.

Aunt Ann had owned the Billie Holiday records that Rosemary had begun to listen to in the early '40s. She had the record "Strange Fruit," and also "Gloomy Sunday." "I was very affected by that," she says. "I couldn't have been very old. And I knew that was a suicide song. Funny, the very aunt who owned that record suicided."

When her uncles' business failed, the family moved again, this time across the river to Cincinnati. Rosemary started as a freshman at Withrow High School. The war was on. Her mother had been coming and going during this time. By the end of her first year of high school, they had moved within the city and were living with their mother. That summer, her mother divorced her father. She had met a sailor stationed in California, and would go off to marry him. Rosemary and Betty learned of the plans in bits and pieces by overhearing them. They also overheard how their mother wanted to leave them once again with their grandmother, but their aunts and uncles wouldn't allow it, arguing that it was too much of a strain on the aging woman, and that Frances's children were her responsibility.

Instead, their mother persuaded their father to come back and move into the house with the girls so she could leave. He was working in a defense plant in Cincinnati by now and earning a good living. Then their mother announced that she was splitting up the children and taking Nicky with her to California. She told the girls that since their father was going to be coming to live with them, they didn't need to worry. Then as they stood there, she took their little brother and got into a taxi and left. They wouldn't see her or their brother again for four years.

Their father did come to live with them and was trying hard. He had a good job, and was on the wagon. They moved into a cheaper apartment, near the streetcar line that they took to school. They had some good times, and would go to hear the big bands that came through Cincinnati, and they'd go down to the drugstore together on Sundays and play the jukebox. When the war went into high gear and their father was making more money, they moved again, this time to a nicer apartment in a better neighborhood. It meant another change of schools, but he tried to make them the best home he could.

They lived this way for three years. Betty, too, was now in high school. President Roosevelt died. The war ended in Europe. VJ Day came. While everybody was celebrating, their father started drinking again. He came home roaring drunk that day, and the girls watched as he gathered up all the defense bonds, worth several thousand dollars, that they'd saved during the war, and got in a taxi and disappeared. They had no idea where or for how long. He would stay away ten days, with no communication.

The girls were loath to call up any of their relatives in the area. They didn't want to be a burden on anybody once again, and they were convinced they could take care of themselves. Their father had left them with no money. So they combed the house, and gathered up all the deposit Coke bottles they could find, and lived off them, budgeting their food, which they ate at school.

It was during this time, in their father's absence, that Betty decided they should audition for WLW radio, and they got the job. The day after they were hired, they called their Aunt Jean, one of their mother's sisters, who lived in Cincinnati, and they told her they had just got a job that earned forty dollars a week between them, and could they come and stay with her? Then they told her what had happened with their father, and she was appalled that they hadn't called her sooner. But it was only when they could pay their own way that they felt it was all right to impose themselves.

That afternoon they gathered up their belongings and dragged the suitcases down the three flights of stairs from the apartment to the street outside, waiting for the taxi that their aunt was sending for them. Dragging the last of their bags, they spotted their father coming up the walk, and they hid around the side of the building until he went inside. They saw he was sober, and they looked at each other, trying to decide what to do. Their cab was there. Then Betty said, "We're not sure if he'll stay sober." And they raced into the cab and went to their aunt's, where they would stay.

The next day, their aunt insisted that they call their father at work and let him know their whereabouts and what their decision had been. He told them to come back, that he could stop drinking if he wanted to, and they could try again. They had to tell him no, they couldn't. They'd heard it all before.

They were starting a new life as singers on the radio, a life that would soon take them out on the road with Tony Pastor. Until they left, their aunt made a home for them. Rosemary and Betty were together, which had always made everything all right. They wouldn't see their father again for a long time.

Outside Rainbow and Stars, there is another snowstorm. In the morning, the first show and most of the second show sold out. All the press has been paying off, and it seems that Rosemary is getting to be the hottest ticket in town. But today's blizzard started dumping snow on the city with such ferocity that for the first time in its five-year history, the club actually considered canceling the show on account of the weather.

Rosemary called the office in the late afternoon, after watching the television preempting all their other coverage to talk about the weather. "This is the thirteenth snowstorm in what has already been the worst winter in thirty years," they keep saying, over and over again, grating on the inhabitants of the city who keep digging out their cars only to have them immediately plowed under again.

"So, do we have a snow day, or what?" Rosemary asks the management, calling in in the afternoon. They wait until the very end of the afternoon to decide; and they decide to go ahead with the show.

At 7:30, Rainbow and Stars, including the adjoining bar, with the windows' uninterrupted backdrop of cascading white powder, has the deathly deserted feel of a science fiction movie in which a nuclear winter has descended on the earth, and the planet's only remaining inhabitants are stranded in a nightclub. Outside, the streets are nearly impassable. Traffic is nonexistent, as is transportation, and the only sound in the eerie, muffled quiet of the city is the occasional snowplow or a car spinning its wheels further into inertia.

But Rosemary's car has made it through, and she arrives on schedule to get ready for her first show. The musicians have all made it in somehow, even though most of them live in either New Jersey or Westchester. They have left home hours ahead of time. By showtime, over half the sold-out room has canceled. In the sea of empty tables, there are perhaps twenty people. "I knew we'd be able to shoot deer in here tonight," Rosemary says to the guys while they're waiting out in the hall to go on.

The management finds the combination of a sold-out house and a blizzard excruciating. Facing the empty room doesn't hold the same angst for Rosemary. "God knows, I've done it for other reasons. This time there was a snowstorm," she says. "It can't be helped. I've done it because I wasn't able to draw the people."

What does frustrate her is that this was the night her daughter Monsita was supposed to come down and see her. Instead, Monsita is stranded in Connecticut, where her three little boys have been having a never-ending succession of snow days, and her nanny has just left her. Rosemary's disappointed. She has been looking forward to spending time with her, and this isn't the first time the snow has kept her apart from Monsita and the grandchildren. In the hall outside the room, as she's waiting to go on, a certain overbearing woman entertainer who has booked a table arrives just before showtime and approaches Rosemary on her way in. "I made it," she says breathlessly. "Well, as I live and breathe," Rosemary says, greeting her by name, and the woman and her entourage go inside to be seated. Rosemary turns to no one in particular. "*She* makes it," she says. "My daughter has to cancel."

She recently had the shocking news that Dr. Gould, the specialist who has been treating her and scores of colleagues for years, has just died. She had been to see him only a few days ago. He had been treating her cold. The funeral is scheduled for the next morning, and there has been a prediction that the snow is going to continue into tomorrow.

She jokes with the audience about the weather. "I want to tell you how much I really appreciate your coming out in all this tonight," she says. "My daughter canceled." It gets a good laugh, and she makes a mental note. She'll use it again in the next few snowstorms, with an addition about her son, who only lives on Seventy-sixth Street, and it will get a laugh every time.

A few people show up for the late show as well. Toward the end of the evening she is ready to start "How Deep Is the Ocean," and nothing is happening. John Oddo, at the piano, is staring out the window. He lives in White Plains. "Hello?" she says, turning to John. "Somebody's supposed to start this; I don't think it's me." The audience laughs. "Are you zoning out on me here, or just wondering how the hell you're going to get home?"

The show ends just before midnight, as usual. She has changed back into her street clothes and is out of her dressing room within fifteen minutes, and wearing her coat, with her brown purse looped over one arm, she chats for a second with each of the few fans who have waited outside her dressing room to shake her hand and tell her how much they love her, before getting past them toward the elevator. Dante follows in his tweed hat and overcoat, carrying a small shopping bag that contains dinner. He's made sure she pulls her scarf close around her neck, which she always gives him an argument about. But outside, the temperature is in the teens, and the hair at the nape of her neck is damp, as it always is from the effort and the lights.

They get back to the hotel shortly after 12:30, the car having inched through the thick powder. Rosemary will have her dinner, which is in the shopping bag. As part of their agreement with Rainbow and Stars, they're entitled to two dinners every night. Dante usually has his between shows, in the cabaret, after people clear out following the first show, if Bismark has a table for him, or he orders his oysters in the bar.

It will be around 3:00 A.M. by the time she unwinds, having her dinner, watching television, reading a little, before she's geared down enough to go to sleep, listening to the radio. The funeral is supposed to start at eleven, which means she'll have to be dressed and ready to leave the hotel by ten. It is going to be crowded.

It snows all night. In the morning, the city is paralyzed. It is still snowing. The sidewalks are calf-deep; it's coming down too fast even to clear them. Moving cars are practically nonexistent, and people wade down the middle of Park Avenue with no interference. Dante calls down to the desk at 9:00 to find out the taxi situation. He's told it is pretty much zero. They probably should have ordered a car. The funeral is to be held at Campbell's funeral home, which is less than ten blocks up Madison Avenue, but to walk it would be impossible. By shortly after 10:00, probably the only empty taxi in New York is obtained, but it can't pull anywhere near to the curb in front of the hotel, because of the drifts and parked cars. Rosemary and Dante are waiting outside, under the canopy, as the driver tries to inch up a little closer, with no success. "Come on, let's go," Rosemary says impatiently, and wearing stockings and delicate black pumps, she wades into the knee-deep snowdrifts and slogs her way to the taxi in the middle of the street. She shakes the snow off her shoes as the cab crawls up Madison Avenue to Campbell's. Again, it can't get anywhere near the curb, and she pushes through the drifts to where the sidewalk has been cleared, stamping the snow off before she goes inside.

The funeral is already crowded. It's being held in the big chapel on the main floor, with the blue walls. In the front, on the congregation's extreme left, a woman plays Chopin on a piano that needs tuning.

The chapel is overflowing with gargantuan flower arrangements, and by the time the room is full and the service is under way, the temperature inside is probably eighty-five degrees. The woman sitting directly in front of Rosemary has doused herself in perfume so strong it's nose-burning. Air is hard to come by.

Dan Rather is one of the speakers. Dr. Gould treated a lot of prominent performers over the years, but it seems most of the other singers are opting for the memorial service later on. Now, the eulogies keep coming. Rosemary prays. She's tired. She hasn't had much sleep, and it's early in the day for her even to be awake, let alone out in the world. Usually, her day begins around four o'clock, when she starts getting ready to go to work.

The service goes on for almost two hours, emotional, draining, and several of his patients keep getting up to sing. By the end, the room is so suffocating that they're all fanning themselves with their programs. Rosemary feels it acutely, with her asthma, which likes it cool, her cold, and the overpowering fumes from the flowers and the woman in front of her. When the service lets out, she tells Dante she wants to walk back. "I need some air," she says. It has stopped snowing. Some of the shopkeepers have started to shovel narrow paths in sections, and holding Dante's arm and trying to protect her bad knee, she picks her way through the snow and ice back to the hotel.

She goes back to bed, trying to get some sleep before she has to get up again in a couple of hours. The extracurricular schedule is really starting to bother her. The press demands are beginning to get out of hand. The next day, she is supposed to be dressed and made up in the morning to do a television interview for CNN. Then she's supposed to be down at the GE building early to be interviewed by Sue Simmons on Channel 4's *Live at Five*, which means she'll have to stay there until it's time for her show. Then there's another TV interview scheduled with critic Joel Siegel, and on Saturday, Charlie Rose is supposed to come and interview her at her hotel for his PBS show. She doesn't know where she's going to get the energy to do two shows a night.

Last year, during the second week of her run, there had been a scare. She was fighting a cold then, too, and in her dressing room after her first show one night, she was a little short of breath. When Bismark heard about it he wasn't going to take any chances, and he called 911, and she was taken by ambulance to the emergency room at New York Hospital. The press learned about it and it immediately became a

"Rosemary Clooney-collapses-between-shows-and-is-rushed-to-the-hospital" story, and it went out over the wire right behind reports of Michael Jackson's latest exploits. Actually, Rosemary lay on a gurney in the emergency room all night, with a woman strung out on crack on one side of her, and on the other, a woman who hour after hour kept singing "The Star Spangled Banner." "She was having a little trouble with the words," Rosemary says, "so I was kind of helping her out." The doctors found nothing wrong, and let Rosemary go home by 4:00 A.M. She went back to work that next night as usual, and that was it.

The afternoon of the funeral, she does get some much needed sleep. Her cold, now being treated by Dr. Gould's woman colleague, has been put on yet another round of antibiotics. She calls David Lotz and flat-out cancels all the remaining press that she is scheduled to do. She will do *Live at Five*, but she has finally decided that she can't keep up daily publicity activities and do two shows a night and make it through the rest of the month. Something has to go, and she puts her foot down. Over the next few days, with the extra rest and her normal schedule restored, she will begin to feel better and more like herself. She was the first person Rainbow and Stars had ever got onto Charlie Rose. It doesn't matter. By the end of the week, Bismark comes in one night with the news that except for a couple of late shows, the entire rest of the run is sold out solid.

* 23 *

"If there's one thing I've learned in all my years in this business," says Donald Smith, "it's that nothing just happens."

In New York, Donald Smith is known as "Mister Cabaret." Most of the energy of his waking hours goes toward promoting it in some form. He is responsible for talking the Algonquin Hotel into bringing cabaret back to its Oak Room. He convinced Faith Stewart-Gordon to institute a series at her Russian Tea Room, and then to install Julie for an extended run last season. He launched Michael Feinstein's career, and is responsible for Andrea Marcovicci's rampant success. He intervened in the legendary Mabel Mercer's semiretirement, and gave her career a new lease that would last more than twenty years. When Julie returned to the scene in the 1980s he took over her management, and has guided her bookings and press ever since. He is the founder and Executive Director of the Mabel Mercer Foundation, an organization dedicated to promoting public interest in American song and cabaret, and is the creator and producer of the annual Cabaret Convention at Town Hall, a weeklong orgy of musical performances by virtually everyone who's ever opened his or her mouth in a club, in front of sold-out audiences who have paid a nominal ten-dollar ticket price.

Above all, Smith is a publicist. He has a profound understanding of the reality that the most brilliant singer can stand in front of a microphone and sing until a nuclear winter, but unless the press is cultivated to cover the event, unless the image is defined before the public, unless people hear about it and their curiosity is piqued, the singer will probably labor in obscurity.

Smith is a big man, middle-aged, with silver hair and a round, Botticelli face. His broad speech reflects his Boston-area upbringing. His father was a superintendent of schools and his mother emigrated from Ireland. From childhood, Donald and his mother would toast Cole Porter's birthday every year. He likes to say that according to his mother, his first words were "When are we moving to New York?"

He lives on and works from two floors of a brownstone overlooking the Turtle Bay gardens in Manhattan's East Forties, near the river. Though an office assistant comes in several days a week, in effect Smith is a one-man operation, on the phone from the time he rises early in the morning, and continuing to do business very late at night, unless he's out at a club or some theatrical function. He is continually juggling the umpteen projects in which he is simultaneously involved, including managing Marcovicci's cabaret exploits and Julie's career, the booking and producing activities, and outside accounts promoting other performers or performance-related events. His pursuit of detail and the fact that he does virtually everything himself means that invariably something always gets left hanging.

When new performers want to establish themselves in cabaret, very often they will find their way to Smith's door. His considerable clout, in terms of both booking and the ability to rally the notice and ears of the press, is the reason. They come to him for career advice, or to get him to come hear them wherever they're singing, or for referrals to others who can help them. If they can afford his publicist's fee, and he agrees to take them on, they begin planning their campaign strategy.

Although people like to think that if the talent isn't there to deliver, all the hype in the world is for naught—and it may be true in most cases—there are very specific formulas for bringing someone—anyone—to public prominence. They are the secrets held by publicists and marketing experts, and the ingredient for optimal effectiveness is a lot of cash. In cabaret, where the financial stakes are not what they are in the mass culture, whoever rises to the top generally must have *something*. But the formula for promotion, with its strategies for getting noticed and their precise mechanical implementation, still holds true.

This season, Smith has taken on the task of manufacturing from scratch an image and stature for an unknown singer who came to him from Atlanta. The singer, in her mid-forties, had sung locally in Atlanta clubs before being interrupted by a troubled personal life. Now she wants to make a splash in the big time, and people have told her that the thing to do is to seek out Smith. But her activity started months before.

The singer, whose name is Judy Argo, is a likable woman, large, with a pretty face and big hair and big jewelry, and her main asset is a naturally big voice. Until recently, she hadn't sung in years, and was working as a cosmetician doing makeovers in a salon. Her manager, a persistent middle-aged lady, owns a wholesale food distributorship, and became her manager after she had convinced her to go back to singing, and is financing the whole operation out of her own pocket. Figuring that managing an artist couldn't be much different from running her business, on a friend's advice the first thing she'd done to acclimate herself was take a subscription to the music industry trade publication, *Billboard*.

They'd decided the thing to do was cut a vanity CD. They calculated that if they hired the most prominent musicians they could find, people would be forced to take notice of it. Looking through other singers' albums, they found a common denominator was often the pianist/arranger Mike Renzi, and they set their sights on him. They got to him through a woman in the recording industry whose name they'd found in *Billboard*, and the manager had called her office three times a day, every day for ten days, until one day the woman had unwittingly picked up the phone and agreed to listen to a demo tape, and was sufficiently impressed by the sound of the singing voice to link them up with Renzi, who agreed to work with them. They were then able to follow through with their determination to hire famous musicians, among them the legendary jazz players Ray Brown on bass, Gerry Mulligan on saxophone, and Grady Tate on drums. The cost of making the CD was over a hundred thousand dollars.

Their calculation was correct. When the CD went out to industry and press, virtually everyone did a double take and thought, "Well, this must mean something," and it avoided the slush pile. Next, they hired the Russian Tea Room's New York Room for a showcase/party, and with Renzi's connections and the musicians in tow, filled the place with music press and other helpful people. One of them was critic Rex Reed, who loved her voice and gave her an enthusiastic quote, which she began to use immediately. Donald Smith, whom they'd already been told they should get on board, had been hounded until he finally agreed to come. He, too, was impressed by the voice, and in a meeting the next day said he'd work with them.

Right away, she was booked onto one of the "Lyrics and Lyricists" evenings hosted by Rex Reed at the 92nd Street Y. Then Smith began calling his press contacts, like writers and radio people, to tell them about her, and he sent out 150 copies of her CD all over the country, with material that included Rex Reed's quote. He knew he had to present her as a performer in New York, and he arranged to book her for a night onto the Russian Tea Room's spring Sunday evening series, to which he attracted about twenty media people, including Stephen Holden of the *Times*, by personally impressing on them his belief that she shouldn't be missed. One of them was Stan Martin, the WQEW-AM radio program director, who hosts a live-guest show on Monday afternoons, and on the spur of the moment invited her to come by and sing a couple of songs on his show the next day. And the next day, she was on the radio.

Smith had immediately set about having the CD repackaged, because the design of the cover and the look of the photo were dated and showed their lack of experience, and they had failed to include information like who wrote the songs that were listed. But in the meantime, the copies he had sent out and followed up on got played over the radio by DJs in the Chicago area, in Massachusetts, and on Long Island—where he also arranged for her to visit the station as a guest. Then a distributor was found for the CD, and while on a trip to London, he arranged for it to be sold over there.

Now Smith is concerned about finding her a real engagement in New York next season. It is a foregone conclusion that she will appear at his Cabaret Convention at Town Hall in the fall. The recent Russian Tea Room night wasn't reviewed. Reviews weren't what he wanted. What he wanted was that when he gets her booked somewhere else next season, the press will remember and already know who she is and come and review her then.

The only problem, of which Smith is all too aware, is that apart from the sound of her big, bluesy voice, the singer needs some work. Or at least, polish. Despite her age and the fact that she's not a novice, her isolation until now from the mainstream music world is evident in a lack of sophistication. Smith wants to work on that, to reshape her choice of material, to rid her style of some things, like the hand motions, that are out of date. Above all, he wants to get her to spend more time in New York—not only to become a recognizable fixture, but to go and sit and experience a lot of other performers doing their thing, from which she can learn.

There is really no question that next season, she will have some sort of run somewhere respectable in New York. (In fact, it will turn out to be a two-week engagement at Danny's Skylight Room, after they'd rejected an earlier plan to open at Eighty Eight's). The major hurdles in terms of recognition have been conquered. Now the writers who cover cabaret are all familiar with who she is, at least as That-Singer-That-Don-Smith-Is-Promoting. She has credentials: she has a quote from Rex Reed. She has appeared in the "Lyrics and Lyricists" series. She played at the Russian Tea Room. Singers working their way up for years can't get to the Russian Tea Room.

The price tag is enormous. Costs include everything from advertising and promotional expenses to the costs of the CD and distribution, to hiring top musicians, to the price of retaining Smith's services. The manager estimates that by the time the singer is launched to a point where she is on her feet, it will have cost her about a quarter of a million dollars.

All of it was accomplished in less than a year (and following her Danny's engagement, she will end up being given a MAC award in the New York Debut catagory). Not surprisingly, this kind of enterprise causes some resentment in certain circles. For the hundreds of performers working their way up through the ranks in New York, visibility comes from years of sending out hand-addressed flyers and graduating to better and better clubs in the hope of landing in a place like Rainbow and Stars, which, to a limited extent, will pay the promotion bills. Or hoping to arrive sufficiently to be able to retain their own publicist. Smith recognizes the situation. "It comes under the heading of 'Life isn't fair,'" he says, and he reflects on what a difference all that available promotion money would have made when he was working with the singer-pianist Steve Ross early on, when he would take a pack of five of Ross's records and carry them personally to the record store.

The reality for performers trying to make their way in the business is that everything costs money, and it is the responsibility of the performer to absorb almost all of it. Playing clubs is not a way for most people to get rich, whether it's a successful young performer in a top room, or the field's highest paid older stars, like Rosemary—who, with her overhead expenses of everything from hotel and transportation to the cost of retaining six star jazz musicians, will just about break even at the end of her run. For the younger people coming to major visibility in this field, the mark of success is not measured by mass-oriented "pop star" equipment like sports cars and forty-room mansions. In many cases (though some make a good living), success is more likely to be defined as the ability to afford to keep on doing what they love.

On the day after Labor Day, Ann Hampton Callaway opened the season at Rainbow and Stars. Actually, the warm Tuesday night, which had come at the end of an interminably oppressive New York summer, marked the official start of the new season in general. "We're kicking summer out on its ass," commented one member of the Rainbow team, and the feeling of regeneration was reflected in the opening night audience, reunited like on the first day of school, watching the dark-haired, attractive young singer at the microphone.

"I want to thank everyone for traveling in from Easthampton and Southampton," she cracked, "to come to Ann Hampton."

Ann, in her mid-thirties, is among those who currently make up the top echelon of younger-generation women singers working in cabaret, along with colleagues like Karen Akers, Mary Cleere Haran, and Andrea Marcovicci. (There are others, like Maureen McGovern, Susanna McCorkle, K. T. Sullivan, Weslia Whitfield, and Nancy LaMott. And there are men, like Jeff Harnar, David Staller, and Phillip Officer, and piano entertainers Steve Ross and Billy Stritch—but the truth is that it's a field overwhelmingly dominated by female vocalists.) They inhabit the top-of-the-line venues like Rainbow, the Algonquin, and the Russian Tea Room (the Carlyle remains almost exclusively a stronghold of older veterans), and thus capture higher visibility and bigger paychecks than their lesser-known contemporaries.

But the younger singers making their way singing classic pop and jazz find themselves in a different boat entirely than their older colleagues from whom they will pick up the torch. Older stars like Rosemary, Barbara, and Julie—or Frank Sinatra, Tony Bennett, Margaret Whiting, Peggy Lee, whoever—though they enjoy popularity today, established their stardom years ago, when the music they were singing was America's mainstream music. Success automatically meant everybody knew you, with all the trimmings. Today, despite the jazz-pop renaissance with its growing audience and hip status, Callaway, Akers, Haran, and Marcovicci—along with Michael Feinstein and other baby-boom, rock-generation performers—begin life as anacronisms. They come of age with a sensibility stretching beyond the top-40 radio habits of their high school peers, usually awakened by the discovery of old movies and Broadway and Hollywood musicals. Set apart from the "in" cliques at school by tastes that brand them as different, they grow up and pursue a career where performing the brand of music they love at once rewards them with audiences and acclaim but at the same time holds them back from the really big money and fame that might come singing rock and contemporary pop.

For years, Karen Akers was followed around by agents trying to sign her to mainstream record contracts. With her powerful, full-bodied alto, and six-foot-tall fashion model look that's all bones and pageboy, Karen in the 1970s was playing Manhattan clubs like Surabaya, Mickey's, and Reno Sweeney, and men in suits from ICM would come and regale her with questions about why she wasn't doing more pop material in a vein that would get radio play. "I just felt silly singing those things," she says. "I mean, I experimented— 'Son of a Preacher Man,' 'The Night the Lights Went Out in Georgia'—but it wasn't me. But on the other hand, if I sang the Piaf song 'Mon Dieu,' or Craig Carnelia's, 'I Met a Man Today'—that *was* me. That was my sensibility, and my heart. The music showed me my intentions; in a sense, clarified them."

Actually, when she was in college, Karen had cut her fingernails and started singing and playing folk music. It was the spirit of Edith Piaf, however, that overrode all that, giving her a direction and inspiration in terms of material and approach to singing that today makes Karen, at forty-seven, stand out as the rare American proponent of European, art-song-driven cabaret. Piaf records were a household staple when Karen was growing up Karen Orth-Pallavincini on Manhattan's Upper East Side and attending a Catholic girls' school. ("Akers" belongs to her ex-husband, with whom she has two grown sons.) Her family was European: her father, from a titled Austrian background, her maternal grandmother, who lived with them, from Russia. The language of the house was often French.

Right now, Karen is preparing for her new show at Rainbow and Stars, where she last appeared about a year and a half ago. She has been among the top younger generation cabaret singers for almost two decades. She's occasionally branched out into acting, like her appearances in Tommy Tune's *Nine* and *Grand Hotel* on Broadway, in Woody Allen's *The Purple Rose of Cairo*, Mike Nichols and Nora Ephron's *Heartburn*, and TV stints like the one on *Cheers* as Cliff the mailman's girlfriend. She has a loyal following that approaches cult status, and she records regularly. She's just now finished recording a new album, *Just Imagine . . .*, and is awaiting its release, which will coincide with her Rainbow date. She makes her home in Washington, DC, where she raised her children after moving there in the late '70s to accommodate her then husband's law practice. "I cried for two days," she says of leaving New York. She recently remarried (her husband, Kevin, is 6'5"), and she is constantly in and out of New York on business, strikingly dressed (she favors big hats), trekking around town to her appointments and making note of health food restaurants she passes on the street.

Onstage, she cuts an austere figure with her brown bangs and regal bearing, singing a mix of standard ballads and songs, like Craig Carnelia's "Flight," by contemporary songwriters, and singing in

French quite a lot. The effect is dramatic, dark-hued, sometimes brooding. Offstage, she's always felt misunderstood by certain critics and audiences, ever since one newspaper in the '70s dubbed her the "ice goddess"—a moniker picked up by everyone else that has stuck to her through the many years since. It was a comment on her apparent aloofness and "high-handed" presentation, like the singing in French, and her reticence at engaging the audience between songs. Karen has long stopped worrying that some people are put off by her image, but it has always stung. In fact, the French songs are closest to her heart, a product of her European background, as is the slight detachment in manner and speech. The rest of the ice goddess persona was born of fear. "It was a totally defensive posture," she says, "just an uncertainty about how people would receive me. Twenty years ago, I was very shy. I was terribly insecure, terribly self-conscious. I had a blushing problem to beat the band. I've never felt superior to an audience, or aloof, but that's the way I must have come across, this hauteur. It makes a whole, very mysterious sort of person—and I'm not like that."

She's still searching for just the right presentation. She's tried to lighten up her image, show the audience that she has a sense of humor ("There is a funny lady behind the bones," she says). She's tried poking fun at her height by including songs like "Daddy Long Legs." Now she's in the midst of trying to decide whether to work on her new Rainbow act with one director who saw her act recently, and afterward proceeded to take it apart, admonishing her that she was wasting her efforts fighting the ice goddess image by attempting to prove to the audience that she's friendly. Karen was immediately unnerved by self-doubt, but started taking notes as he talked. She still isn't quite sure what she's going to do. She's never worked with a director before, but feels she could use some help with things like connective tissue—what to say to the audience between songs—and she's gravitating toward working with him. "It may not happen," she says. "It depends on whether he'll be willing to work for almost nothing. Because I have no money right now. I'm barely paying bills."

Karen, at the top of her field, accepts gracefully the consequences wrought by choosing to follow her passion over pursuing a mainstream recording career. "It does pay my bills, but barely," she says. "And if something goes wrong . . . And things happen. And it's tough right now, things are very tight. I'll be in better shape after Rainbow and Stars. Not much better, but better enough not to have to agonize."

Big money and national fame for a singer come out of major recording activity. Most younger generation singers who make a living singing jazz-based music in clubs or concert also record. But the irony of the business is that with a few breakthrough exceptions (Michael Feinstein, picked up by Elektra, caught on in a mass-oriented way; Harry Connick, with CBS Records to create and hype a persona, also broke from clubs to mainstream) most of the major recordings that have brought standard pop to the forefront of baby boomer mass culture have been "crossover recordings"—that is, by artists like Linda Ronstadt, Carly Simon, or Natalie Cole, known and established for their rock and mainstream pop success, now shifting their attention to something different. Their status as recording stars is responsible for turning their uninitiated fans on to this "new" music, thus creating audiences to go and see Karen Akers or Ann Hampton Callaway perform. Yet frustratingly, those rock-generation performers who've dedicated their professional lives exclusively to this same music have a hard time breaking through to the mass market, with its infinite material and personal recognition. But as Karen Akers says, "I'm very lucky to make a living doing what I like."

Her sentiment could be written in Latin on a banner flown by most of her younger generation colleagues, who recognize they've made a trade-off, but whose allegiance is to performing the material they love, that feels right for them.

Mary Cleere Haran is a lithe redhead, who in the last few years has been securing herself in the top echelon of younger cabaret performers. Her voice, a smooth, supple alto, and her jazz-inflected rhythmic sense have allowed her to be likened to Anita O'Day, with shades of Doris Day. This season, Stephen Holden of the *Times* will call her Rainbow and Stars show ". . . more than simply the best-sung cabaret act of the year; it is also the wittiest." The act, called "An Affair to Remember," is a compendium of movie songs from the 1950s, with commentary. Last season's act (which formed the basis for her just-released second album) was movie songs from the 1940s, with commentary. Mary's passion doesn't show onstage. Onstage, couture dresses skimming her figure (she trained as a dancer), she exhibits a cool charm and the Irish gift of gab, hanging back in her singing, reticent toward—rather than soaking up—audience adulation. Her heart is in the pop classics, uncomfortable with contemporary material. The considerable press she's captured loves to tout her retro image, a throwback, they say, to the screen heroines of '30s and '40s screwball comedies. She kind of likes all that, but it says little about who she is.

To witness Mary's passion, you have to observe her talking about her work. With a narrow face and pale, freckled skin, she's edgy and more intense than she lets on. She talks fast and low, and will make a deadpan quip followed by a hushed, restless laugh. It's the "with commentary" that drives Mary's talent. At forty-two, she gears herself toward her own generation, craving to introduce, or ignite, the same feelings for the romance and subtlety of the material that she herself feels toward it. She painstakingly writes her act as an "act," not preparing it as a group of songs, but choosing and threading the songs with anecdotes and information in a historical context in such a way as to lead her audience—many of them other rock-generation people—into cozy acceptance of the material. With wit and a formidable mimic's ear (her vocal impression of Marilyn Monroe singing Irving Berlin's "Lazy" is uncanny in its nuances) she prepares the culture of the room as if she is doing an organ transplant and wants to make sure nothing will be rejected as foreign. "Rather than just present them with, 'Look—isn't this a great song?'" she says, "you have to go a little bit of a journey, because you can't depend on whether people will be there, or understand. I want to help them discover it in a way that I discovered it."

Growing up in San Francisco in a large family (her father was a teacher, her mother emigrated from Ireland) she was weaned on *The Jack Benny Program* and awakened to old movies by her older sister, which developed her tastes in a way that made her something of an oddball among her peers. She spent her hippie days (she lived in a Haight-Ashbury commune at one time) in basic conflict between the movement's principles and its rock concerts: "So loud, so tedious, so macho," she says. "Except for Janis Joplin, no women were up there doing anything. Everybody looked like a slob. It was, 'This is expression? This is romance? No! This is a drag. This doesn't speak to me at all.'" Her life was irrevocably changed the night she saw Miss Peggy Lee, wearing white chiffon, perform at the Fairmont Hotel. Her mother disapproved—of Peggy Lee, of Mary's desire to follow in her footsteps, the whole thing. "It's an Irish-Catholic thing," Mary says, "not to make a display of yourself; that it's vulgar for a woman to get up there and be a feminine object." An ardent feminist, Mary is a strong proponent of the notion that cabaret is really a women's medium, primarily because it utilizes and celebrates the things that in our society (like it or not) women are most comfortable with—emotions, intimacy, the universal wisdom of childbearers.

Though she began performing in church basements as a teenager, she spent a lot of time doing things like working as a researcher on various PBS documentaries (particularly one on Doris Day), before finally putting her performing career into high gear when she was in her mid-thirties. Appearing in small clubs around New York and in stints like *The 1940s Radio Hour* on Broadway, her real success has come over the last few years. She lives in Brooklyn with her husband, Joe Gilford (actor-comedian Jack Gilford's son), a struggling theatrical writer/director, and their three-year-old son, and she grapples with trying to make a living doing what she likes. "Nobody said it was going to be easy," she says.

She's a walking illustration of the dilemma faced by many others. The root of it is that the mark of a major career is a major engagement in New York. She has that. A month at Rainbow and Stars in the spring. The problem is that then what do you do? Four weeks, give or take, even at Rainbow and Stars, can't support a person, let alone a family. There have to be other jobs for the rest of the year. Except, if you're an artist affiliated with a major club like Rainbow (or the Algonquin, the Carlyle, or the Ballroom) those other jobs can't be at other clubs, say the contractual and unwritten rules of the game. Work, hard to come by anyway, has to emanate either from outside New York (difficult, with a small child at home), or from specialty, one-night engagements in the city, like a private function, an industrial show, the Russian Tea Room. Mary feels the pressure. "I've got to figure out a way to make more money," she says.

Recently, her quest to get more work within the system blew up in her face. She's been with Rainbow and Stars for two years, since Rainbow spirited her away from the Algonquin, where she landed after coming up through the ranks. It has been the Rainbow gigs that have established her in a major way, and in return, her four or five weeks a year on the 65th floor are among their biggest draws. The time came recently for the Algonquin to celebrate the seventy-fifth anniversary of the Round Table, and it was arranged for Mary, who has a Dorothy Parker show, to go into the Algonquin for a week, in combination with other people, and do her Parker show as part of the festivities. Joe Baum, Rainbow and Stars' owner, reportedly was furious (he is a notorious stickler for exclusive relationships), but allowed himself to be convinced that her appearance there, which followed shortly after the close of her Rainbow show, was a special commemorative event that wouldn't hurt anything. Next thing, it's announced in the newspaper that Mary will be reprising her Dorothy Parker show at the Algonquin for a month in the fall. Baum hit the ceiling. "My agency was aware of the whole thing," Mary says, "and they thought they would deal with it in time. I thought they'd cleared it with Joe Baum. But apparently they hadn't."

In the brouhaha that followed, the booking for October at the Algonquin was dissolved, and the slot given away. It was made clear to Mary, who was in disgrace at the Rainbow head office, that her future at Rainbow was questionable; that Baum was so angry he didn't want her back. "It was implied that he'd never gotten so mad," she says. "It was bad. People told me, 'He's never behaved like this,' that it was very, very iffy that I was ever going to get booked back. I thought, 'My whole world is going to be destroyed, and I worked so hard to get there.'"

Long since having given up the idea of the additional work at the Algonquin, which would have paid handsomely, now she scrambled only to save her Rainbow job, which means everything to her. "I wrote him a letter," she says of Baum. "I had to write him a letter." Her explanation/apology and cool heads eventually prevailed. The situation salvaged, she's back financially where she started, worrying about the family bills. "You're between a rock and a hard place," she says with her restless laugh. "There's nothing you can do. And you just have to accept it." More and more, she's exercising the writing aspect of her talents, and was recently retained to write Leslie Uggams an act for Uggams's engagement at Rainbow and Stars next season. She's also writing herself a one-woman show, for which she has lined up a workshop production off-Broadway next season.

The yen to impart information to an audience as an integral under-pinning of the act is the mark of many women singers raised in the feminist era—and the talk, far beyond a songwriter credit or a con-nective anecdote, is mainly what separates them from their predeces-sors. That, coupled with the intense emotion she pours out over her audience, is what has spurred Andrea Marcovicci to her remarkable success. Marcovicci is something of a phenomenon, able to pack in audiences to sold-out houses, night after night, for runs lasting sever-al months. When she's in town, she reigns over the Oak Room at the Algonquin, which some in the business have begun referring to as the "House of Marcovicci."

Thin, dark, intense, dramatic, she radiates focused passion with everything she does. Although vocally she's struggled at times with intonation, in performance, her gift is always to reach out to the roomful of people surrounding her and will them to be caught up in her spell. The forcefulness of her bohemian-chic personality, the all-out raw feeling she emotes, and her penchant for articulating everything from researched material about the music to poetry that complements what she's singing, gives her a magnetism that is formidable. Whether she's doing a show celebrating spring, or one commemorating the songs of Irving Berlin, she exerts an emotional pull on people, and audiences are regularly swept off their feet. Nightly, there is a stack of letters left for her at the desk in the hotel lobby, from people who take time after the show to tell her how she had moved them.

Marcovicci, who's forty-three, has been around for years, as a folk singer originally, and as an actress on the stage, in movies like *The Front*, with Woody Allen, and on television. (She still acts, and appeared earlier this season on Broadway in Frank D. Gilroy's play *Any Given Day*). She, like Karen Akers, was raised on Manhattan's Upper East Side, the daughter of a physician and a singer. She recently married, and lives primarily in Los Angeles. With bobbed hair and a gaze that focuses solely on the person with whom she's talking, her manner is forthright and dramatic. While the occasional inattentive audience member is the bane of every performer, Andrea has been known to confront the person in the lobby when she's finished singing and ask, "Why did you find it necessary to ruin my show?"; she often gets an apology.

She only came to the fore of the cabaret scene several years ago, in the late 1980s, mostly by the design of Donald Smith. Marcovicci was living in California, and developed her act after talking the proprietor of the Gardenia, a Los Angeles club, into letting her have the place Saturdays at midnight. He practically gave her the key, and she held court and quickly started to catch on. Smith was introduced to her at a party while he was on a trip to San Francisco, and she was in the city appearing at the York Hotel. She communicated with him using a pad and pen, since she had put herself on complete vocal rest (a practice she still maintains today, not uttering a sound between her last show on Saturday and her first on Tuesday). Smith stayed over in San Francisco an extra night to see her act, and was instantly taken with her. Arranging on the spot for them to work together, within a few months he had booked her in New York at the Algonquin. Her reception there, aided by her instinct for promotion and that star quality of seeming to grow toward a responsive audience like a plant to sunlight, prompted her return year after year with four-month

The Rosemary Clooney of her fans' collective memory: the young star c. *White Christmas*.
(Photo courtesy of Gabriel Ferrer)

Mama Rosie, with husband Jose Ferrer and three-fifths of her children: Miguel, Maria, and Gabriel (on her lap) . . .
(Photo courtesy of Gabriel Ferrer)

. . . and today, backstage after a Betty Clooney Foundation benefit, with
(left to right) Rafael, Maria, Miguel, Monsita, and Gabriel. (Photo courtesy of
Gabriel Ferrer)

Rosemary and Dante.
(Photo: David Lotz)

Old friends: Rosemary
and Tony Bennett.
(Photo: David Lotz)

Barbara Cook at the height of Broadway stardom: as Cunegonde in *Candide* . . .

. . . and dancing with Robert Preston in her Tony-winning role, *The Music Man*'s Marian the Librarian. (Photos courtesy of Barbara Cook)

With her son, Adam, around 1960.
(Photo courtesy of Barbara Cook)

Barbara taking stage today. (Photo: Mike Martin)

Julie Wilson in her nightclub heyday, with three admirers: Noel Coward, George Raft, and Danny Kaye.
(Photos courtesy of Donald Smith)

Julia Mary Wilson, age 6.
(Photo courtesy of Julie Wilson)

Julie with sons Holt (l.) and
Mike (r.) in the early 1960s.
(Photo courtesy Julie Wilson)

Today, the reigning
Queen of Cabaret,
dressed for the office.
(Photo courtesy of Donald
Smith)

The unsinkable Annie Ross.

Barbara Carroll (backed by the Cafe
Carlyle murals).

Bringing standards to a wider audience: Linda Ronstadt (photo: Robert Blakeman)
and Michael Feinstein (photo: Sharon Weisz).

Four from the next generation: Karen Akers (photo: Paul Greco);
Ann Hampton Callaway; Mary Cleere Haran (photo: Hans Neleman);
Andrea Marcovicci (photo: Andrew Brucker).

engagements. From the beginning, with Smith's guidance, she generated a lot of press, and her cult status was on its way. ("She's been on everything but bread wrappers," Smith says.) She has used her visibility to champion young songwriters, and she regularly includes and records new work. Her projects edge toward the funky, like the concert she gave on Manhattan's Upper West Side made up of street musicians she'd rounded up. Her audiences span the yuppie set of her own generation, discovering cabaret for the first time, and older patrons who seem touched that this young woman feels so deeply for the music of their youth. Marcovicci loves that. "Every now and then, you see a twenty-year-old and an eighty-year-old, sitting side by side, enjoying the same song," she says. "Few musical forms can boast that."

At Ann Hampton Callaway's show opening the new season at Rainbow and Stars, Ann is singing one of the songs she wrote herself. The song has a Brazilian feel, and in the glamorous club, with the city laid out and glimmering behind her, she sings wearing a black dress cut low and gold filigree drop earrings, and she sways and tosses her dark hair to the sensual rhythms. Then mid-phrase, one of her dangling earrings drops down into her cleavage. She opens her green eyes a little wider without missing a beat, and the audience laughs, and when it's the musicians' turn to play a few bars, she turns away and discreetly pulls it out, and finishes the song. When the applause quiets down, she stretches out her hand toward a middle-aged woman, seated in the front, who bears a family resemblance. "Mommy," she says, "could you hold this for me till I'm done?"

Ann has really been coming into her own as one of the major young cabaret performers only in the last couple of years although at thirty-five, she has been around for a decade and a half, since she arrived in New York with her sister and talked her way into her first piano bar job. She'd been in New York three days, and she and her sister, Liz, had left their tenement hotel and gone to Sharma's, a piano bar on Third Avenue. They overheard someone make a request for the piano entertainer to play "Sometimes When We Touch," and he didn't know it. "I know it!" she piped up, and sat down to play, and her career started right then and there (the song was a favorite request when she sang with wedding bands back in Chicago). The cavalier *joie* with which she approaches life in general didn't permit her to worry that her ability to play the piano was limited, and what she could do was self-taught; she just methodically set to teaching herself hundreds of songs. "When I first came to New York, a friend of mine said to me, 'If you want to become a star, you have to do contemporary music; if you want to just have a nice life, you can do what you're doing now.' I walked into a scene that was not at all welcoming of who I was, except for a few places that would hire me. But there was no cabaret convention, there was no MAC; there wasn't the word 'cabaret.' Eventually it became that I was doing this work in, quote, cabaret. I'm just lucky that it turned into a community where I could find a home."

She managed to work steadily, in piano bars and restaurants like Les Tuileries on Central Park South, the Supper Club's Blue Room, and the Oak Room at the Plaza, with the requisite appearances at breeding rooms like Don't Tell Mama. Early on, Ann was singled out as one remarkably gifted. Blessed with an extraordinary, three-octave vocal instrument and the technique and musical instincts to support it (there are influences from artists like Streisand, and from Liza Minnelli, who befriended her), her creative facility extends to writing music and lyrics to songs she then performs. In today's cabaret scene, she is probably the closest follower of the poet-singer-songwriter tradition that her generation grew up with, people like Joni Mitchell, Carole King, Carly Simon, and Paul Simon. In performance, it's only recently that she's fully emerged from behind the piano, letting musical directors like the venerable Richard Rodney Bennett take over so she can just be there in front of the mike and sing. She's still getting used to it—and standing 5'10", she still grapples a bit with attaining physical ease onstage. A romantic's romantic with heartfelt ballads a strength (though she's cultivating the jazzier repertory, and she likes to scat), she exudes the coltish, earnest passion of a love-struck schoolgirl, and audiences are affected by the sterling quality of spirit that comes through when she performs. "When I sing, I feel like I'm going to cry any second," she says. "But when I'm happy, I feel like I'm going to cry any second. I once had an acting teacher who said, 'You cry and laugh more than anybody I know.'" She couples that with an off-the-wall sense of humor and ability to think on her feet, which has led her to develop onstage antics (from her days in noisy bars where she struggled to get the audience's attention) like having the crowd call out random words and phrases, and after praying to the cabaret God for inspiration, writing a song incorporating them on the spot. Hokey—but peculiarly successful. (She doesn't do this at Rainbow, where she represses it for a more sophisticated image.)

Growing up in Chicago, her father a television and radio journalist, her mother a singer/pianist/voice teacher, Ann had always felt like a misfit among her peers. Writing poetry and songs on the guitar her parents gave her for her tenth Christmas, struggling to express the emotions inside her, she was understood, she felt, mainly by her teachers. "It was very lonely, a lot of my childhood, I missed people who were concerned about the end of the world, or who seemed to be in love, or awed by nature." She read a lot of philosophy and poetry. "It was like, 'Books are the only things who understand who I am!'" she says, and laughs. "Or I'd go to the library and get a million symphonies: 'Rachmaninoff knew how I'm feeling—he understands!'"

Financially, Ann makes out better than a lot of her colleagues. One reason is that with her piano skills, she's a self-contained act, without need for an accompanist if the job doesn't warrant the expense, and she works all the time, all over the country. Recently, she wrote and can be heard performing the title song for Fran Drescher's CBS-TV sitcom, *The Nanny*, one of this season's hits (she'd submitted songs to other of Drescher's projects over the last years, and this one just caught). TV royalties would make any cabaret singer's life seem worthwhile. Last season, her first album was released to enthusiastic reviews, and she is currently working on another, to be released next fall, which will include a number of her own songs as well as standards.

Still, Ann probably has felt the glass ceiling more than a lot of her colleagues, mostly because her abilities and style make her seem the likeliest candidate to break through into the mainstream arena for a national success along the lines of Michael Feinstein's. She's felt the pressure over the years from people who have gushed about her talent. "A lot of people had this expectation, 'Oh, she's going to be a star,'" she says. "Then when I wasn't a star by the time I turned thirty, it was, 'Well, why aren't you a star?' I don't know! I'm doing what I do, and I'm working hard at it, and I'm working in lovely places." (The pressure was increased, because her younger sister, Liz Callaway, struck success early on Broadway, appearing in shows like *Miss Saigon*, and earning a Tony award nomination for her performance in *Baby*.)

Over the last few years, Ann has altered her sensibility to concentrate more on the work itself, less on what others expect of her career arc. She practices meditation, yoga, and free associaton, keeps a journal, writes poetry, and meets periodically with her friend Barbara Feldon (*Get Smart*'s Agent 99) to read it over lunch. If she wakes up to a beautiful morning and her schedule permits (she recently bought a condo on the Hudson in Dobbs Ferry, outside the city), she'll spontaneously get on a train for someplace like Croton Falls and spend the day hiking.

Ann, like many of the others who have chosen this field, is driven less by the lust for a megamillions success than by a burning need for self-expression. She always remembers one ladies' room attendant she encountered during her sister's Tony nomination party at Gallagher's. "She had every lotion, every perfume, every hairspray," she says, "and she was just in there doing her job, and she was so proud of what she did. And she was singing—she was singing up a storm. And you couldn't walk out of there without feeling very touched by this person's soul. And I just felt, there's this whole other way of being an artist. I was born with a level of fire, and the ability to funnel it, and a passion for expressing myself. I'm sorry for people who don't have that passion."

25

*B*arbara goes into the bedroom of her dressing-room suite and changes out of her gown. It's closing night for her at the Carlyle. The last show was a zoo, packed to the rafters with a mixture of the regular Saturday night audience and theatre and show business friends, standing two deep by the bar in the back as the waiters tried to squeeze through with their trays of drinks. The whole show had a kind of free-for-all, festival atmosphere that made it seem more like an overdressed Village piano bar than the Carlyle.

When she emerges from the bedroom in her silk caftan, the people have already started to ring the bell, and the living room is filling with friends who have come up to say hello. People love loitering in that suite. Her manager, Jerry Kravat, arrives, a big man with dark hair, a club business veteran who books the Cafe the rest of the season. His blonde wife is with him. They make themselves at home and talk to

Wally. John Beal, the bass player, is also there, having changed out of his tuxedo into a black turtleneck and pants. Barbara alternates between talking to the guests and calling to Louise, who is in the bedroom, starting to pack up the accumulation from their seven weeks of residence.

Other friends come into the suite, and a succession of awestruck fans who for some reason or other have made her acquaintance or are with others who have. They are introduced, and they shake hands, and she looks directly at them and gives them a big smile and a friendly "Hi, Bill," or "Bob," or whatever, and says, "It's nice to meet you," with the slight twang that remains of the Georgia drawl. Then one of the group takes out an instant camera and she poses smiling in the midst of the others.

Barbara's fans, almost more than any other group of a performer's fans, have a life all their own. They are a reminder that the word "fan" is derived from the word "fanatic." Her fans fall into two categories. There are the regular fans, people who come for an evening out, who know her records or who used to go to see her in the theatre all the time in the old days when she was on Broadway. They're always plenty enthusiastic and the husbands blush when they go up to her in the back of the Cafe after a show and tell her how they saw her in *The Music Man* when they were first married, and the wives tell her tonight's their anniversary, and how come she doesn't sing more of the old things, like "Till There Was You"?

Then there are the groupies. Barbara has hoardes of groupies. Real groupies, rabid groupies, who are passionate in their devotion to her, who deify her as a kind of earth mother goddess, and who are the ones who have made her a cult figure. A lot of them are gay—mostly gay men, some gay women—and a mix of straight men and women. They can recite all the lyrics from every show she's ever been in, in chronological order, or cross-referenced by the number of performances it ran. They travel hundreds, sometimes thousands of miles to hear her perform. You can always spot them during one of her shows, their heightened emotional excitement as they watch and listen approaching ecstasy. Louise was one, before she went to work for Barbara. She had worked, as she still does, in the theatre archive of the Library at Lincoln Center, and she first saw Barbara in the mid-1980s in a television special on the all-star concert version of Stephen Sondheim's *Follies*, from Lincoln Center. She began to go again and again to hear her sing, until she'd been to hear her seventy-seven times. When Barbara took the mother's role in the musical *Carrie* in

England and it was announced she would be leaving the show rather than come to Broadway with the company, Louise bought a ticket and flew to London on the spot. There, she saw *Carrie* eleven times. Then she wrote Barbara a letter, which is how they eventually met.

Carol Sargent has come into the suite with a couple of other people. A graying woman in her forties with steel-rimmed glasses, Sargent is the president and founder of the Barbara Cook International Appreciation Society, her fan club. Sargent also discovered Barbara on the *Follies* broadcast, and found herself obsessed. Having trained as a singer herself and currently working as a fundraiser for a private school in New Jersey, she decided to found the Society partly out of the need to do something constructive with all her newfound adulation, and partly out of the compulsion to somehow get closer to Barbara.

It wasn't hard for her to find like-minded fans, and they advertised charter membership in theatre journals. They have become a close-knit band of compatriots, accumulating a formidable music, audio- and videotape, and publication archive on Barbara's career, which they make available to music and theatre researchers. Once a year they publish the B.C.I.A.S. newsletter. It's impressive. It looks sort of like a black and white *People* magazine with only one subject. It comes out in September, along with Barbara's Carlyle engagement, and goes out to members spread across the United States, Europe, and far-flung places like Australia. The 1993 journal is forty-seven pages. It includes no fewer than sixty-four photographs and illustrations, and forty different features—reprints of reviews, articles, and references in the general press, and heartfelt testamonials from members covering everything Barbara's done over the past year. They also issue a fully photo-illustrated, black and white, twelve-month wall calendar.

People have long speculated why Barbara is a cult figure, attracting such passionate groupies with an attachment to her that in emotional excess goes far beyond the average fan admiration. Barbara's status emerged long after her ingenue days, when she had reestablished herself as the person she is now. People compare her position to that of Judy Garland, especially in their role as icons of the gay community. Garland, in fact, is one of the people Barbara cites as a musical influence (Mabel Mercer, with her attention to lyrics, is the other). From Garland, she says, she learned that every song has a beginning, a middle, and an end. Like Garland, Barbara is a highly emotional singer, and it is the suffering that both women so obviously went through that people seem to respond to. There is a kind of raw empathy about Barbara, a poignancy in everything she does. Like Garland, she exudes a dual image, and it appeals to both sides of her audience's psyche—at once the veteran, nurturing, seen-it-all mother and the uncertain, hurting little girl.

*B*arbara can bisect her childhood into two distinct parts: the sunny days before she turned six, and everything after that. She was born in Atlanta on October 25, 1927, two years before the Depression hit. Her father, Charles, was a traveling millinery sales-man, making his living on the road, selling ladies' hats. An upbeat, personable man, he was away from home a great deal of the time, and he used to call on the phone two or three times a week and ask his lit-tle daughter to sing him a song.

Barbara doesn't remember a time when she didn't sing. It was something she always did, the most natural thing in the world to her. "It was just a part of being alive," she says. "I breathed, I sang."

The family, of English-Scots-Irish descent, lived on the third floor of a small apartment house in town, which in the early '30s was far from the metropolis Atlanta would become. At that time, Barbara was a happy, confident child, who would get up to sing and dance for anyone who asked. When she was very young she was taken to her first stage production. "I was so excited when I got home," she says. "I felt such joy. I was dancing around the house, I was singing. I was thrilled. And I was having such a wonderful time because they were enjoying what I was doing so much. I was showing off, as I love to do, very early on."

Though she would grow up as one, she wasn't always an only child. She had a little sister a year-and-a-half younger, a baby with blonde curls on whom her parents doted. The baby caught pneumonia at one point, and almost died. Those were the days before antibiotics, and the doctor told the mother that if the baby were to get it again, she might not be so lucky. When Barbara was three and her sister one and a half, Barbara got whooping cough. Her sister caught it from her and died. Barbara remembers her mother, in her grief, telling her that if she hadn't given her sister whooping cough, the baby would have lived.

She remembers the day of her sister's funeral, to which she was not taken, and how to stop her from crying, her father had taken her over to the kitchen window, picked up a bottle of Mercurochrome and drawn a funny face on the palm of her hand with the red liquid, telling her that would cheer her up during the day.

She adored her father and loved his buoyant salesman's good humor and penchant for telling stories. When she was six, her parents would separate, then divorce. It was 1933, the depths of the Depression. Divorce was uncommon then, and a child from a broken home was an oddity, in the eyes of society an outsider with a faint whiff of disrepute. From the day her father left, everything would be different. What she remembered as a golden time would turn gray from then on. Reasonably comfortable before (considering the Depression), now they found themselves in dire financial straits. Barbara and her mother left their apartment and moved in with her maternal grandmother, who lived in half of a two-family house with three of her other daughters, one of whom was an invalid. Crowded into close quarters, there was often a lot of tension in the house, the adults constantly worried about money, the anxiety taking its toll on Barbara. The house was uncomfortable—cold in the winter, with heating from coal stoves and a cast-iron stove in the kitchen for cooking. Although the house was wired, the family couldn't afford electricity, and Barbara did her homework by kerosene lamps. (When she tells her son about it today, he thinks it sounds picturesque; at the time, it was anything but.)

In school, she felt like an outsider. The other kids came from families that were intact, and because of the poverty in which Barbara's family was living, she was often forced to wear the same clothes to school every day, for which she was ridiculed. From the really sunny, carefree little girl she was before her father left, she became insecure and ashamed of her family's situation.

"I think it's possible to have lived through all of this and not felt that I was poor. A lot of people talk about that, maybe because of the adults around them. People say, 'I never felt it.' Well, I did feel it. And I was embarrassed."

Though there were playmates, she became somewhat of a loner, beginning to enjoy solitary time with books, or listening to music. In her overcrowded living situation, she savored the hour and a half between the time she came home from school, when there was only her grandmother and invalid aunt in the house, and the rest of the family had yet to return from work.

Though Barbara saw her father occasionally as she was growing up, it was never for any significant length of time. But she continued to idolize him. "He had a tremendous personality, really, really sunny," she says. "He could hold you rapt with a story—a true salesman's personality. I probably wouldn't have idolized him so much if I'd grown up with him. But as it was, he was my hero. When I saw him, it was like Christmas had come to town." A few years after the divorce, he moved to Charlotte, North Carolina, and he remarried when she was eight or nine. Barbara saw much less of him. They spoke on the phone, and he wrote letters. When he'd come to Atlanta he would see her, but it would only be for short periods of time, and in between other things. "I always felt that I was being sort of fitted in," she says. "Like first he's going to do this, then see me, then do that. So even to this day I hate it when I see somebody in the early part of the evening, then they're going to go off and do something else. I feel so utterly abandoned."

After the divorce, her father's family began to disappear from her life. "With the exception of my grandmother and grandfather," she says, "I think the rest of my father's family didn't know how to deal with it. So I just saw less and less of them. Even in retrospect, it's still very painful."

Of all Barbara's close relatives, it was her maternal grandfather, Charlie, who had a real love for music and theatre. He had been divorced from her grandmother, and he was an alcoholic. (There was alcoholism on both sides of the family.) She didn't see her grandfather too often, but every once in a while he would come to visit. He doted on Barbara, who adored him. "He was a very gentle, placid, sweet man," she says. "My granddaddy would always want me to sit on his lap and sing 'Indian Love Call.' He loved me to sing to him."

They wouldn't always live with her grandmother. When tensions ran too high between her mother and the family, they moved out, only to move back in again later on. Her mother was working as a hotel switchboard operator, so Barbara was left alone a great deal of the time. It was up to her to make her own dinner and take care of herself while her mother worked the evening or night shift. Sometimes Barbara would be alone when she woke up, and would get herself off to school.

"It was a really lonely situation for me," she says. Her sense of feeling different only added to her insecurity and nervousness. "And I wonder how in God's name I managed to be in this business."

The only time, in fact, that Barbara was not nervous was when she was performing in front of people. From a very early age, singing in front of people was always the time that everything was all right. It was what people had always admired her for, and what she could do better than everybody else. It was the one thing she could do that she knew brought joy to others as well as to herself, and amid the bleakest of family tensions, somehow, for the moment, she could always make everything all right. "I could always hold an audience," she says, "even though I didn't know that's what I was doing."

She wanted to be Jeanette MacDonald. It was the barber in town who arranged singing lessons for her. She always had a dutch-boy haircut as a child, and when she went to the barber, her mother would have her sing for him. He knew the family was poor, and he convinced a woman he knew, who had some money, to pay for singing lessons and the carfare to get to and from them. The woman wanted to remain anonymous, and to this day Barbara has never found out who she was. "I hope she knew that I'd gone on to things," she says. "I hope so. It would be nice if she knew. I'm sorry I never had a chance to thank her."

When she would get up in front of the class in school for a song or recitation, immediately it felt right to her. From the age of seven or eight, she had sung in kiddie shows around Atlanta. The first work she got paid her 50 cents for doing a tap dance. Before long she was getting $2.50 for a show, and had joined two separate troupes that performed at army camps in the area, like Fort Benning in Columbus, Georgia, and for organizations like the Elks and the Rotary Club. On Saturdays, they performed in local movie houses, doing five vaudeville shows between the serials. "I loved the way people looked at me after I performed," she says. "They looked at me with a new admiration. It was some of the first feelings of respect I'd ever felt."

She remembers the day in school, when she was about fourteen, when she consciously realized she could hold an audience. "I was reading a poem or something, and I guess I had a good reaction. And I had that feeling—like when you're doing something you know is right. You know you're good at it. It was the first time I really thought, 'Shit—I know how to do this!'" Her mother came home from work, and Barbara kept her new knowledge to herself until dinner was over, because she had this big announcement to make. Finally, when they had settled down, she said to her mother, "I have something to tell you, something very important. I learned something today, something really, really important. I can act." Her mother, probably like the mother of a lot of teenage daughters, said, "That's nice," and suggested they clean up the dishes. But from that day on, Barbara knew she had something.

Apart from the singing, high school was no easier for her than grade school had been. In many ways, she felt even more isolated. Added to the stigma of her family situation was now the fact that with her interest in music, art, books, and the finer points of movies, she didn't have that much in common with anyone else. "Most girls I knew in high school were interested in boys and getting married and gossip," she says. "Not that I didn't like gossip, too. But they just didn't have an artistic bent. I finally found one friend, Jo Forrester, and she was a year ahead of me at school. And it was like the two of us against the world. She was really the only one I felt close to, who understood my interests."

The lack of money was still a big problem, and it added to the difficulty of making friends. She was living right at the edge of a wealthy part of town, Druid Hills, and a lot of kids in the high school she attended were well off. "Atlanta's a very social town," she says, "and high school was very social." The big thing was to be in a sorority, and she was chosen for one, which she loved. She had to pull out of the sorority, though, when they were raising money for a dance and the girls had to either sell out their tickets or come up with twelve or thirteen dollars. At the time, her mother was making thirty dollars a week.

She didn't date a lot, but she was always falling in love. Every week. Passionately. "God, I had awful crushes, very early on. I was in love constantly. It took me a long time to break that habit. I'd keep diaries. If Joe Kelly gave me a little piece of Dentyne, I'd keep the wrapper. I'd put it in my diary. I still have some of these things."

Actually, there were very few boys around who were interested in ideas, as she was. In the Georgia of the '30s and '40s, racial prejudice was part of the atmosphere everybody breathed, and Barbara had been submerged in it her whole life. It had never made sense to her, and it outraged her, although, as with her penchant for listening to classical music, there was no direct influence that would suggest why. As a child and teenager, it fed her disgust with Atlanta and her determination to leave it as soon as she could. "I was surrounded by people who thoughtlessly were extremely prejudiced," she says. "And I don't have any idea why I couldn't buy that, because I didn't know one person close to me who didn't believe that. I guess there were teachers, but nobody talked about it.

"I fought against it, I'm sure in some stupid ways. I would sometimes get on the bus and go sit in the back with the black people. I was militant about it, I was making a statement. But I'm sure that in doing some of those things, and trying to be friendly with black people, I was only making them more uncomfortable. And I wasn't ready to be comfortable with them myself. But I knew I didn't want to be put into that southern racist mold."

She finished high school just as the war was ending. She had taken typing in high school, and her mother wanted her to get a job with the civil service as a secretary, which she would do when she went to work for the Navy Materiel Redistribution and Disposal Office. It had never seriously occurred to her mother that Barbara's talents could earn her a career in show business. She just wanted to insure Barbara's security, and a job with the government was one way to do it. At one point in high school, there had been a choice between taking French and taking shorthand, and mother and daughter locked horns. The romantic teenager, who was enamored of all things French at the time, somehow convinced her mother that while she would someday have a use for French, she would never have one for shorthand. (Sure enough, today she'll occasionally sing in French.)

Even so, it took a while before Barbara could fully believe that she would really be allowed to make a life out of music. "I held two thoughts at once," she says. "That I could do this thing—but positive I'd never get a chance to do it. The idea that I would have a chance seemed so remote; it was like the dream of the world. Things like that didn't happen to me. It wasn't until later that I thought, 'I have to really try. At least try.'"

After the Navy job and one following it at a government housing agency, she and her mother packed for a trip to New York. It was supposed to be a two-week visit, but Barbara was packing for a much longer stay, having decided to try for a career on the musical stage. "I must say, I never, ever thought I'd go back to Atlanta," she says. "Not ever. I wanted to get away from Atlanta almost as much as I wanted to be in New York to see what I could do."

The Broadway Hour is a radio show in New York that tapes every Thursday at five o'clock off the lobby of the Sheraton Hotel on Seventh Avenue. If you look through the window from the street, you can see them there, sitting around a table with microphones. Barbara is being interviewed by the entertainment critic from television's Fox News, Stewart Klein, who also hosts this show. He's asking Barbara about the good old days in *The Music Man*, and how she liked working with Robert Preston (she loved it) and about the success the current revival of *She Loves Me* is having (she's happy) and what she thinks of the new Broadway production of *Carousel* (not much—but then, she only saw it in London).

Passersby in the lobby stop to watch the proceedings. When her segment is done and they break before going into the next segment with the priest who is doing some charity event, Stewart Klein shakes hands with her and tells her how nice it was to have her on the show.

She steps down the two steps to the main part of the lobby, and looks at her watch. She's dressed in pants and a turtleneck and a scarf, with a gold pendant. Right now she's supposed to head uptown because Dixie Carter is opening at the Carlyle, but she's still got about an hour to kill. She turns to the two other guests who were on the segment with her. "How about if I buy you kids a drink?" she says. They start for the bar, where she will order a Perrier and lime, her usual drink. On the way across the lobby she's stopped by a family of tourists who ask her for her autograph. Then they ask would she mind if they took a picture with her, and she poses with her arm around them. She asks where they're from (Ohio) and are they having a nice visit to New York (yes) and are they seeing any shows (*Miss Saigon*, tonight). They tell her how they love listening to her albums ("Well, thaaaank you," she says with her hint of a drawl) and that they recently saw her on television performing at the White House. She tells them to enjoy the rest of their stay. They smile and blush a lot.

Since her closing night at the Carlyle, she's been to California to recuperate and stop by Pritikin, gone to London for a club date, and played a run at the Terrace Theatre in Washington, DC, before coming home to her orchids and perpetually disorganized paperwork in her Riverside Drive apartment. She's gone on a strict diet and exercise kick, walking several miles a day on the treadmill.

She'll be leaving town again soon, to go back to London for a series of concerts at Sadler's Wells, where she'll record a live album. The Dorothy Fields album has been doing so well, the DRG label wants her to do another, so she and Wally have begun to talk about what to include.

Before this year she hadn't thought about it much, until the publicists and record people and her manager brought it up, but it's going to be her and Wally's anniversary together. It will be exactly twenty years since her career was reborn in cabaret.

In the second half of her Russian Tea Room run, Julie recovers her bearings. When she finally shakes her cold and has performed all the new material enough to feel sure of it, she settles in, and the patrons who come in to see her show in the last two weeks see the old Julie—secure, magnetic, in masterful control of her audience. Beginning Cole Porter's "Down in the Depths, On the Ninetieth Floor," she holds the microphone in both hands quietly in front of her, to the accompaniment of somber block piano chords. "'With a million neon rainbows burning below me,'" she intones with a desolate edge, and then closes her eyes. Relating the empty sophistication of an isolated woman imprisoned in a gilded penthouse, she stands very still, her facial expressions by turns weary, snarling, ironic. "'While the crowds at El Morocco punish the parquet,'" she continues with bitter restraint, allowing herself to move her head from side to side as she gathers steam, spitting out the words, building emotionally until she finally engages her right arm in motion, briefly— before returning it to join the left once again, holding the mike. At the song's climax, her face is pained, intense, desperate, but she still doesn't move, and she finishes quietly, ruefully, with voice and eyes lowered: "'Down in the depths, on the ninetieth floor,'" she sings, and bows her head.

Julie's intensity in relating to people is the source of her magnetism. With her opalescent eyes, she doesn't just look at you when she's talking to you—she sort of looks into you, as if she can really see what's under your skin but is too polite to mention it.

The penetrating attention she gives an individual in conversation comes out onstage in the laserlike focus of energy directed at the audience. The result is that it's impossible to take your eyes off her.

The reason is that Julie has a highly developed, innate mastery of the art of attraction. In today's world, spellbinding—the nuances of captivating people (the skills that Gigi's courtesan aunt tried to impart to her ingenuous ward)—is a lost art. For Julie, it has nothing to do with phoniness, or putting on an act, or trying to be seductive. Behind the sequin gown, the feather boa, the gardenia in her hair, and the smoky voice, Julie's flat accent of the prairie is there without cosmetic surgery, her pioneer underpinnings there for anyone who cares to look. What she does have is a subtle command of the ability to fascinate. And she fascinates everybody—men, women—but especially men. It's the intensity, the way she makes one person at a time feel like the only person in existence, the crack in her voice when she talks, the slightly off-color shadings she will give to a comment or a lyric, with only a hint of amused seductiveness. It's a mastery honed by so many years of experience that it's just become the way she is.

Onstage, Julie refines sex appeal to high art. Men find her very sexy. All kinds of men. Young men, come to her show from their yuppie jobs, older men, who remember her from her Maisonette days, or just men enraptured, watching her for the first time. Age is not an issue. She turned sixty-nine the week before her run started. It's true that when she walks into a room, dressed for the evening, she is stunning to look at. But actually, the fact that she's an older woman, exuding the languorous, implied mysteries of all her experience, is what makes the attraction so powerful.

In her Russian Tea Room show, she's about to do a song that's one of her signature numbers. It's a campy little piece of special material that she bought outright for a thousand dollars in 1954 from an English music-hall performer who needed the money. She reaches over and puts her hand on a blue feather boa that lies on top of the piano. She looks through slightly drooping eyelids out into the audience. "I'm going to need the help of one of you gentlemen," she says. She looks around, and fixes her gaze on one of the front tables. "How about you, sir?" A middle-aged businessman gets up and blushes, and eagerly steps up to the platform. "One should always have help getting into a feather boa," she says seductively, and gives him the end of the enormously long boa. "Now just hold that," she says, and as he holds the end, she turns around toward him until it envelops her. "You've done this before," she says, and he blushes and the audience laughs. "What's your name?" "Uh—Jim." "Well, thank you, Jim," and she gives him a kiss and sends him staggering back to his seat to a round of applause. Then, holding the boa around her, she starts to sing, "I'm a bad, bad, bad, bad, bad, bad, bad, bad woman/But I'm good, good, good, good company . . . ." (Julie buys her feather boas either in New York's wholesale feather district, on the West Side, or in a shop on West 14th Street that is also a major supplier to drag queens. Ostrich feathers are among the best, but hard to come by. She usually settles for turkey.)

Julie has a repertory of songs that are right for an older woman. Her favorite opening number, which she likes to think of as her theme song, is "Don't ask a Lady (what the lady did before, ask what the lady's doin' now)," which Cy Coleman and Carolyn Leigh wrote for the revival of *Little Me*; its basic message is time is short and plastic surgery is fragile, let's get to it before everything drops. Another of her specialties is Stephen Sondheim's "Boy, Can That Boy Foxtrot," an ode to a younger man, its double entendres delivered by Julie with delicious understatement and an elongated "f" on "foxtrot." A few years ago, a woman came up to her after a show at the Carlyle and said she was a singer from the Midwest, and she loved the way Julie did the song but whenever she herself tried to sing it, it came out sounding dirty. Julie told her, "It isn't a dirty song. The way you're approaching it in your mind is making it that way. All you're saying is that you're having a most enjoyable time with this young man who you're obviously very attracted to and is obviously a very good lover. But there's nothing wrong with that. You have to have a sense of humor about it; you must have fun with it; you must enjoy it."

When the material is serious, facing the issue of being an older woman is more uncomfortable. One of the new songs she put into this year's show is one she first heard from the songwriter/piano bar entertainer Charles DeForest, when they were sitting around the piano one night at Danny's Grand Sea Palace on 46th Street. He said, "Julie, I have a song for you. I want to play it for you." It was "He's the Kind of Man . . . ." It's a sort of gigolo song about a young man and a lonely older woman, and she was instantly taken with it. When she began to dig into it to perform it herself, she found it was a little close to the bone. "It's a terribly personal song," she says, "about needs, and being human. I've never verbalized in a song before that particular part of living. You know, it's easy to kid about sex, to be tongue in cheek about sex and sex appeal, if the song is fun, and naughty and blatant, and putting it on the line. But that song gets close to home. There are some things that are very personal, that you might express quietly to a very intimate friend. Then all of a sudden you find yourself singing about it to a roomful of people. I guess I could edit my material, but I really don't want to do that."

After the Tea Room show, Julie goes up to her dressing room to change out of her gown into the dress she'll wear between shows, and she comes back down to the front dining room outside the cabaret, where people are waiting to greet her. Coming into the room, before being noticed, she sits down abruptly at a table with two very surprised diners to put her shoes on, because her feet hurt her, as usual, and she's come barefoot down the stairs, carrying her shoes in her hand. Then, in the bronze colored gown, the gardenia still behind her ear, she gets up to greet her public.

A bald man in his sixties comes excitedly over to her, with his wife, and waits for her to finish talking to someone else. She finally turns to him. "Miss Wilson," he says, "I've been a fan of yours for forty years." "Well, isn't that nice," Julie says, extending her hand, and smiling. "We drove all the way in from Pound Ridge to see you." She shakes his hand. "What's your name?" she asks him. "Uh—Philip." She holds onto his hand, and looks directly into his eyes. He blushes, and looks like he's about to hyperventilate. "Thank you, Philip," she says. "I'm so glad you could come."

★ 29 ★

It's a rainy Sunday afternoon in Greenwich Village. The rain has alternated between coming down in sheets, and just sprinkling in a dreary mist. Julie comes down the street from the subway, and goes into Eighty Eight's, a club on Tenth Street, just off Bleecker, that serves as a showcase for wall-to-wall performers, many of them young or starting out in their careers.

Julie has finished her Tea Room run. She has come in from New Jersey on the PATH train to see two separate people, one scheduled to go on at 5:30 and one at 8:00, who have come to her in the past for advice and who very much wanted her to come and see their shows this evening. In her performing mode, Julie might be considered cabaret's reigning queen. The rest of the time she is widely held to be the Mother Teresa of the cabaret set, tirelessly trooping out night after night to encourage the young and minister to the sick of heart and talent.

The bar is virtually empty downstairs. Later on, at 9:00, or 10:00, or 11:00, it will be jammed as one of the hoppingest piano bars in the Village, with the singing waiters belting show tunes, and the crowd joining in. But now it's only 5:15, and the only people there are three young men at one table drinking seven and sevens, and the bartender, a good-looking thirtyish man with a long blond ponytail and an earring, wiping the bar and singing along with jazz singer Diane Schuur, whose voice is coming over the speakers.

"Hi, Julie," the bartender says when Julie comes in. Everybody knows her there. She's there at least once every week or two, usually more. She's come in with her customary large black tote bag over her shoulder, her purse, which she sometimes puts inside the tote bag if she's on the train, if it fits, another shopping bag, and an umbrella. She leaves the umbrella in the wastepaper basket by the front door, and she goes up the curving, carpeted stairs to the cabaret room. "Hi, Julie," says the sound and lighting man. She goes through the glass door into the gray-carpeted room. "Hi, Julie," says the dark-haired waitress, Helen Baldassare, a singer and comedienne, who also works there. Julie has greeted them all with a crackly "Hi, darling, how're you doin'?" and really listened to what they said back.

It is five minutes before showtime, and except for two waitresses and the pianist, who goes over to fix some music on the piano (and says "Hi, Julie" on his way back), there are only four people in the entire room. They sit huddled and damp with their coats beside them on empty chairs. Julie is shown to the round table right in front of the microphone, and she begins the reverse cocooning process, opposite from the covering up she does when she goes off to the Port Authority and New Jersey late at night. She piles the tote bag, the shopping bag, and her purse on the empty chair beside her, and takes off her wet raincoat and puts it on top. She takes off the babushka, folds it, and puts it inside the tote bag for later, and takes out a pair of black shoes, which she swaps for the tattered running shoes on her feet. The running shoes go in the bag, and she begins to rummage for the earrings that she knows are in there somewhere, and she takes out a sweater, a bulging address book, a wallet, checkbook, token purse, and several things wrapped in Kleenex, one of which turns out to be the gold earrings. She has a habit of wrapping certain things in Kleenex—jewelry, keys, what-have-you—which she has on at least one occasion thrown out. She puts on the earrings by feel, and then takes out a compact and lipstick and fixes her makeup. She smooths her hand over the front of her hair, which, it being a casual occasion, is in one braid down her back, a "Pocahontas day," as the guys in the bar like to refer to it. She's fully emerged, chic and together in a black slacks suit with a loose jacket.

The singer is hovering nervously in the back of the room. Two more people have straggled in. The pianist seats himself and announces the singer, and she comes down to the platform, wearing a black cocktail dress. She is not the prototype of the usual beginner who looks to Julie for support. She is a fifty-four-year-old professional woman with grown children who always wanted to be a cabaret singer. She has taken some voice lessons, and a few years ago got into the summer Cabaret Symposium at the Eugene O'Neill Theater Center in Connecticut, where Julie serves on the advisory panel. Last year, she did her act for a couple of shows at Eighty Eight's. When she steps up to the microphone, Julie applauds loudly and cheers the woman's name. The act lasts an hour. The woman is very earnest, and has worked very hard on a lot of strung-together medleys and special material—familiar things with clever or "relevant" lyrics added, and specially tailored things not in the familiar repertory. (Jean Harris is the subject of one number this afternoon.)

"A lot of work went into that," Julie says after one long, dramatic segment, and when the show is over, she applauds louder than the other five people in the audience, and when the woman comes over to her after taking her bows and looks at her needily for approval, Julie points out several things she liked in the show, and the ways in which she was stronger than in last year's show.

Erv Raible comes over to Julie's table. Raible is the owner of Eighty Eight's, and the founder and president of MAC—the Manhattan Association of Cabarets and Clubs—dedicated to the promotion and advancement of cabaret as an art form. Most notably, they sponsor the MAC awards every March (which, through their efforts, has been designated "Cabaret Month" in New York). Raible is a short, square man with sandy brown hair, a thin moustache, and an outgoing, upbeat disposition, dressed in black pants and a black tee shirt. Back in his native Cincinnati, he'd been a schoolteacher, teaching visual arts and art history to fourth through twelfth graders.

He came to New York with his friend Rob Hopkins, also a teacher, in 1978. They'd had the idea they wanted to go into the nightclub business, and for a year, they drove the 700 miles from Cincinnati, and then back again, almost every weekend. They settled on the Duplex, on Grove Street in the Village, a club where in better days people like Woody Allen, Joan Rivers, and Dick Cavett started out. When Raible and Hopkins opened the piano bar, Raible waited tables, Hopkins poured drinks. Soon they'd turned the upstairs room into a cabaret with a piano they bought from a neighbor in Brooklyn, cultivating a following and press with bookings and public relations they did themselves. With its success, they opened another club, Don't Tell Mama, on West 46th Street, and another, Brandy's, on the Upper East Side. They had caught the cabaret resurgence that was on the upswing in the early 1980s, and they presented slews of young hopefuls, including, early in their careers, Ann Hampton Callaway, Mary Cleere Haran, Phillip Officer, Jeff Harnar, Nancy LaMott and others who went on to prominence in the field. Hopkins fell ill, and the clubs were sold off, though Raible held onto Don't Tell Mama until some time after Hopkins's death, before parting with it in 1989. He opened Eighty Eight's in the spring of (what else) '88. There, he tries to keep up with the number of (mostly) young performers clamoring to be booked and with the club's schedule of shows: two a night, Monday through Thursday, two or three on Friday, three or four on Saturday, and usually four on Sunday. Unlike the uptown clubs of the Carlyle or Rainbow variety, each show belongs to a different performer. If a performer is to play more than one show, it's usually something like Wednesdays in April at 8:00 P.M., for example. Or every Friday night at 11:00, a slot that the female impersonator Miss Coco held for two years. (Another of the club's biggest draws, Long Island-born Baby Jane Dexter, a large, raunchy-humored blues belter with wild blonde hair and eye shadow, has played there for Saturday night runs that have lasted seven months.)

Raible estimates that for every three to five slots per month he has open for new talent, twenty-five performers a month beg to be booked. Most come to him through recommendation by others in the business; he does little auditioning. For the ones who do get the slots, the club's arrangement is not a bad one. Raible provides a sound and light technician and a two-hour technical rehearsal. In exchange, the club takes one dollar off the cover charge (soon they'll have to raise it to two), which is around ten dollars, and the performer keeps the rest. The room seats sixty-five comfortably, eighty-five if absolutely necessary. The club makes its money on the two drink minimum with each cover. ("I don't know," Raible says, laughing. "I thought I would get rich. You know, that TV thing that shows nightclub owners in a silk suit . . .")

Raible still does all the press himself, but it's mostly up to the performer to fill the seats. As in every segment of cabaret, the performer absorbs the cost of everything. People starting out often pour thousands of dollars into getting an act together. (There is a mini-industry of people who make a good living fueling the career ambitions of the talented and not-so-talented.) In an average scenario, the money goes for postcards and fliers, plus mailing costs, and a musical director/accompanist, who averages between $100 and $150 a show, plus anywhere from $20 to $50 dollars an hour for rehearsal (however, sometimes singers and pianists make a special ongoing financial arrangement). Then, some use a stage director to shape the act and help with things like patter, and they earn a similar hourly wage. There are things like wardrobe, props, hair and makeup, and publicity photos . . . . "I know people who spend $10,000 to $15,000 a run," Raible says. "It could be six or eight shows. I don't think it's anything for a performer to spend $2,500 or $3,000 for a shot at it."

The talent pool (excluding areas like comedy and impersonations) is a mixture. There are singers of the traditional variety who are there primarily to get up and sing songs. Then there are the requisite dilettantes

(Raible prefers the word "dabbletantes") who want to sing and have the money to do it, and may do one or two shows a year, with an audience comprised of their friends.

Eighty Eight's and other mid-level, piano-bar-type rooms like Don't Tell Mama, Danny's Skylight Room, and Rose's Turn are also breeding grounds for a lot of musical-comedy-style acts: revues or acts derived from a Broadway show idiom—both in musical material, and in their structured theatrical conceits. There are lots and lots of young performers who fit into this category, and as they perform in the various rooms, often forming one another's audiences, they have become their own self-referential culture. In this stratum of cabaret, theirs is probably the dominant culture, providing lampoon material and "in" jokes about the personalities who work in the business, largely feeding on itself. Some of the performers are mediocre, a few are exceptionally talented. Many of them have gone to the O'Neill Center's annual "cabaret camp" to be coached by performers like Julie and Margaret Whiting (as well as directors and professionals like Raible and Donald Smith) about how to put together and market a cabaret act. Even so, you often can't help feeling a pall of futility over much of what one sees, no matter how engaging, because you wonder where they can take it next. The more traditional club-style singers, even with a carefully constructed act like Mary Cleere Haran's or Andrea Marcovicci's (their "construction" is largely about annotating the musical material), will move up into rooms like Rainbow and Stars and the Ballroom and the Algonquin. Apart from jobs on- or off-Broadway in musical comedy itself, there is no longer much of a track in the real world for what a lot of these other performers are doing.

Raible estimates that over the last fifteen years, in his various clubs, he has presented about fifteeen hundred young performers. Out of that, he estimates that maybe one or two hundred make a living per-forming—which he thinks is a generous guess. Out of those he fig-ures that maybe fifty people are actually able to make some kind of a living in cabaret.

Raible's job is tinged with the bittersweet reality that those he nur-tures early in their career generally fly away, because his is a club from which, in most cases, people move on as they move up. He doesn't mind that, because it's the way things are, as long as they remember their roots. It irks him when they don't, just as it infuriates him when sectors of the business, especially the press, put down Eighty Eight's and rooms like it as being tainted by amateurism. "It would be nice if everybody arrived full-blown out of the Algonquin," he says. "Then I'd want to own the Algonquin. But it doesn't happen that way. A lot of people act like these rooms never happened. But these are the rooms where people start."

✳

Julie has never discouraged anybody she's come across who wants to sing, even when other people tell her that in certain cases she should. "I don't think that's my place," she always says. It goes along with her philosophy that life is short and if you really want to do something, you should give it your best shot and go for it. So she holds onto the scores of fliers her novice acquaintances send her, asking her to please come and see them perform. Most of them are in their twenties or thirties. She tries to get to as many of them as she can, often going to two or three of their shows a night, several nights a week, paying the full cover charge (which goes to the performer) unless the performer comps her first. When they ask her for a comment, any comment, on their work, it soon afterward shows up on their next flier as a quote, with "–Julie Wilson" after it.

That, and benefits, is part of the reason that even when she's not working, Julie is running all the time, driving herself constantly, never coming to rest. She often goes alone, which she doesn't mind, and she knows people wherever she ends up, anyway. "There's so much to do," she always says, "and not enough time to do it all." She feels a responsibility to go out to see the kids perform. It's a priority with her; she feels it's something she can give back. That's also the reason she does more benefits a year than she can keep track of. She doesn't have the money to give away, so she feels it's all she can do.

As a result, most days she leaves her house in Jersey City in the early afternoon, and doesn't get home again until well after midnight, as she will tonight.

First, she will see the eight o'clock show at Eighty Eight's, a young European man she coached up at the O'Neill. Then she'll take a subway up from the Village to 57th Street and the Russian Tea Room, where Helen Schneider, a young singer who has been getting some attention, especially in Europe, is doing a Sunday night.

Julie gets there just in time for the second show at 10:30, and the staff of the Tea Room is delighted to see her. One of the young managers from the restaurant, who lives a few minutes away from her in New Jersey, asks her how she's getting home, and says he'll drive her after the show, which is a relief, because it means she won't have to drag herself down to the Port Authority bus terminal. Jackie Krull, a young, long-haired singer who is the Tea Room's cabaret coordinator and is standing at the entrance to the room, embraces her and shows her to a table in front. A middle-aged man who's a friend of a friend comes over to say hello, and asks her if she needs a ride home to New Jersey, because he lives right near there. She thanks him and says she already has one. Starving by then, Julie orders a steak, and gives the rest of the audience a living example of how to eat a full meal while seated directly in front of a performer and not be noticed (it's all in the timing—when to cut, when to lay your knife down, and when to raise your hand to your mouth, synchronized to the music).

As it turns out, by the time the show is over shortly before midnight and the rest of the audience has gone home, the young man who was going to give her a lift has learned that because the menus are to be changed the next day, he'll be kept there for two more hours. Julie takes it in stride, and tells the young man not to worry about it, and starts to gather her bags together for the bus ride home. Julie's used to the Port Authority in the wee hours, her cocoon of the old raincoat and running shoes and babushka hiding all but the makeup on her face. "The drug dealers don't bother me," she says. "They just think I'm an old prostitute who's had a bad night." Jackie says she'll drop her in a cab.

It's been a long day for Julie. Before her club hopping, she spent the afternoon grocery shopping for her son Holt, who has the flu. She went through the kitchen of his apartment on the Upper East Side and was horrified at how ill stocked it was, and that he didn't own a can opener. Even though he makes a good living as an actor, it goes against her Depression-bred, touring-veteran thrift that he spends so much on ordering out. So she went around the corner to D'Agostino's and bought him some supplies and a can opener.

Now, at half-past midnight, she and Jackie walk downstairs through the deserted restaurant, to the front door. "Goodnight, Julie," the coat-check girl calls, as they step out onto 57th Street, lit up and motionless except for the hustler who accosts them, shaking his cup of change.

*M*aking the best of whatever was to be had is how Julie grew up in Omaha. Born on October 21, 1924, of primarily Swedish farming stock, she came from a long line of disciplined workers who did for themselves. Her father, Russell, who sold coal, came from Stanton, Iowa. He was a drinker, impatient, with a hot temper, who was out of the house at six-thirty and in his office at six-forty-five every morning of his life. When he wasn't working at the office, he worked around the house and the yard.

Her mother's maiden name was also Wilson—Emily Bennett Wilson. She was originally from Missouri, the seventh of twelve children. "People always say, 'Where do you get your energy?'" Julie says. "I think I was born with it. I think it's my heritage. My mother's and father's people were farmers, they all worked hard. My mother started when she was seven, out in the fields, hoeing beans. My mother's mother, Grandma Elizabeth Wilson, would like have a baby and two hours later, she'd be out helping."

From the age of twelve or thirteen, her mother had gone to work for a schoolteacher in Nebraska as a housekeeper. She cooked, she sewed, she canned, she baked bread, she cleaned the woman's house and did all the washing and ironing, until she was sixteen. "Of course, the schoolteacher did nothing but correct her English and her grammar," Julie says. "She adored my Mom. And my mother always spoke beautifully."

A thin, pretty woman with black hair, Emily decided to learn to be a hairdresser, and went to beauty school. It turned out, when she went to work in a beauty parlor, she had a knack for marcelling hair, the marcel wave being the rage at the time. "You'd heat the iron in a little stand," Julie says, "so you'd have this hot steel curling iron with a handle, like a fork. And if it was too hot, you'd burn the woman's hair. You had to know what you were doing. And she made these waves for all the wealthy women. My mom could really twirl that iron. And if somebody had a problem, it was 'Go get Emily.'"

Russell Wilson chased her in a Model T Ford, which his father had indulged him with when he was twenty, and the two were married.

Julie grew up with her brother, Russell Jr., who was a year and a half older, and the two were inseparable. Later, she would have another brother, Lawrence, who was eight years younger.

She was christened Julia Mary, Julia for her father's sister, who had died of tuberculosis at the age of twenty-one, and Mary for her mother's sister. Before she was in kindergarten, she had changed her name to Mary Lou, because there was a song that went "Mary Lou, I love you/Cross my heart, yes I do," and she had a doll cradle with "Mary Lou" on it. Her mother went along with it, and she would be Mary Lou into adulthood, when a public relations man told her it was corny (and there was jazz pianist Mary Lou Williams, which would be confusing), and she should use Julie. None of it really mattered, because at home, she was always called "Sis." (Her brother Russell was always "Junior.")

When the Depression hit, the family moved outside of town, to a house with a few acres. Her mother went to the bank and asked to borrow fifty dollars. "It was the only time in her life that she ever borrowed a penny," Julie says. The bank asked her what she wanted it for, and she told them it was to buy a cow. They gave her the money, and she did buy a cow, and some chickens, and the family sold milk. That area of the country suffered hard in the Depression. People who were homeless or hungry were always coming to the door of the Wilson house and Julie's mother would take them in. "She never turned anyone away," she says. They also took in boarders.

Julie and her brother made some money, one summer, by ordering firecrackers by mail and selling them at a stand by the side of the road. They each made enough to buy a bike. After a few years, they moved to a house her parents built inside the city limits. She grew up there, and she still owns the house.

"It's funny," she says, "but I never felt poor." She attributes that to her family's heritage of doing the best with what they had. "My mother had always been poor, I guess, coming from a family of twelve children, and being farmers. But she had never felt poor either. They grew everything they needed. They cured their own hams, they grew their own corn and potatoes, and they canned hundreds and hundreds of jars of peaches, and corn, and relish. They baked their own bread every day. So there was always that sense of having enough." Julie's first job was selling pens at Christmastime at a little local shop.

Although her childhood was far from luxurious, it was a relatively happy one. She was close to her mother and brother. She learned from her mother's wizardry at baking pies. She had friends at school, and went on to attend Benson high school. When she would get ready to go out on a date, her mother would do her hair. "Friday night," she says, "that was the big date night. I'd wash my hair, and Mom would get out the old curling iron and make all these curls on top." In her high school yearbook, under "goals and desires," Julie listed first, being an actress and second, being a schoolteacher.

Julie has always felt the drive to perform, as long as she can remember. She began at the age of six, with a song she learned called "Josephine," in which she first exhibited her characteristic penchant for the dramatic for those around her who would listen. "'There never was a gal I could love/Like my Josephine/She's a flirt, she's a scamp, she's the vampiest vamp/ I've ever seen.'" "I did it with all the gestures," she says. "Don't ask me where I got that, or why I was attracted to a song called 'Josephine,' with those vampy lyrics."

By the time she was fourteen, she was singing with local bands. But she never had that much confidence in her voice, which was the reason that when she rose to the top of the nightclub scene, she would largely confine herself to witty, naughty special material. After high school, she enrolled in Omaha University, majoring in drama with a minor in music. She had only been there a short time when one day her aunt Nora called her and said that Earl Carroll's Vanities had come to town and one of the girls had gotten pneumonia, and they were looking for a replacement, and they were going to make her a star.

Julie called them up, and introduced herself as Mary Lou Wilson. The man asked her if she could sing, and she said, "A little." He asked if she could dance, and she said, "A little." He told her to come down, and she put on black-cherry lipstick, fashionable at the time, and auditioned with a scale and a timestep. She was told to see Minnie about a costume, and she came back out in the scanty top and little skirt. They said, "You're a little hippy, but you'll do." She was in show business, with a paycheck of forty dollars a week, and when the company finished in town, she left Omaha with them and started life on the road.

Part of her was embarrassed by what she'd done. The revue had burlesque-type comics and in her sketchy costume she was part of a trio that sang songs like "Morning Glory." ("'Morning glory, morning glory/Lift your petals to the sky,'" they sang). When she left the university, she was ashamed to tell them why. The job of informing the school was left up to her mother when the dean of women finally called the house to find out what had happened to her.

Though she had always gravitated toward sophisticated material and had the show biz bug, the girl who left Omaha for the often seamy world of nightclubs and show business was a naïve, wholesome, cornfed thing, to whom people would repeatedly say for the entire early part of her career, "You're a nice girl. Why don't you go back to Omaha and get married? You're too nice for this business." She was so naïve compared with the other Vanities chorus girls that although they did five shows a day, she kept taking off her makeup after every show. Ironically, she would go on to become the toast of the after-dark world, the personification of supper club sophistication, as she remains today. But there's a part of Julie that always feels she should be back in Omaha, baking pies.

* 31 *

At Eighty Eight's, another one of Julie's novice acquaintances is singing. Julie has already had a long day. She was out until 2 A.M. the night before, and left the house around midday to catch the PATH train and make her daily voice lesson with Keith Davis, before trudging around on various errands and stopping by her makeup man, Steve Herrald, as she does every day that she needs to be somewhere in the evening.

Following the show she will go down the street to a bistro where the husband of the woman who's singing is hosting a small dinner party for a few friends, and she will sit there captivating a wealthy businessman from Palm Beach, who will suddenly remember that when he was thrown his bachelor party at the Plaza's Persian Room in 1954, she was there singing. Then after dinner she will ask that the rest of her steak be wrapped up (also her hostess's), and she will take it home for her dogs. She can't stand to see food wasted. But all that won't be for another couple of hours.

When she came up to the cabaret room at Eighty Eight's from the bar downstairs, lugging her customary baggage, she looked tired. Now, she sits on the banquette, listening to the red-haired singer. In the semidarkness, with the overflow of stage lighting from the front, she suddenly doesn't look drawn anymore, but luminous and glamorous. From day to night, light to dark, Julie is like changeable silk, or one of those 3D picture cards that changes before your eyes if you turn it slightly one way or another. She is thoroughly a creature of the night, blooming at late shows, at peace in the smoke and clatter and rippling jazz chords of the clubs. That's why she objects when managements forbid her listeners to smoke while she's singing. "I grew up in it," she says. "So maybe the air wasn't pure, but it wasn't antiseptic. It was earthy, and smelled like booze and cigarettes, and it was a saloon." And to Julie, no matter what you want to call it—regardless of the fancy venues or the sophisticated presentation, or the lofty descriptions of her artistry—in her heart, what she is and always will be is an authentic, true blue, dyed-in-the-wool saloon singer.

*I*t's Rosemary's night off from Rainbow and Stars. She's agreed to do a benefit for the National Academy of Recording Arts and Sciences, which is jointly honoring the memory of puppeteer Jim Henson and songwriter Joe Raposo, who wrote a lot of the material for the Muppets and *Sesame Street*. It's being held as a cocktail reception at the Regency Hotel on Park Avenue. The party has a *Sesame Street* theme. Big Bird is scheduled to attend. So her daughter Monsita comes down from Connecticut with her oldest son, Nathaniel, who is nine and dressed up in a blue blazer and a tie and gray pants. The organizers have reserved a table for Rosemary during cocktail hour, but she has opted to stay in the dressing-room suite upstairs with the kids, Dante, her manager, Allen, and saxophone player Scott Hamilton and his wife and two-year-old son. They all come down when it's time for the formalities to start. They show some old clips on the TV monitor of a young Rosemary on 1950s television singing "On the Street Where You Live" as a duet with Kermit the Frog. Then Rosemary, wearing a black dress, comes in from the back of the room and up to the microphone and sings two songs, the first one being "An Ordinary Dog." Monsita stands in the doorway watching her mother, her hands on her son's shoulders, making sure he can see his grandmother.

By the time she's done, Big Bird is hanging around the anteroom waiting for pictures. At the Regency, it's kind of an alarming sight, but it's New York. The photographers are there. Picture time. First Big Bird and Rosemary. Rosemary puts her arm around Big Bird. Big Bird puts his wing around Rosemary. Rosemary smiles. Big Bird just kind of looks the same. The photographers flash away. Now the kids get in the picture. Now Rosemary gets out of the picture, and Big Bird poses with just the kids, who don't seem to be jarred at all by the unlikelihood of the situation. "OK, honey," Rosemary says to Nathaniel, "now look up at Big Bird. Look up at him." The grownups have a great time watching the kids and the bird.

They're going on to dinner at her son Rafael and and his wife, Sylvia's, house, where Sylvia's mother, who's visiting from Italy, has cooked dinner for the family. But Monsita has to start back to Connecticut with Nathaniel, because he has school tomorrow. They say good-bye in the lobby of the hotel. Rosemary says a private good-bye to her grandson, stroking his head with her hand and telling him how on the weekend, he'll either come down to stay over with her at the hotel, or she and Dante will come up to Connecticut to see him and his two little brothers. They don't know yet that more snowstorms are going to keep any of that from happening, and she will get to see him only once more for the rest of the time she's in New York, when he comes up to see the show with his parents the night before closing.

Rosemary and Dante wait out on the street in front of the hotel for the car that will take them to Rafael's apartment. It's cold, and Dante tries to get her to put a scarf around her neck, as he always does. She says no, and he tries to insist, and she waves him away. They're into their Burns and Allen act again: "Now—cut it out, honey—just—just, never mind." They stand out on the street under the light of the hotel canopy, and the car still hasn't pulled up. Dante playfully steps up close to her, faces her, and opening his coat, stands there holding it around her to keep out the elements. This softens her up, and she lifts her face when he bends down to give her a little kiss on the mouth.

Rosemary and Dante feel like they've been together forever. When someone recently said to her, "So you've been together twenty years?" she laughed and said quickly, "Oh, no, it's much longer than that." Then she started to count, and realized it's been just over twenty years, though they've known each other much longer. They always say they'll never get married. They've both been married before (Dante was married to a French chorus girl), and they're happy the way they are. He can tell when she needs her quiet time alone to recharge and regroup, and he stays away; he also knows when to be around. Dante is like a large kid—part of which is that he rises to the occasion with the offbeat things he knows people are expecting from him, like the booklet he sent away for showing a hundred different ways to use garlic; or his detailed idea for a nightclub in space; or how he fell asleep on the couch in their flower-filled suite just before Rosemary's opening and woke up amid the blooms thinking he was dead. They bicker constantly, and she finds a comfort in that, partly because a lot of it is done for its entertainment value.

She's relieved that the youngest grandchildren now know to laugh when they see them arguing, instead of asking her, "Are you really mad at Poppa?" and she'd have to tell them, "No, no, no, no." And when one of the grandchildren is sleeping over and there is a thunderstorm, Rosemary and Dante will wander independently into the child's room and they will sit there together by the bed in case he or she should wake up frightened.

Dante never had any children of his own, but since he came into the family at a time when Rosemary's children were still school-aged and at home, he's close to them and is a grandfather to their children. "It was always comfortable with Dante," Rosemary says, "always. It's wonderful, because we have the same history as far as memories are concerned. The same music, the same things, the same time frame. With Joe, I always had to be careful. He was sixteen years older than me. I always felt I had to be cautious. But with Dante, I don't bother myself about that. If something's on my mind, it comes out of my mouth. And he'll say, 'OK, Rose-*may*-ry.'"

At Rafael's apartment on the West Side, his mother-in-law has spent the day preparing dinner. Rosemary has always been a big fan of Italian food. She settles onto the couch, and Rafael brings her an Absolut martini. Rafael, her baby, is an actor. He has blond hair and blue eyes, and he looks very much like her. He has his father's deep voice, which serves him well, because he's made a success doing commercial voiceovers. He's landed some big American Express commercials to run during the Winter Olympics, and for the last two weeks he's been going around repeating "Don't leave home without it" in Norwegian. The walls of his apartment are hung with a number of paintings by his father, and some by his artist brother Gabriel, who's married to Debby Boone and lives in California.

"You look very homey and cute today," Rosemary tells him, as he plays host. Being there is a chance for her to unwind, before going back to work tomorrow. She gets very focused when she works, especially in a long run like this, where the physical demands are so great. Usually, if she's doing a single concert somewhere, she'll prepare, and then when the concert is finished, she'll relax and go out with the people closest around her for some dinner; she always treats. But with this run, where there's always another show hours away, there's no room to do anything but keep up the regime. As much as she loves to be with friends and family, Rosemary needs a lot of time alone. People around her know the signal, because she partially shuts down communications. To unwind, she watches television (a lot of CNN and Court TV, to which she's addicted), and she reads and writes letters, usually all at the same time.

Since her breakdown and recovery, she's tried consciously to break old habits like needless worrying, and dwelling on anger and guilt and her natural tendency to feel responsible for fixing everything for the entire world. In her reordered thinking, she tries to minimize the annoyances that are out of her control, and concentrate on what's really important to her. Her philosophy is that if you can control it, do something about it, and if you can't do anything about it, don't get hung up worrying about it. It doesn't always work, but she tries, and she'll occasionally get impatient with someone close to her who's belaboring something that is finished with or can't be helped. She has also learned the value of being in control of the things you can control, that can make life more comfortable and less stressful, leaving unencumbered energy to do good work. Rosemary, like Barbara and Julie and others who have reached her stage in life, knows too well that there will be plenty of things to come along that nobody has any control over, so it's good to take charge of what you can.

Of course, she still worries. She worries about her children. "I really wake up in the morning and say, 'Who's where? What are they doing? What are they thinking? And what are the things that maybe could go wrong, what are the dangers out there?' I still do it, every day of my life." She also worries about her grandchildren, and Dante, and her brother, and what's happening around her and if she's hurt someone unintentionally. She tells the group at Rafael's about how a few nights ago she ran into one of the kids from *Saturday Night Live* outside the GE building, where they both work. He told her he was a fan of hers, and she returned the compliment, referring to the obnoxious character he has on the show and saying, "I love you, you're so ..." and searching for the right word ... "snotty." She immediately felt she'd said the wrong thing. He said something like, "You know, it's really only a character," which of course she knew and she said so. But she really felt bad that maybe she had hurt his feelings, and it's still bothering her. She's thinking of writing him a note.

*I*n a sweltering auditorium at P.S. 41 on West 11th Street in the Village, four hundred people sit fanning themselves with sheet music. They have two things in common with one another. They can all sing, and they're all gay. They're called the Unity Choir, and they're made up of part of the Gay Men's Chorus, and others, both men and women, from around the city who have come together to participate in the weeklong celebration honoring the anniversary of the Gay Liberation Movement, touched off in the Stonewall riot twenty-five years ago, on the night of Judy Garland's funeral.

Tonight, they are rehearsing an anthem written for the occasion by classical composer John Corigliano and playwright Bill Hoffman, which the chorus will perform in the opening ceremony. For their soloist, they could have asked any number of people to stand up beside them in the stadium tomorrow. They wanted Barbara.

Barbara is a little late, as she usually is, only because in trying to get all the loose ends organized, Barbara is always running about fifteen

minutes behind life. The conductor starts to rehearse the chorus anyway, and while they're singing, she comes in from the back of the
room, unnoticed. She is wearing a long black tee shirt and pants and
silver jewelry, and her brown purse is slung diagonally over her
shoulder. Standing in the back by the door, she joins in singing her
part, her voice soundless under the din of the chorus. Nevertheless,
she stands there, her mouth moving, rocking back and forth as she
sings, until the conductor notices her, and stops the chorus. The conductor stretches out his arm toward her. "Folks," he says, "Barbara
Cook." Four hundred people whip around in their chairs to look.
Then they begin an ovation that will last almost five minutes. First
they applaud, and the applause won't stop, then somebody rises to
his feet, and in waves, they follow, and the applause grows louder,
and they start to shout, until the room echoes with the roar. She
stands there, drinking it in, moved, smiling and saying "Thank you,"
even though nobody can hear her.

After rehearsal is finished, at about nine, a group including the
composers, her secretary, Louise, and her son, Adam, walk through
the streets of the Village looking for a good place to get some dinner.
Barbara comments on the arrival of the World Cup soccer fans in
New York coinciding with the Stonewall anniversary events. "I hope
there won't be any incidents," she says, "all that testosterone running
rampant." She pauses to admire the architecture along the street and
stops by the window of a hair salon to marvel at an orangy-yellow
hibiscus tree visible through the glass. "Isn't that beautiful," she says.
"My favorite color hibiscus, too." The group settles on an Italian
restaurant that's down a flight of stairs. They talk about the concert
tomorrow. "*Oy vey*," Barbara says to Louise. "I still don't know
what I'm gonna wear."

After the performance at the opening ceremony, Barbara and the
chorus are supposed to repeat the same thing for the closing ceremony, a week later, at Yankee Stadium. The singing will go well tomorrow, but there will be a number of problems with the way the people
running the whole event handle things—like leaving her name out of
the press release and therefore the *New York Times* blurb, doing the
same thing in the program (the composers have also been over-
looked), and giving her bad placement in relation to the cameras so
she is given short shrift on the stadium's big-screen TV and generally
can't be seen. Even though Barbara won't particularly notice the
problems, it will make the people around Barbara very angry. They'll
ask that certain things be fixed if she is going to do the closing perfor-

mance. The person running the event, of which the chorus is only a small part, will get so abusive with Jerry Kravat, her manager, that Barbara, because she believes in the cause, will call up herself to try and smooth things over, only to have the person tell her, "I thought you were doing this because you're idealistic."

That's the problem with doing benefits. Barbara is giving her services free of charge, because she wants to help out. But it's still a performance in front of an audience, where her abilities are being judged. If she's not presented well, the audience won't know or care that she's doing it for free, they just see what they see. But because it's a benefit, there's less control over what they do see. Barbara will fret about the situation and try and decide whether to pull out because the guy is so obnoxious, or whether to see it through. "The thing that's upsetting," she says, "is that if you do pull out, the performer always comes off looking bad. Especially a woman performer. There are things you need to have a certain way, because you're the one out there being judged—and they say, 'What a bitch.'"

In the end, she will do the closing performance, and everything will be in place, and it will go over well. But tonight at the Italian restaurant in the Village nobody's thinking about any of that. Because O. J. Simpson, who has recently been accused of slashing the throats of his ex-wife and her male companion, has just evaded arrest and taken off in his white Ford Bronco, threatening to blow his brains out. As everyone digs into their linguine, he is leading police on a chase across the freeways of California. Every few minutes the waiter comes in from the kitchen, where the television is on, and goes from table to table giving a progress report. Several tables of people have recognized Barbara, and a middle-aged woman comes over and says to her, "The music is still going on in my head," and when the woman realizes nobody understands what she's talking about, she explains by telling her how she remembers seeing her in *The Music Man*, and what a big fan she is. But every time the waiter comes in with the next installment, attention keeps turning back to O. J.

Finally, they are the only ones left in the restaurant, and on the way out, everybody crowds into the narrow kitchen with the dishwashers to look at the tiny black and white television on the wall. The white Bronco is still rolling down the freeway, and nobody seems to be able to do anything about it. The little Italian proprietress, crammed in the kitchen watching with everybody else, says in her heavy accent, "I feel sorry for poor O. J.," at which point Barbara answers, "Well, I don't—he'd been beating up his wife." Opinions, for Barbara, are not things to be bottled up. "I never had a gray opin-ion in my life," she says. "I feel strongly about things, and I almost always overstate my case. I certainly can come on strong."

As they leave the restaurant, the proprietress takes Barbara aside and, in broken English, explains that everyone has told her she's somebody famous—and apologizes for not having recognized her. Barbara smiles and mumbles something about being a singer. "You know who come here all da time?" the woman says. "Hildegarde." "Oh, she's a darling," Barbara says. "She eighty-eight year old." "Yes, isn't she amazing?" "She celebrate her eighty-eight birthday at Eighty Eight's." "Yes." Barbara is trying to get out now, because she wants to get back home to her apartment to watch the O. J. Simpson events. Like Rosemary, she is a CNN addict. "You know who else come here? Charles Kuralt."

Barbara will get home in time to see Simpson taken into custody. And pick out what she's going to wear for tomorrow's performance.

* *34* *

*I*n between shows at Rainbow and Stars is about an hour and a half. The first show is at 8:30, the second begins at 11:00. With getting in and out, it leaves a little over an hour to kill every night. For Rosemary, it's less time than that, because of the people who come to say hello. First, there are the people she knows, some of them old friends she may only get to see once a year. They'll knock on her door and walk in, or she'll come out into the alcove by the phones.

Then there are all the other people. She doesn't know them, but they know her. To them, she's family. They call her Rosie. They wait for her to come out of her room, and they stand there smiling and nervous, and when she's done talking to whomever she's talking to, they go up to her and tell her how much she means to them, and take flash pictures with her arm around them. They tell her that

"Tenderly" was playing the night they got engaged, or that their cousin once sat next to her on a plane; and once in a while they'll tell her that they, too, suffered some sort of breakdown and that her story has lent them courage; and Rosemary will give them a hug.

Rosemary is an object of universal public affection. Everybody somehow feels she belongs to them personally. It's not only because she's homey and direct and accessible. It's because she's been a part of their lives. Rosemary never takes her fans lightly, even when she's exhausted at the end of the night, and she's got her coat on trying to get down in the elevator so she can go home, and they continue to engage her in conversation. She feels a very strong sense of obligation to them, never forgetting that they're the reason she is where she is. She is also sensitive to the nostalgia she elicits. "Very often I'll run into a guy my own age, or perhaps a little older," she says, "and he'll say, 'We danced together in the Philippines.' Now, I never went to the USO things during the Second World War, because I was too young. But I worked with Bob Hope, and all these people, so the perception is there. And you know, the first time that guy said that, he knew it wasn't true. But now it's become true; now he believes it happened. So I say, 'I was there. I remember it very well.' And they look so relieved, sometimes. Because they're standing with the wife who doesn't really believe it's true, anyway. You know, it's only a moment for me, and I walk away from it. But it's part of their history."

It's between shows, and Rosemary has chatted and extricated herself from well-wishers, and is spending the remainder of her between-show break in her dressing room reading and relaxing, as she usually does. Outside in the lobby, people on their way out of the first show, on their way in to the second, or on their way to or from the rest room are glued to the bank of TV screens watching the Winter Olympics, as they have been for the last week and a half. A few days ago, it was to watch speed skater Dan Jansen break his long streak of mishap and tragedy and win a gold medal. Tonight, Tonya Harding is skating her final program, and there is a crowd gathered to watch as she skates over to the judges and hoists her leg onto the rail, explaining with tears and pantomime how her shoelace broke and she should be given another chance to try again later in the lineup. Several patrons get into a heated discussion about the issue of whether she was responsible for having Nancy Kerrigan clubbed in the knee (someone points out that Peggy Fleming would never find herself in that situation).

Rosemary, who has lost the bet with her manager that Harding wouldn't be permitted to skate, has already written out a check.

Between shows, Rosemary's musicians hang around together in the side lounge just past the cabaret room, or if they get restless, they wander around the lobby or go over to the bar to get a drink before going back to the lounge. In their tuxedos, they are constantly being stopped and asked directions to the men's or ladies' room (as is Dante). More often than not, rather than just tell the person, they'll walk the person over to the spot and point it out. In the chairs scattered along the edge of the lounge, they sit with their back to the view and schmooze. Mostly, the three veterans, guitarist Bucky Pizzarelli, drummer Joe Cocuzzo, and bass player Jay Leonhart, hang out together more, joined by John Oddo. Bucky, Joe, and Jay work together pretty regularly. They've just cut an album together, with pianist John Bunch, that the record company has dubbed *New York Swing.* Joe had been a little put out because on the first album they did in the series, his name, "Cocuzzo," came out mangled into something else entirely.

They talk about Musician Things. Like parking. What rate they're getting at the garage. Or the union rule about getting reimbursed. Or how they know what the parking rules are for the different streets where the different clubs are so they know where and for how long they can leave their car. (The Algonquin, on 44th Street, is great, because of the way the meters work.) Or how they'll be playing a set somewhere and know that by a certain number their meter is running out, and they'll have to run out between sets and put in more change. Or they talk about other jobs they're doing, or just did, or are about to do, and who else is going to be there, and they gossip about whoever it is. They talk about the different bandleaders they've worked with.

Joe Cocuzzo is thin, with high cheekbones and curly gray hair, and he stands very straight and has a habit of putting one hand in his side jacket pocket, and he always puts his glasses on when he's ready to play. Originally from Boston, he used to play drums with Harry James's and Woody Herman's bands, and for a number of years, he played with Tony Bennett, when Bennett was using a thirty-five-piece orchestra. He writes a little, as well. He commutes to work every night from New Jersey.

Jay Leonhart is tall and lanky and very loose-limbed at the bass, and when he solos, he closes his eyes and scrunches forward and sings "ba-do-ba-do-ba-ba" in unison with whatever he's plucking out. He's from Baltimore. With his round, professorial gold-rimmed glasses, he always has a sheepish look on his face, and he writes a lot of droll songs that he performs and records, like the one about sitting next to Leonard Bernstein on a plane, or the one about playing night after night at Rainbow and Stars and knowing that everyone is really only looking at the view behind him—which he says Rainbow's management found less than appropriate, and requested that he not do that one there anymore.

Bucky Pizzarelli used to work in this same building some thirty years ago, when for a while he was a studio musician at NBC. Now his son, John Pizzarelli Jr., has been having much performing and recording success as a jazz guitarist/singer. Bucky has a heart-shaped face, silver hair, wears glasses, and is dapper, always with a red silk boutonnier in the lapel of his tuxedo. He also lives in New Jersey, and with all the snowstorms in the last couple of weeks, he's been stranded in the city once and stayed over with one of his kids; a few nights ago, the blizzard was so bad he couldn't get into work at all, and the band had to do without him. On the other hand, last week, he was scheduled to play for the lunchtime series at St. Peter's Church at Citicorp, and he arrived at noon to find that the concert had been canceled because of the weather. But he was there, and so was one person in the audience, so he played for an hour and had a great time.

If he's not eating his dinner of oysters ("I'm gonna lower my cholesterol," he says every time he orders them), usually Dante wanders into the lounge between shows. He knows where there's a cappuccino machine in the back kitchen, and he and Bucky know how to use it. Then Dante tells his stories, about how his mother brought him to Hollywood from his native Denver when he was a very little kid, because he was a whiz tap dancer, and how she took him to audition for the movies, dressing him for the audition in a top hat and tails because that's what Fred Astaire always wore, and until she saw all the other kids at the audition in rehearsal clothes, she thought that was what dancers wore. Or about how he went on to dance in a lot of the MGM musicals in the '50s, like *Seven Brides for Seven Brothers*, or his days doing Monte Proser's Tropicana nightclub show in Las Vegas, or about when he replaced Bobby Van on Broadway in *No, No, Nanette* in the early '70s.

On the night of Tonya Harding's shoelace incident, everybody's wandering around waiting until it's time for the second show to start, intermittently checking out what's happening on the TV. Dante and Bucky are standing across from the bank of TV screens, against the wall where Benny Goodman's photo history begins, and Bucky is telling Dante about a recent discovery he's made. "Mane and tail shampoo," he's saying. "What?" Bucky says it slower. "Mane and tail shampoo. Like for a horse." "Naw . . .," Dante says. "Yeah," Bucky says. "It's terrific stuff. I heard about it when I played this gig in Dallas. All the rich society ladies use it down there." "Mane and tail shampoo?" Dante says. "Mane and tail shampoo. It's great, look at my hair. But you've got to get it at a tack shop. It was funny," Bucky continues, "I went to a tack shop near where I live in Jersey, and I asked the girl there for mane and tail shampoo. And she said, 'You're not going to shampoo a horse in this weather!' But I'm telling you, it's the best stuff. I've got to get some for Rose."

When Rosemary comes out, ready for the second show, she stands outside the room with the musicians waiting to go on, as usual, and she's a little shaken. "You know what just happened to me?" she says to the guys. "See that girl?" She points to a young woman in tight pants, high heels, and a gold sequin vest, who has just walked by and gone in to be seated. Then she tells how she was in her dressing room reading. She hadn't locked the door, because suddenly it opened, and this girl came in, and closed the door behind her, with a wild look in her eyes. She told Rosemary, "I just wanted you to know that tomor- row I'm going off to Minnesota for rehab, but tonight is my last night out, and I'm doing cocaine and drinking Courvoisier." The girl wouldn't leave. "And I'm sitting there in my curlers trying to look cool," Rosemary tells the guys, "and I'm thinking, 'Aha. Where's Dante?'" He did walk in, by chance, and pleasantly escorted the woman out of the room saying, "OK, we've got to get ready for the show now." When he had closed the door on her she stood outside the dressing room and started knocking again persistently, but they didn't answer. Finally she went away, though she's now sitting inside with a man for the second show. During the show she will sing along quietly, and get up a couple of times to leave and then come back. And after the show is over she will go back into the bar, where eventually she will lose all control and at 1:00 A.M. be taken away by ambulance.

On the whole, Rosemary has had good luck with who has come in to see her. At different times during this run, the tables in front of her as she sings have been visited by people like Helen Gurley Brown, Joanne Woodward, Bob Mackie, Jane Powell, Joey Heatherton, Gloria DeHaven, and Barbara Walters, who came with Senator John Warner.

When she stood up to sing after her breakdown in 1968, it was another story altogether.

*W*hen Rosemary emerged from her illness and hospitalization, she found herself playing at the Holiday Inn in Ventura on weekends, where people who had stumbled in off the street would talk through the show. She needed the money. But virtually nobody would hire her. The word was out. After twenty-five years of building a reputation as a thorough professional, the incidents surrounding her breakdown had branded her a bad risk. "Is she still drinking?" club owners would wonder, assuming that had been the problem.

The bills from her treatment were already amounting to exorbitant sums, and although her psychiatrist gave her consideration by cutting his hourly fee almost by half and instituting a very modest payment plan, it was out of necessity that she went back to work, before she felt she was really ready. Though Ferrer had been paying some child support, she had a lot of people depending on her.

She was off any drugs now, with the exception of the mood elevators prescribed by her doctor. But it was only about six months after her release from the hospital, and she resented that it was all too soon. She had begun to gain a lot of weight, and was no longer the girl from *White Christmas*, the Rosemary that people expected to see. From an audience perspective, it was as if overnight she had become a zaftig maternal presence instead. She had not yet regained any pleasure in singing or entertaining, and it showed. When she did work (she had begun with the Tropicana in Las Vegas), she went in on time, but unenthusiastically, recited by rote the material that she was programmed to do, and collected her paycheck. The word that spread damaged her professional viability even more, and employers and audiences alike stayed away in droves.

But a change was taking place in her. At home again with her children, the oldest of whom was turning fourteen, she began to reorder her universe. For the first time in her life she was off the treadmill, and was able to prioritize, from scratch, what was important to her. She planted a garden. "Now I know what fish emulsion is," she says. She'd gotten into decoupage, with its thereputic value, and to this day she remembers with undying affection the friends to whom she gave the trays and trinkets, who appreciated just how much the activity had meant to her at the time. She got hold of a book called *Cook, My Darling Daughter*, and she learned to cook. "My mother didn't know how to cook," she says. "And I read it, and they had a chapter, 'Souffles Aren't Scary.' The first paragraph said 'Anybody that comes in the back door and is hungry, sit 'em down and do something like a cheese souffle; use leftovers.' And it was just this great thing—so I did that. Because I now had the time, and the inclination, I was getting down to some things that I'd never done in my life. And I loved it— absolutely loved it. And it was a good time to do it, because my kids were growing up then."

It was during that time that she found something else. One day she pulled up to a red light on Santa Monica Boulevard, on her way home to fix dinner for her kids, and another car had pulled up beside her. She had a scarf over her head and some old jeans on. A man's voice said hello, and she said hello back without really looking. It was Dante, who had been out of her life for some twenty years, and when she realized who it was, she suddenly found herself wishing that she wasn't looking the way she was looking on that day. He said he'd like to see her, and as the light changed, she called out her phone number and he wrote it in the dust on his dashboard.

Rosemary and Dante had first met when they were both on the lot at Paramount, in 1953. She was working on her second picture, *Here Come the Girls*, and Dante had been given the task of making a dancer out of her (for Rosemary, unlike her sister, Betty, dancing had never come naturally). She and Dante hit it off instantly and began seeing each other, something that would continue up until the time she married Ferrer. Since they were the same age, it was a much different relationship than the one with the man she would marry, in which she felt she had to watch every move. "Dante and I used to have water fights," she says.

An hour after the chance meeting at the stoplight, he called her, and she invited him to the house for dinner a few days off. It was the end of 1973. He, too, had been married and divorced. From the day he showed up for dinner, he would never leave the family. He forged a friendship with her children. In the scaled-down operations of Rosemary's new lifestyle, he showed her that there was life beyond needing the seven people in help whom she had always maintained in her life with Ferrer. "He would say to me, 'I'll paint the hall,'" she says. "I said, 'Can you do that?' Sure you can. All these things people have been doing all their lives, I didn't know you could do. He can fix the toilet, even. He showed me you don't have to have all that. And anyway, it's just an extra layer of baggage." Over the next few years, in the small places she was playing, Dante would join the act in which her oldest son, Miguel, was now her drummer.

She had come back to her enjoyment of the music a few years after working just because she had to. She had a job during the summer in Tivoli Gardens in Copenhagen, and suddenly, it was as if something lifted. She began to find pleasure in her work again; found a joy in her singing that she had not felt in a long, long time. It was then that her doctor took her off her remaining medication.

The irony was that now she was ready, the jobs weren't coming. Money continued to be a problem. She would go back to court to get alimony from Ferrer, something she hadn't asked for at the time of their final divorce because she was still making a star's salary. When her mother died, a few years into Rosemary's recovery, she would not have the money to fly herself and her children, who were very close to their grandmother, back to Cincinnati for the funeral. She asked her ex-husband to pay for the children's tickets, but not viewing the occasion as a priority, he declined. Finally, Rosemary's relatives got together and chipped in so they could attend as a family.

During this period, because she was out of the limelight, Rosemary had a chance to rethink her relationship to her music. "Because I didn't have the high pressure of a big career for those years," she says, "I could approach the singing freshly, in a way that I could now really understand every word I'd ever sung. I got right back to basics. I had a chance to do things I hadn't had a chance to do before. And I was interested in it."

She didn't mind that she was working small, out-of-the way rooms where people were surprised to see her. She was just glad to be working. "The reconnecting with an audience was something that came to me after everything," she says. "The reconnecting, and having things really work, was part of starting to enjoy singing so much again. The audiences were small. Sometimes they stumbled into a place accidentally. But there were always people who liked to listen to what I did. And it was very worthwhile."

New to her was the ability to express deep emotion, something that had been difficult for her going back to childhood. "There were so many changes in my life as I was growing up," she says, "that I couldn't let myself get really emotionally attached to almost anybody. I could love them, but I couldn't really say, 'I don't think I'd be able to live without this person.' Because I would have to learn to.

Because I'd never be sure of where I'd be living the next month, the next year. I only knew that as long as Betty and I were together, we were going to be all right."

She'd always had the ability to express humor; she could cry at a movie, because somehow that was "safe." But she remembers, as a child, not being able to cry at the death of her grandfather, whom she adored. Now everything was changing. Interestingly, the chief hallmark today of Rosemary's personality and image is one of unconditional warmth. In life, she will sincerely tell someone "I love you" the way some people will say "Have a nice day." It came to her late, with her recovery, and it quickly began to show itself in her work.

In her early career, because of the shallowness of a lot of the material that she was made to record, and because of a deceptively casual style that lacked the flash or drama of, say, a Peggy Lee, Rosemary had long been artistically relegated to the realm of the "pleasant." "Sometimes I wince when I listen to some of the records that I've made," she says. "Because it gets terminally cute. Jesus. I get a little embarrassed by that stuff. But that's OK. I like some of the long lines, the purity of it."

With the control to really choose the material that meant something to her, and the greater depth she was now able to bring to it, she began to establish her second career as the one that would eventually earn her recognition as an accomplished, serious artist. She would begin to record again, sporadically at first. Then in the late '70s, she would enter into an association with the small Concord Jazz label, from which has come a string of albums now numbering eighteen, from a tribute album of Billie Holiday songs, to albums of show tunes and various composer songbooks, to the Grammy-nominated efforts of the last couple of years.

But in the early days after her recovery when there were no jobs, neither could she get a major record contract. During that time of minor appearances wherever she could find them, a few of her friends who could help her stuck especially close by her. One of them was Merv Griffin, who had his talk show and would have her on television whenever he could, getting her before the public again and showcasing her work. Another was Dinah Shore, her close friend for ages, who also would give Rosemary as much exposure on her television show as was possible (and would compare notes with her on growing corn). Additionally, Rosemary's baby brother, Nick, who was by now a writer and talk-show host in Cincinnati, would arrange to fly her back now and then to appear with him. She did commercials for Coronet paper products, singing their jingle. She was making ends meet, and she was beginning to reestablish herself with the public.

When she was just getting back on her feet, something happened—the farthest from anything she could have imagined—that would devastate her. She was playing Virginia Beach, in 1976, and she returned to her apartment to find a message that her cousin had called and that she was to call back immediately. She knew it must mean an illness in the family, but she was not ready for what she heard when she got him on the phone. He said, "Betty's had a stroke." It had come suddenly, and without warning, and Rosemary couldn't believe what she was hearing. Betty was in Las Vegas, preparing for the wedding of her daughter the following week, and she was standing by the pool and just slid to the ground and lost consciousness. She was forty-five. As her cousin told her, Rosemary felt a wave of weakness draining her. "I remember my cousin saying 'It's bad.' And I said, 'It's all right, because whatever it takes, I'll drop everything, and I'll just go with her, and I'll stay with her; wherever she has to stay, I'll stay with her, and she'll learn how to talk again, and she'll—' And he said, 'No, it's worse than that.' And then you know."

Betty had four children, and had never been sick a day in her life. They found two aneurysms, and Rosemary was at the other side of the country. She waited by the phone for the calls from her family at the hospital. The doctors would try to operate, but it looked bad. Then the call came that they had operated, and there was nothing to be done, and that Betty would probably live only another forty-five minutes. Rosemary sat there as the forty-five minutes ticked by, thinking that these were the last minutes she was going to spend in the same world with her sister, and the time was slipping away. She was flooded by all the memories from their childhood, from their days on the road with Tony Pastor and the matching plaid taffeta dresses their grandmother had made them when they left, the time they'd argued and she'd thrown green ink at Betty and then, shocked that Betty actually was covered in green ink, had stuffed her in the bathtub and tried to scrub her off. And how even after they were grown and lived apart, both in troubled marriages and raising their families, their bond had never lessened. And she thought about how her whole life, the fact that Betty was there had been the one thing that had always made everything all right. The phone rang again, and Betty was gone.

Leaving her engagement in Virginia, Rosemary flew to Las Vegas for the funeral, meeting her brother, Nick, at the airport. They rode together in the car to the funeral home. "Here we are in this garish town," she says, "with this horror, this tragedy. And we're driving down this strip. And we didn't say anything for so long, and then Nick said, 'Isn't this the most ridiculous place in the world to die?' And there she was."

Rosemary had to leave her sister's funeral halfway through to fly back to Virginia because the club owner had been so considerate, she couldn't annihilate his Saturday night business by canceling. Betty's death had shaken her to her foundations. She didn't know how she was going to be able to go on without her. Though the pain has lessened with the passing time, to this day Rosemary has really never got over it. She has become much closer to her brother in the time since, and they take long vacations together in exotic places, like Singapore. "All the places we never went with Betty," she says. "Betty used to explain me to Nick, and Nick to me. She was the one who could handle it. She was so funny, that was it. And she was so pretty." (She has since established the Betty Clooney Foundation for Persons with Brain Injury, for which she leads annual fundraising benefit concerts.)

The shock was a test to the mental stability she was beginning to feel comfortable with. But there was no repeat of the Robert Kennedy delusions; there was no falling back on the pills, though the temptation was there. She knew at that point that she was really going to be all right. "I'd been sick just a few years before," she says, "and when it happened, I watched people around me watching me, to see how I was doing."

It wasn't the first time she had felt people watching her behavior since her recovery. "There are times when people are watching you so carefully, that you really have to act—'Now is this too far? Is this too much?' You have to watch yourself intensely. It takes a while before you get back to even feeling as though you can say something that sounds the least bizarre—something that in normal circumstances would be acceptable." Shortly after her recovery, she would write a book about the experience and her life to that point, one of the reasons being that for her children's sake, she wanted the facts of her illness out in the open rather than have them face the conjecture that was still bandied about the entertainment world. Eight years after she began treatment, she finished her analysis and group therapy. "Dr. Monke said, 'You're terminated,'" she says. "And if you need a brush and polish, he's always there."

Her comeback had started in earnest just before her sister's death, when her old friend and mentor, Bing Crosby, asked her to do a big benefit at the Dorothy Chandler Pavilion in Los Angeles, to honor his fiftieth year in show business. Then he asked her to accompany him on tour. She had first met Crosby when she came to Paramount for a screen test, at the time he was filming *Road to Bali* with Bob Hope and Dorothy Lamour. Crosby was on a bicycle, and they were introduced, and Rosemary was so awed that when she said something about their being scheduled to work together on a radio broadcast toward the end of the month, it had come out garbled, as being "sometime in the twenties." She had felt like such an idiot afterward that she'd gone to his dressing room and knocked on the door and explained that she wasn't stupid, she had just always been in awe, and from then on she would try not to think of him as "Bing Crosby" anymore. He had laughed and invited her in for a drink, and they had remained close friends ever since. They were always friends, never anything more, and they enjoyed a compatible musical and personal relationship that would take them through movie, television, radio, and recording collaborations over the decades.

He was a very private man, strange in many ways, who was often uncomfortable with intimacy. In severely troubled times, Rosemary would not hear a word from him, but then it would filter back to her that he had been anxiously asking others how she was doing. Now, when she was at a professional low, he would come to her rescue. With his motion picture, recording, and radio work, personal appearances were not something Crosby had had time for since his early days with the Paul Whiteman Orchestra. In what would be the last few years of his life, he embarked on a series of concert tours, discovering that he loved the feeling of performing before a live audience. He invited Rosemary to join him, and they traveled around, playing places like the Palladium in London. There would be other jobs for Rosemary, like in *Four Girls, Four,* a show she'd go on the road with intermittently over about seven years, with Margaret Whiting, Martha Raye, and Helen O'Connell. But it was the touring with Crosby that gave Rosemary back her visibility.

Although Rosemary achieved tremendous stardom as a young woman, it is in her second incarnation that she's found herself, not only as an artist, but in her personal image. She seems right as a hip mama; she's comfortable with that. With her previous public image as a 1950s-style perky young thing, she was never comfortable; she had always been unsure of everything but her singing, trying to live up to what she thought people expected her to be. Now, in her maternal role, she surrounds herself with younger people. (The nature of her earth mama image is different from Barbara's, perhaps because although Barbara's attitude is certainly maternal toward young people, it is tempered by her childlike quality. Rosemary, surrounded by family and young friends, is more of a with-it matriarch.) She has always related to young people, whether it was speaking out against Vietnam and covering her Cadillac with flower decals, or stopping by her kids' rooms to listen with them to their rock and roll albums, never criticizing their music (she's a big Linda Ronstadt and James Taylor fan, and is friends with both), or having a serious conversation about Good-and-Plenty candy with her three-year-old grandson. In group therapy, she always sided with the young people against those of her own generation, wanting to get closer to them. Young people, whether it's those she works with or audiences, are drawn to her in return.

It's really only in the last five or six years that she has come so strongly to the fore with artistic and popular recognition as a leading icon of standard pop and jazz. What paved the way for the critical attention that put her in that category was the start of prominent appearances in New York clubs—first, at the Blue Note in 1987, and then at Rainbow and Stars, every year since its opening in 1989. Without that to spearhead her artistic persona and draw critical attention to her albums, despite the depth and excellence of her present-day work, she might very easily have met the fate of other '50s pop personalities, like her nemesis Patti Page ("How Much Is That Doggie in the Window"), people who may indeed work, and may indeed make a living and draw an audience—but who are wafting in the realm of Nostalgialand, their value only in the memories they evoke in their audiences; their place in the scheme of the current music world, nowhere.

She's glad to have reached the 65th floor. She loves the Rainbow and Stars job, and is always saying how it's the most important thing she does all year. But in the reordered universe that evolved with her recovery, something happened. She started caring not so much about getting places careerwise, as about simply wanting to relate to the people—whom she sees as just people, no matter where they are. In other words, she sees singing up at Rainbow and Stars as not that much different from playing the Holiday Inn in Ventura, once she'd gotten her joy back in singing. Rainbow is nicer; the musicians are better; the pay is better, and so is the notice. "But my work is not that different," she says. "The top of the Holiday Inn—that part never bothered me. It's still people in front of you, reacting to you. It's nice if you can have Carnegie Hall or the Hollywood Bowl . . . but it's the work. You know?"

*I*t's Saturday night, and Julie is at home in Jersey City, sorting through the papers stacked up on her dining room table. She's never at home long enough to get any kind of order in her house. When she gets home in the wee hours, usually her machine is filled with phone messages that she'll try to answer, but is always behind on. Her mail lies around in piles and some of it she won't get to for months. Sometimes she gets home at one or two, and spends until six or seven in the morning going through things, trying to sort out her life. Then she grabs a couple of hours' sleep, and is back on the PATH train by the early afternoon into the city for her voice lesson and another day where she will probably get home no earlier than midnight.

She would like to have people over for dinner, and get a chance to cook for them and take out the Crown Derby. Cornish hens are something she cooks really well, and rhubarb pie for dessert. But it's been years since her house has been together enough to have a dinner party. She's lucky if she can just keep up with the things that come at her every day that need attention.

A couple of months ago the water main broke in front of her house. She was informed that because it was on her side of the line, it was not a city problem and she was responsible for fixing it. She had not the foggiest idea of whom you would even begin to call to repair a broken water main. Finally one of her neighbors suggested some people to call. It cost her two thousand dollars.

She lives in a brownstone townhouse that is one of a row of brownstones, connected to each other on the sides, in a working-class neighborhood of Jersey City, which is just across the Hudson River from lower Manhattan. Recently a tree in front of her house was struck by lightning during a thunderstorm one afternoon. She didn't even notice until one of her neighbors told her. She gets home so late, it's always dark, and she really would have no reason to notice unless someone pointed it out. Now a limb of the tree is dangling over the front door of the next house. She's not sure whether she's supposed to do anything about it.

She bought the house the month she returned to New York from Omaha in 1984. She had been looking at apartments in Manhattan, and found that the rent for a studio apartment on the East Side was a thousand dollars a month. "I said, if I'm paying a thousand dollars, I'm going to put it into equity in a home, a building—so if I die, my kids have something in their hands, not just rent receipts." Every month she meets the mortgage payments.

She has more property, also with a mortgage: acreage in the Adirondacks, with a house and several outbuildings in need of repair. She hasn't had a chance to get up there and visit the place in almost two years. She has a fantasy that one day, when she's in her nineties or something, she'd like to open a tea shop in one of the buildings at her country place. She'd bake two kinds of cake and appoint the room with the unmatched cups and saucers and pieces of china that she's been collecting for years. Whenever she goes by an antique or junk shop or garage sale, she can't help rescuing these things. "When you think that each cup belonged to someone," she says, "that it meant something to someone who had a life and who loved and had a family, and for whatever reason—they died, or they got old, these things are being sold off . . . . I love having things that you know have so much of somebody's lifetime behind them."

But her fantasy is not for the foreseeable future. Now she concentrates her energies for the disciplines of work and everyday life and getting back and forth to the city, starting each day by getting down on the floor with the yoga exercises she's been doing since she was in high school.

She's recently returned from an engagement at Chicago's Goldstar Sardine Bar, where she got a slew of press and business was so good they extended the run. Before she left, the city had declared a "Julie Wilson Day." She had returned home to the usual pile of mail and flood of phone messages, and on this Saturday night is trying to get out from being so far behind.

But when midnight comes she stops what she's doing. She's already walked the dogs and had some dinner, and now she changes into a black pants suit and puts on some makeup. Locking up the house, she heads out into the dark to walk to the subway and take the PATH train the three stops into Manhattan. It will let her off down the block from Eighty Eight's, where a young performer named Ricky Ritzel is doing the 1:00 A.M. show. "I knew if I didn't get there tonight, I'd miss it," she says, "I've got all these benefits coming up." When she does get there a little before 1:00, greeting the bartender and waiters on her way in, there are only two other people in the audience. "It's so heartbreaking," she says.

Shortly after she closed at the Russian Tea Room, Julie had a job for two weeks working a Caribbean cruise. She did four shows. The rest of the time, for two whole weeks—without places to run to and obligations to fulfill and domestic business to catch up on—she did absolutely nothing.

*J*ulie was sitting at home in Omaha after her mother's death in 1983 wondering what to do with herself. "My mom died, and Holt was in Paris, and Mike was in California, and there I was," she says. "I had been so busy with being needed and caring for everything, I didn't even miss the business. It was like I was never even in show business. Now, it was like, 'What do I do? I'm in limbo, and I don't have anything to do.'"

One day around Christmastime, the phone rang. It was the press agent Henry Lehrman. Barron Polan, it seemed, had been on the bus and run into the illustrator Hilary Knight (of *Eloise* fame), who had told him that Michael's Pub was looking for someone to do a Cole Porter show to run in conjunction with the publication of Robert Kimball's new Porter book. Polan had suggested Julie, and now Lehrman was on the phone as she sat in Omaha asking her whether she'd like to do it. The catch was that she had to be ready to open on January 3. It was now two days before Christmas. She wasn't sure if she could get herself together in time. But she allowed herself to be talked into it, and accepted the date.

Then she found out that Billy Roy, who had been her musical alter ego for some years before her absence, was already booked. She asked the club for the names of some pianists. "I said, 'Which one's the oldest,'" she says, figuring that would be the safest choice. She was paying $1,000 dollars out of her $3,500-a-week salary. She found minimal enthusiasm from the accompanist she'd chosen. Julie was an hour late for the first rehearsal. When she got there, they rehearsed for a little while, and then the pianist said he had the flu, telling her, "I have to go home." He went on to say that if she wanted to rehearse, she'd have to come out to Port Washington, on Long Island, where he lived. "So the next day I went out to Port Washington. We worked an hour and a half. He'd say, 'Excuse me,' and he'd go take some pills, drink some tea, then we'd go another fifteen minutes. Then he said, 'Sorry, I can't do anymore. I'll see you tomorrow.' The next day was Saturday. We're opening Tuesday. So I went out there on Saturday, and we have like an hour rehearsal, and he says, 'I can't work tomorrow.' I was so angry. But I didn't know if I could get anybody by Tuesday.

"I mean, this guy was such a bummer—he didn't even know 'Why Can't You Behave?' Can you believe that? A man, sixty-five years old, doesn't know 'Why Can't You Behave'? It all came down to, 'Well, what *do* you know? Let's find some of the Cole Porter songs that you know, and we'll work around it.'"

Tuesday came, the day of the opening, and they were supposed to rehearse at Michael's Pub in the afternoon. But a press call had been set up for the afternoon, and Julie had gotten into a gown and gotten made up, and the press came and took pictures and asked questions. Then when they left, the piano tuner came to tune the piano for the show. He stayed an hour. Then it was time for the restaurant doors to open for dinner. There would be no rehearsal at all that afternoon, and when they went onstage in the evening, they'd had a total of about five hours' rehearsal.

Julie was petrified. "I could feel my knees shaking," she says. "I'm up there forgetting practically every Cole Porter song I ever knew. Billy Roy had finished his show and come down to hear us, and during the show I could see him sinking under the table. And I thought, 'Oh God.'

"Then after the show, Gil Wiest, the owner, starts screaming at the pianist. Then the pianist comes to me and says, 'He's screaming at me.' And I said, 'Tell Gil Wiest that if he has anything to say, say it to me.' So I walked up to him and said, 'Mr. Wiest, if you don't want me here, I'll pack up right now and get out.' I said, 'I will survive with or without this job. It's not the end of the world.' And he said, 'No, no, no. I like you very much, you're a very nice girl. I just don't want the critics murdering you.' I said, 'Mr. Wiest, I've been murdered before.

But I survive, I keep going.' He said, 'Take it easy, take it easy.' I said, 'The pianist has been sick, he's had the flu; we've had very little rehearsal; we're doing the best we can.' He said, 'OK, OK.'"

Luckily it had been arranged for the press to be held off from Tuesday until Thursday, leaving the two shows on opening night and two more the next day before they would see it. "It began to fall into place, bit by bit," she says. By the time the critics saw it, they would rave. She would be held over for fourteen weeks, go off to perform in Boston with Bobby Short, and return to Michael's Pub six weeks later with a Sondheim show.

She had been away for eight years. Now that she was in show business again, she began slowly to work her way back into the public consciousness. John S. Wilson, the *New York Times* jazz and pop critic, helped start her off by doing a feature on her. Although eight years by itself doesn't seem like a long time, Julie was coming back to a different world from the one she had left, and doing it as a different performer. She didn't feel the readjustment herself, and once she got her bearings after the rocky opening at Michael's Pub, she felt as though she'd never been away. "The only way I can explain it is that the feeling was like meeting an old friend you haven't been in touch with for a long time. Yet the friendship was there as strong as it had been from the last time you saw him, and you picked it up where you left off—with no embarrassment, no apologies, no discomfort, no, 'I'm sorry, I should have written . . . .'"

When she'd gone back to Omaha, she was leaving the decaying wreckage of a world that had long since seen its heyday. Now she was coming back into one where standard pop music was enjoying a rebirth, and with it, the club scene—now being labeled "cabaret." Into this rejuvenated new order, at the age of fifty-eight, she reemerged as a de facto doyenne of the business. The Julie of the second coming was not the same performer who had entranced nightclubgoers of yore with naughty special material. There was now another side, a darker side, that had taken over.

She had begun a fascination with more complex work, especially the work of Stephen Sondheim, which has become her favorite material to perform. The one that she seems to feel the most profoundly is that perennial survivors' anthem "I'm Still Here." She begins it quietly, relating with matter-of-fact pride how she's seen the good times and bum times, and is around to tell us about it. By the end, she wrings her hands and defiantly thunders in a hoarse shout that seems to come from the depths of her soul, "'And I'm here!'"

She has since done an album of Sondheim songs, one of the four songbook albums she's recorded in recent years (the others are Cole Porter, Harold Arlen, and Kurt Weill). "You have to be chemically attracted to a song," she says, "like people. And there are songs that you hear and say, 'Oh, I'd love to sing that.' But if you haven't been around the block enough times, then there's no point." With the depth of the more difficult material and the intensity she brings to it, the knife-edge of wit and tragedy has become sharper. That edge, and the power it brings with it, has become the hallmark of everything she's achieved since her return.

Quickly, after the Michael's Pub run, she was once again absorbed into the top echelon, playing extended engagements at the Algonquin, the Cafe Carlyle, and Rainbow and Stars. Apart from her old fans, who found her again, a generation newly familiar with the music thought she was the coolest thing they'd ever seen.

The one thing Julie has never had is a hit record. She has recorded albums over the years, but never a hit single. She introduced "The Coffee Song," but Frank Sinatra had the hit record of it. Because of that, while she has fans and a reputation and work, she has never been afforded the luxuries that come with mass identification. Rosemary has "Come on-a My House," "Tenderly," "Hey There," and a string of others. Mention Barbara's name and people will invariably say *The Music Man* or *Candide*. Mention Kitty Kallen, and if you get a puzzled response, mention her number-one hit, "Little Things Mean a Lot," and hear the sigh of recognition. "I never had anything where somebody would say, 'Oh, that's the gal that sang such and such,'" Julie says. "'Oh yes, she did *that* song.'"

The price is more than just lost record royalties. It affects her ability to sell herself on a scale that goes beyond localized club settings. It doesn't preclude her doing so. She makes occasional television appearances, including the PBS special in 1992. She records, and people buy her albums. She has come back to Broadway since her return to the business, in the part that Peter Allen wrote especially for her in his show, *Legs Diamond*. (It was through one of her albums, as a matter of fact, recorded live from the St. Regis, that Allen had become a fan of hers when he was a young man in Australia.) She continues to get newspaper and magazine coverage on a national scale, as a reigning legend of cabaret.

But the big money isn't in cabaret. It's in concerts in regional America, where people of her own generation would be buying tickets saying, "Remember when she sang . . . ."

Also, she's forever being confused with other singers, particularly Julie London. People regularly come up to her and tell her how much they loved "Cry Me a River," London's hit song. She made an appearance on the *Perry Como Show* where, coast to coast, Como actually introduced her as "Julie London." Retribution came three months later when he had Julie London on the show and Como announced her as "Julie Wilson." Julie, who was playing a hotel in Lake Tahoe at the time, got calls from people she knew all over the country telling her.

She takes the confusion in good humor. "I get called Julie Andrews, and Julie Harris. I was once playing in a show in Denver and got reviewed as Julie Harris." Recently, a novice doing a cabaret act, who knew full well who she was, was so flustered that Julie had come down to see her that she said, "I can't believe that you're here— Julie Harris!" and then immediately horrified at what had come out, tried to correct herself. Julie just said, "It's all right. I answer to Julie Harris, Julie London, or Nancy Wilson."

Like most things, Julie accepts it as reality. In life, she is very much a fatalist. "I consider myself very lucky," she says, "one of the fortunate people. And I'm just chugging along; go with the flow, go wherever it takes me." Her philosophy is never to expect too much, because then you won't be disappointed, and you might find an unexpected bonus.

Julie is not a worrier. She never has been. She just doesn't worry about things because she knows they're out of her control anyway, so whatever happens, happens. Other people know that, too, intellectually, but they worry all the same; not Julie. In that sense, she is not in the least neurotic, compared to a lot of people generally, and almost everybody in show business. She's steady, she's logical, she's never been nagged by uncertainty. She may also be unique among performers, who are prone to self-examination, in that she's never been in therapy.

Actually, she went once. She was married to McAloney, and her children were very young, and the marriage was going through a tremendous upheaval. Her dentist, who was also a friend, told her she should really talk to somebody. "He said, 'If I make an appointment for you, will you go?'" she says. "I said, 'You mean a shrink? An analyst?' He said, 'Yes, I think you should.' I said, 'All right.'

"So he made the appointment, and I went. The doctor asked me a lot of questions, and I answered them. He asked me about my family, and I told him. I told him my older brother, Russell, eighteen months older, fell out of a second story window at the age of twenty-four months and lit on his head on a cement driveway. And the analyst said to me—you know what he said? He said, 'Did you push him out the window?' I said, 'What? *I* push him out the window? He's two years old and he's eighteen months older than I am. I'm a little baby. *I* can push him out the window?' I couldn't believe it, and I thought, 'Are you for real?' Then the analyst said to me at the end of the session, 'Young lady, you don't need me, I don't want to see you again. But would you send your husband in?' And that was it."

Julie doesn't believe in pampering herself. She just keeps pressing on, going through her daily routine, working to make money to meet her bills and monthly mortgage payments. She often says she would have made a good pioneer, that she was born in the wrong era (though she probably would have ended up singing in a frontier saloon). In terms of discipline, she thinks a lot of people today are too spoiled. "That's just my own humble opinion," she says. "You know, like a lot of people walk around complaining about the weather. So it's hot. And in the winter, it's cold. But I mean, that's what weather does. What about all those people who had no central heating, no indoor bathrooms, no nice, soft toilet paper, or whatever? How did they manage? They lived. They loved. They did whatever they did, in spite of it all. Like now, if there's two inches of snow, they close the school. I think that's utterly and totally ludicrous. But I'm just an old-fashioned tomato, I guess."

But apart from the stoic self-discipline, Julie has a heightened empathy with other human beings. She is easily moved by the human condition, and cries readily. About how hard her parents' families had to work; about how much Billie Holiday means to her as a singer. Not often about herself. Her nerves and emotions run so close to the surface, she is so lacking in armor, that she in turn elicits empathy from others. Perhaps it's the great tiredness that creeps out from beneath all the energy and strength.

In the summer of 1991, her younger son, Mike, who for a long time had been battling alcohol abuse, died suddenly in his sleep. The precise circumstances remain shrouded. He was twenty-six. Troubled, he had been gifted and artistic, and of his flailing, Julie just recently said she thought that maybe he was starting to find himself. The funeral was in Omaha, and Julie went back with her son Holt to attend to the arrangements. When she returned to New York from the funeral, she had an engagement that weekend in Connecticut, which she honored: two concerts, Friday and Saturday, both sold out, that she refused to cancel, because people had bought their tickets and were counting on her. "You've just got to keep going," she says.

She did both concerts, and except for the few people around her who knew what had happened, the audience would never have recognized it by her performance. But it wasn't as if nothing had happened. Music is unforgivingly transparent; everything shows up, filters through. "The more that happens to you, the more experiences that you have in life, it gives you a richness and understanding of things that you perhaps failed to understand before," she says. "I'm not a very analytical person, I just sing from my guts, from my heart. And I try to be as honest as I can. I think audiences want to be moved. They want to be provoked into thinking and remembering. Nothing does that like music. Music is incredibly disturbing and moving, so moving."

In the three years since her son's death, Julie has not yet got around to answering the outpouring of cards and letters that came to her from everyone she knew. It bothers her deeply that she hasn't answered them; she wants people to know what their thoughts meant to her. But time is the one thing there's never enough of, and she is always running.

"Life is strange," she says. "There are no answers. Life is the unexpected. So you're grateful for what you have and the gifts that are given you. I feel extremely lucky to have been given whatever this drive is that I've felt since I was a child, this drive to perform."

38

*B*arbara is starting to think about her upcoming London concerts at the Sadler's Wells Theatre when she gets a call that Steve Allen, who is scheduled to go into the Cafe Carlyle with his show, is having a back problem, and could she go back into the room for a week. She does.

She did the same thing last year, as well, when Eartha Kitt had some scheduling problem and they asked Barbara if she could do a week then. Both years, on the Friday of that specific week that Barbara is filling in, horrendous crimes are committed on the block, spectacular, terrifying crimes where, ultimately, no one is killed, but cause police to cordon off the street in front of the Carlyle—and the outside photograph of Barbara, holding a microphone, singing in a sparkly dress—with yellow tape and parked police cars with flashing sirens; there are news cameras and reporters and rubbernecking crowds—all of it disbursing in time for Barbara to go on and sing.

Madison Avenue and 76th Street is probably one of the safest chunks of paved ground anywhere in New York City. Last year, gunmen went into the art gallery across the street from the Carlyle on Friday afternoon and took hostages, holding them at gunpoint into the evening.

This year, also on the afternoon of Barbara's Friday night shows, there is a shooting at the Vera Wang Bridal House, located in the Carlyle building, its entrance farther up Madison from the Cafe/Bemelmans Bar entrance, toward the end of the block. Vera Wang has been in the news lately because she designed Nancy Kerrigan's Olympic skating outfit. This time, well-dressed gunmen follow two tourists, a husband and wife, into the shop, where they are preparing for their daughter's wedding. In the ensuing robbery, centered on the wife's jewelry, the gunmen shoot both the husband and the wife, and walk off casually into the crowd on Madison Avenue. The husband and wife will eventually recover and sue; the gunmen, responsible for a series of similar crimes, will be caught, but not for a while; and the story will capture headlines for a long time.

It doesn't affect Barbara's business at all. This Friday night, in a black, jeweled gown, she sings the show she sang for seven weeks, earlier in the season, to two full houses.

✳

Across the foyer in Bemelmans Bar, the Carlyle's other Barbara—jazz pianist Barbara Carroll—has commenced her run. With its whimsical murals by the artist and writer Ludwig Bemelmans depicting scenes from Central Park, the place is dark, with leather banquettes lining the walls, and at the center of the small room, next to a pillar, stands a grand piano. Bemelmans Bar is not a "listening" room—it's the hotel bar—which means that whether or not someone is performing, very often people talk, so very often it gets noisy.

Carroll is used to it. For about six months of the year—in a fall and a spring season—Carroll can be found seated there Tuesday through Saturday nights from 9:30 to 12:30.

Carroll is a slim woman in her sixties, with red hair slicked back, brown eyes, and a pale complexion, and when she is absorbed in her playing, she gazes down at the keyboard with a half-smile. She is one of the preeminent progressive jazz pianists to come out of the 52nd Street small club scene of the 1950s. Her style is crisp and swinging, her improvisation infused with the fugues and impressionist harmonies (Ravel, Debussy) of her classical background. Growing up in Worcester, Massachusetts, the daughter of a plumber (who also played the trumpet), she began playing the piano at age five and was trained classically through high school. But she worshiped artists like Nat Cole, Art Tatum, and Teddy Wilson, and as a teenager, she joined combos that played weddings, bar mitzvahs, and other local functions, and later, area clubs. "I was always the only girl," she says. "My mother's friends said, 'How can you let her do that? Hanging around with these crazy musicians?'" She was making enough money to pay her tuition at the New England Conservatory, which she soon left for a career in clubs—first in Boston (she played with a lot of nightclub rhumba bands), then arriving in New York in the late '40s.

On 52nd Street, she quickly made a reputation as a swinging bebop pianist in a field overwhelmingly dominated by men. "In retrospect, I remembered that it was much more difficult for me because I was a girl," she says. "But at the time, I was so focused on what I wanted to do that I never even thought about that." To the fraternity, she was at once "the chick piano player," and also a musician-colleague worthy of respect. She loves musicians as a breed, for their communication in a language that has always defied barriers of race and sex (even in times when American society was considerably restrictive), and for their intrinsic civility. She got early jobs through a helpful friend, who would recommend her as "Bobby" Carroll. Then she'd arrive for work (female, to everyone's surprise) when it would be too late to replace her. Before long, the tricks were no longer necessary. She got a regular gig with a trio at the Down Beat Club and performed opposite Dizzy Gillespie. She led a group throughout the '50s at the Embers, and later married the trio's bass, Joe Shulman. She has recorded extensively, appeared on Broadway in Rodgers and Hammerstein's *Me and Juliet*, done jazz festival, concert, and television work. She took time off in the '70s to raise a daughter with her second husband, agent Bert Block (the jazz scene had dried up along with the rest of the nightclub scene when rock and roll took over). When she returned to work, the Carlyle job became her professional home base. It started out as a two-week engagement; this is her sixteenth year there.

The Carlyle recently gave her a dinner to honor the release of her new album, *This Heart of Mine*. After a dinner of salmon and spinach and sorbet in the dining room, Bemelmans Bar began to fill up with friends, admirers and press, who huddled in the dim light around the piano and sipped their drinks while Barbara played, joined by Frank Tate on bass. Dressed in black with a sparkly top and dangling earrings, she spun out her take on "The Way You Look Tonight," Billy Strayhorn's exotic "Lotus Blossom," a rollicking "I Won't Dance," her own compositions like "Barbara's Carol," and she sang (she's begun to do that in the last years) songs like Cy Coleman and Carolyn Leigh's "I Wanna Be Yours." Tony Bennett, sitting near the piano, got up to join her in a song, singing without a mike, turning from side to side to include everybody gathered around. Young professionals at the bar, talking throughout the rest of the evening, were finally prevailed upon to quiet down. "My old pal Tony Bennett," she said, remembering him as a kid in the old days, when he'd hung around the clubs on 52nd Street where she was playing, asking for a chance to sing.

She loves the Bemelmans job, because working alone (the bass is special, that night), she has complete freedom—to improvise, to free-associate (she'll go from "This Heart of Mine" to "My Foolish Heart" to "Heart and Soul"), to choose her repertory. She likes getting requests, but she only plays the ones she wants to. She lives in an apartment in the 60s, near the East River (her husband died some years ago) and she's ecstatic because her daughter just gave her her first grandchild, a baby boy. When she finishes her season here, she'll go and fulfill a few dates in California. But apart from the Carlyle and other New York appearances like the occasional Sunday night at the Russian Tea Room, where people sit clustered around the piano (moved to the middle of the room for the evening) and hang on every note she plays, she's been doing more work in a concert format lately. For almost fifty years, she has been a creature of the clubs, but she enjoys concerts. For one thing, the patrons aren't so inclined to talk.

*

Upstairs in the hotel, Barbara Cook is between shows, sitting in her dressing room suite, when she suddenly realizes how long she has been in New York. It starts in front of the baked potato that room service has sent up for dinner, when she picks up the roll that came with it and raps it on the tray and says to whoever is around, "God, I'll never get used to your Yankee rolls. They're so hard." To which Wally says incredulously, "Our *Yankee* rolls? How many years has it been that you've been living among us Yankees?" She stops to figure it out. "Forty—I came here in 1948," she says, and counts. "Can you believe it?" she says. "I've been here forty-five years."

*

> "Barbara Cook is a fresh-faced, trim young blonde who sings even better than she looks—and that's going some. She invariably extends drama critics to use words like "delicious" and reporters who interview her to come away employing similar adjectives, words like "supple" and "button cute."
>
> –From *The Music Man* program, 1957

In 1974, Barbara was still in a deep depression, near the height of the weight gain that had recently been exposed to public scrutiny when financial pressures had forced her back onto the stage. The year 1974 would eventually be remembered as her comeback year, the year she began a new lease on life as a cabaret artist. But she wasn't thinking that way then.

It would be a couple of years before physical collapse would turn her around toward recovery. But even during her worst days, things were happening for her that would take root later on, things forming the personal and professional groundwork for the Barbara Cook who would emerge.

For the first time, she was beginning to feel ready to look at the world around her instead of just looking in on herself and her career. She was greatly concerned about the Vietnam War, and harbored a desire to put it in a greater context, to understand. "I'd always felt lacking in terms of a higher formal education," she says, "because it was something I never had." She started to read the *New York Times* within an inch of its life. When she had got her son off to school in the morning, she would start with the front page, and keep reading it right through to the back. It took pretty much the whole day. It was very new to her. With a curious mind by nature, she had never paid much attention to news and current events when she was younger and engulfed by her Broadway career. As a young wife, opinions on "important" subjects were often things she had trusted her husband to formulate.

"I needed to learn about myself," she says. "I needed to make up my mind about things in the world. I needed to grow up."

Now she was deliberately starting to educate herself, and she liked it. "See, I didn't go to college," she says, "and I felt inferior because of that. I don't at all anymore." She became fascinated by politics and world affairs, informed herself, and developed a strong point of view. "In large part, it's in relating to the world that you find out who you are," she says.

"One of the things I often say to students is 'Read the newspaper.' Because if you don't know who you are, you're not going to have anything to say in a song.

"I had a friend who was very bright, and I said, 'Give me a reading list'; and another friend, 'Give me a reading list.' You know, I didn't even recognize that there was any good part to this difficult period until the friend who gave me the reading list said, 'You really ought to understand—this has been a good time in lots of ways.' I didn't think he was right at the time. But he was right."

To this day, Barbara's curiosity about everything extends far beyond the front page. "Because the world is filled with wonder, still, and miracles," she says. "It's thrilling. I cannot understand people who fight space exploration; or the SST; or computers. They study why some plant has some particular characteristic—and in the meantime, they find a cure for God knows what." Unlike many women of her generation, she has no fear of technology. She carries with her one of those wallet-sized rolodex electronic address books, punching in names, numbers and memos, and showing it off to friends. She wants to buy a notebook computer she can travel with to keep track of her performing and business affairs.

The biggest change in her life at that time came when she met Wally Harper. Juilliard graduate, arranger, conductor, and composer, he had worked on Broadway in shows like *Peter Pan*, *Company*, and *Irene*. He and Barbara had never worked together in the theatre, but had met socially a couple of times, though Barbara wasn't really too sure what he did.

When Barbara toured in summer stock with *The Gershwin Years*, Wally went up to Connecticut to see her in it. "I hadn't heard of her for a long time," he says, "because she'd just dropped out of sight. And she sounded great. And she was very fat, and it was the first time she had sung since she'd become really big." Shortly afterward, he caught up with the show again, in Massachussetts. He talked to her afterward and told her she should think about doing a concert or something. He wasn't sure exactly what, but something.

They ran into each other back in New York at the Grand Finale, an Upper West Side club, and with a mutual friend, Wally began talking to her again about putting something together, telling her that she should depart from the strict show tune repertory and try some contemporary material. "Barbara's kind of a skeptical person," he says. "She was skeptical, but interested."

The next day they got together at his apartment at three o'clock in the afternoon, and they worked until three or four in the morning. They would do the same thing every day for the next three months. Exercising their muscles, they tried out a lot of different kinds of material and ideas, some of which worked, some of which failed miserably to gel. "We did a lot of indulgent things, musically," he says, "and we'd tape it. And then we'd listen to it the next day and just scream with laughter; it was just awful. However, out of that came the germ of some really good things."

It was all in the timing. Wally, who had *Irene* running at the time, and therefore an income, was at a personal and professional crossroads, trying to figure out for himself what was next. Barbara was at an all-time low, with no idea where to turn. "We were kind of two lost souls," he says, "both hiding out, and it was like, 'Well, at least we have these songs.'"

They had hit it off, and immediately become very close friends. Sometimes they'd sit and talk for eight hours, then begin working late at night, for four more. They weren't particularly thinking of cabaret at the time, just putting together some material that would give Barbara the freedom to communicate in a new way, having been tied up for a great deal of her earlier career with performing in character onstage.

From her background in lyric singing, she says Wally taught her to swing. Wally says her sense of rhythm and blues-oriented ability is inborn, and he only drew it out. But she made an effort to stretch herself. "Singing soulful ballads is really my strength," she says. "But you can't make a whole show out of soulful ballads. Even though I used to feel that's what I'd like to do." Instead, they tried out a mix of contemporary things with a rock feel, and jazzy arrangements of standards, and straight classic and contemporary ballads. The main thing was that in large part, they stayed away from the theatre music that had been the bedrock of her past.

After a few months of working, Wally called a friend of his at the Eugene O'Neill Theater Center in Connecticut, and they arranged to try out fifty minutes of material up there, in front of an audience. It was the first time they'd ever worked together in front of people. It was nerve-racking, and Barbara was terrified, but they got through it. It went all right; not spectacularly, but all right.

The mid-seventies were a time when cabaret was starting to undergo a grass-roots revival after the bleak years of the sixties and early seventies, and there were small clubs springing up in New York, a number of them on the West Side. One was a place called Brothers and Sisters, where several other personalities from musical comedy's better days, like Helen Gallagher and Karen Morrow, had done their acts. Barbara and Wally were invited to do a show. It was the first time Barbara had played a club since her date at the Blue Angel in the early fifties, when she was first starting out in show business.

They would play Brothers and Sisters seven weeks, and public memory of the event would take on mythic proportions in theatre and cabaret lore, retold by fans with the same awed reverence reserved for transcendent experiences like Judy Garland's legendary Carnegie Hall concert. For Barbara, the reception she got at Brothers and Sisters—overpowering waves of love that came at her from the people crammed into the small room—was an epiphany. Not only because it signaled her comeback and the fact that there were people out there who loved listening to her. It was also because in the intimacy of the setting, she was connecting to the audience directly, personally. She was giving, and they were giving back. It was eye-opening because in her life spent in the theatre, for all the excitement that being a character onstage had held, the audience had always been something removed from her. "At Brothers and Sisters," she says, "people reached out to touch me."

A lot of people came to see her during the Brothers and Sisters run who had wondered what had happened to her over the last years. One of them was the artists' manager Herbert Breslin, who saw the act and signed her up for concert and symphony bookings. Almost immediately, there was to be a concert at Carnegie Hall, set for January 26, 1975. It would be recorded live and issued by Columbia Records. "I was so scared," she says. "It's like you need to invent a new word for it; 'scared' doesn't say it. Wally was, too. We'd put together a whole lot of new stuff that we thought was good; and I was singing all this stuff that I'd never sung in public before, and it was being recorded."

One of the things they did, which they still do whenever they put an important show together, is try it out in front of a room full of people. "We ask friends to come in and lend us their ears," she says. "You can learn only so much about a song in rehearsal. You can do just so much work, and the rest of it is done in front of people. It's something about baptism by fire. I always think I've done what I can to find what there is in a song, but invariably, I learn more in front of people. It doesn't have to do with doing it another twenty times. It's that finally, when your life is on the line with a song, you just find it."

Her life was on the line as the Carnegie Hall date approached, and she tried to get her terror under control. "I didn't know whether I could pull a hall like that together, fill it with my personality, make it an event. Making the decision to do the concert, I remember breaking it down to life or death. Like which way is the positive, which way is the negative. And if you can do that, the answer is clear. If you're scared—so what? Everybody's scared. You just do it anyway. It isn't going to kill you. Although you think it's going to."

About a week or ten days before the concert, she began to calm down enough to believe she could get through the singing. "I thought, 'Wait a minute. You've been singing all your life. You know you'll be able to sing it.' And also, the show-off part of me took over and said, 'It'll be nice to show people this new stuff.'" Whether she'd be able to make it work as an evening, beyond the singing, she still had no idea. For the first time in all her extensive performing experience, she was going onto a vast, world-famous stage to face a hall filled with people—and she was going to be just Barbara. She didn't know if just Barbara was going to be enough. "There's nothing to hide behind," she says. "There ain't no forty girls, forty. There ain't no hat and cane."

It more than worked. The evening of that Carnegie Hall comeback concert would go down in theatre and music annals, again, as one of those monumental events of cult status. The Columbia live recording is now a collector's item. The audience, packed to the rafters, went wild with the hysteria that one has come to expect from Barbara's fans.

In his review of the concert, John S. Wilson of the *New York Times* affirmed the new place she was taking up as the person she had become. "As she swirled around the stage in a loose, flowing pastel gown," he wrote, "with full, jaggedly cut sleeves that made her look like a sun goddess when she raised her arms, it was evident that her new body fits her new, expansive personality. In fact, it is difficult now to think of her in any other form."

But despite its success, the Carnegie Hall concert had thrust her back into the major limelight at a time when physically and psychologically she was still at a low. Suddenly, the press was all over her, and all they wanted to talk about was her weight. Everywhere. Mercilessly. Interminably. There was barely anything written about her during that time that didn't at some point mention the "trim, 106-pound figure" of yesterday. There had been the "before" and "after" photos side by side in the Sunday *Times* the day of the concert. The smirkiness of much of the press commentary (the *Times* aside) took bad taste to the level of cruelty, like the *New York Post*'s headline, "Barbara Cook Returning as a Much Bigger Star," with an article that began "Barbara Cook got fat."

She fielded question after question with a mixture of grace, openness, and sass about How much had she gained, How much had she gained this year as opposed to that year, How long was she planning to stay this way, and on and on. It was as if in the public sense, her reemergence marked the official death of "that neat little, pert little thing," as she referred to her former image, and everyone wanted dibs on the autopsy.

"If you're an artist, or a creative person," she says, "part of the gift is to be able to use all the bad stuff, mix it up and somehow get it back into your work; to use it in a positive way. Because we've all had pain. That's what being alive—part of it—is all about. And you know, you can't sing when you're fifteen the way that you can when you're forty. You just can't. Because you don't have the stuff to do it with. And you can't sing when you're forty the way you can at sixty."

It wouldn't fully happen for a while yet, but, in fact, for the first time in her life she was beginning to feel comfortable with who she was as a person. As she gradually began to work her way out of the bad times, she gained strength from her newfound education and interest in the world around her. She also found a freedom and confidence in being herself that she had never even known existed. She was no longer able to conform to the "perfect image" that she knew everybody wanted to see, and she stopped worrying so much about how she was coming off to the people around her. "For so many years I felt like the little girl pressing her nose against the glass on the outside," she says.

Ongoing therapy had helped her sort out a lot of things that had been tormenting her since childhood. "I've always been in therapy," she laughs. "Like eighty-two years." Actually, it was around 1951 that she first sought help, and she went for twenty years steadily, and sporadically after that. "I mean, unbelievable," she says. Eventually, she decided she'd had enough, and she simply stopped. "I haven't been in therapy for a long time. If I have, it's been for something that disturbed me, I'd go and talk about it and get out."

After the Carnegie Hall comeback, she began to appear in public regularly again, playing dates at clubs like Reno Sweeney, the Bottom Line, the Ballroom, and Michael's Pub on the way to her current affiliation with the Carlyle. There were more and more concerts, including another concert and album at Carnegie Hall, "It's Better With a Band," and concerts at Town Hall, the Hollywood Bowl with the L.A. Symphony, the Boston Pops, Kennedy Center in Washington, and throughout the United States, Canada, and Europe. In 1987 she went to Broadway with "Barbara Cook: A Concert for the Theatre." She started regular visits to England for club and concert dates, and maintains an avid following there. She also began to record again. For her part in the 1985 all-star Lincoln Center concert revival of Stephen Sondheim's *Follies*, she won a Grammy award.

Barbara is a star of cosmopolitan, more than middle, America. Her fame was born when Broadway produced theatre stars of the stature of Ethel Merman and Mary Martin and Gwen Verdon, and it is carried on by her old fans, generations grown up on her cast albums and theatre lore, and audiences introduced to the concert, cabaret, and albums of her more recent years.

Only two words kept her from being a household word outside major cities: Shirley Jones. Shirley Jones, through no fault of her own, was probably the prize of every musical comedy ingenue's voodoo doll collection. During the '50s, she starred in all the big, technicolor Hollywood musical adaptations of the homey Broadway repertory. *Oklahoma! Carousel.* And *The Music Man.* Barbara was sent out to Hollywood and tested twice to play Marian the Librarian, her role, which she had created from scratch and that had won her a Tony. But in the end, the part was given to Jones because they said Jones was "a movie name." (Robert Preston, however, immortalized his Professor Harold Hill on film, although previously he had actually been a Warner Brothers player whose real stardom was only defined by *The Music Man* on Broadway.) Not getting the chance to recreate the part on film was a blow to Barbara when it happened. It's something she's long since stopped worrying about. Still, it's one of those issues that, even now, people love to dredge up in interviews.

Barbara's second incarnation, after Carnegie Hall, would not just be a deeper version of a career started early on. It would be a new and different expression of life for her entirely. She had gone back to the New York musical comedy stage once in 1971, playing a spinster in *The Grass Harp*, based on Truman Capote's novella. It ran only a few performances, though her reviews were typically glowing. In 1990, she was talked into playing the mother in the musical production of *Carrie*, which opened in Stratford, England. It was such a mess that she left the show before it came over to bomb on Broadway. But apart from those ventures, in the last two decades she has defined herself solely by her music.

When the mature Barbara emerged, it was evident, as it still is, that her years of trials had done nothing to harden her outlook. There is nothing world-weary about Barbara. There is nothing namby-pamby about her either, nor was there ever in her youthful theatre days. Then, as now, she had edge, and fire, and temperament. Time has added to that the patina burnished by fifty years in the business, with all the savvy and deftness that goes with it.

But accompanying the veteran with the raunchy sense of humor, the unjaded little girl, equal parts joy and hurt, has never disappeared. She seeps through every day, in small ways, especially in her instinctive joy as a born performer, the "show-off" side of her. Turn a light on her, and she's on, clowning for friends or reveling in moving an audience to laughter or tears; and then when she's finished, her face lights up with a half-smile of delight, like a small child who knows she's just done something wonderful.

With her clear blue eyes and sweet tone, she wistfully sings of love and romance edged with a purity of heart that evokes the Atlanta schoolgirl held at arm's length by her peers, falling in love passionately every week, belying the mature woman whom to this point, everlasting romantic love has eluded. Onstage and in life, tinged with the wisdom of her experience, she remains an optimist.

"You depend on the dream so much," she says. "What happens is, you fall in love with the dream. And then when the man doesn't work out, we think we miss the man. It's not the man you miss, he screwed you up. The pain comes because you miss the dream. You miss the hope."

Earlier, she used to think about getting married again. Now she just thinks it would be nice to have someone who would be a close companion. She likes to think that in light of how far she's come, she would not make the same mistakes she has in the past. "But knowing me," she says, "if I fell in love with somebody I would just be bonkers, probably. I don't do things by half-measures."

She still has fears, not like she used to, but they're still there around the edges. However, it's her basically sunny nature that pilots a great deal of her outlook, her insecurities usually eclipsed by her humor, enthusiasm for the world at large, and passion for expressing herself, be it in song or opinion. There is no comparison with how life used to be for her, when a call to the long distance operator meant panic. The professional success she's had in the last fifteen or twenty years has built her confidence in herself, as did the period she spent reordering her life. Now she feels an ease in living and working as she pleases that in her younger days was not accessible. "I'm so much more comfortable now in the world," she says. "It's so hard to imagine how I felt before, how uncomfortable I was, how I never felt equal. The last time I went to the White House, my dinner partner was Henry Cisneros, the Secretary of Housing and Urban Development. I had a wonderful time conversing with him, talking about the problems in the cities and all that kind of stuff. And I felt really comfortable. There was no way on God's green earth that would have happened twenty years ago."

Though she loves to be with people, she also needs a lot of time alone to recharge. "I always have," she says. "I think part of it's because I do have such a one-track mind and I'm an intense person. I'm most comfortable when I can just deal with one person, or two, at a time. I don't particularly like cocktail parties for that reason, or big dinner parties, because I don't know how to split my concentration. Relating to people is tiring for me. If I went out every night for five nights in a row, I'd be exhausted. It's not that I wouldn't enjoy doing it, or wouldn't enjoy the people I'm with. But it's like, it's all going out. Then I have to sit back and fill the bucket up again."

In her apartment on Riverside Drive, the living room window is filled with what seems like hundreds of orchids. She says it's more like thirty or thirty-five, although at one time she had as many as fifty. Usually, one of the first things she'll do in the morning is go out into the living room and take a look around, water them, and see what's happening. "They're wonderful plants," she says, "because they'll tolerate a lot of not being taken care of." She loves making things grow, she always has, and it relaxes her. When she was married and living in Port Washington, she had a garden. In her various apartments, she always had pots in the window. "I haven't any idea why," she says, "but it comes to me easily. For me, it's simple, it's a matter of finding out what they need and giving it to them, as much as you can."

When she grew her first orchid, the plants intimidated her. She drove herself crazy trying to get everything perfect for them, trying to do everything just right, worrying it to death. A few months later, when she was getting ready to do "A Concert for the Theatre" at the Ambassador, she went up to the producer Manny Azenberg's office. "In the middle of the conversation," she says, "I looked up and I saw ten thousand plants, and I thought, 'Oh my God, they're all orchids, and they're all about to bloom—or blooming.' I had mine, and I was worrying, and I didn't feel like it was doing anything. And I was like, 'How do you do that? What did you do?' He said, 'Put 'em in the window. Water 'em every now and then. If you're really conscientious, feed 'em now and then. They'll be fine.' And they were."

It was a lot like what was happening with her. As soon as she stopped worrying so much about everything, she found that things began to take care of themselves. "The first time an orchid bloomed for me," she says, "I felt like God. It's thrilling. They take forever to do anything. Months. And in the beginning I kept thinking, 'The damn thing's not doing anything.' And they're really weird-looking plants before they bloom. But when they do it—boy, they really do it."

On the evening of Barbara's master class at Juilliard, the Juilliard Theatre off Lincoln Center Plaza is jammed with students, faculty, and fans. Last year when she gave a class, it had been held in the small hall, open just to a few students and faculty. But word had traveled, and this year they moved it to the large theatre, opened it to the public, and every ticket to be had has been sold.

If the people came to see *Barbara Cook*, they may have been disappointed. She hasn't come here today to be an onstage personality, and it is apparent the moment she trudges out in black pants and turtleneck and a black silk over-tunic, with a beige tote bag and the rectangular gold-rimmed glasses she wears all the time, except when she performs. Master classes are notoriously ripe opportunities for star teachers to play to an audience they know has really come to see them. Not today. Barbara's here to tell the students what she can in the space of two hours, and with Wally seated at the piano, she's ready for work.

A thin young woman with short dark hair comes onstage. She's a drama student, and she's singing Irving Berlin's "How Deep Is the Ocean?" and she's terrified. Barbara retreats to the shadows at the back of the stage as the girl sings it through once, her voice quavering a bit. It turns out this is the first time she's ever sung in public. When she's finished and the audience applauds, Barbara comes forward and hugs her. Then she tells her to start again. "This time," she says, "don't perform it. Just sing the words as if you were speaking them."

Barbara retreats as the girl starts over again. When she comes to the line "How far would I travel/To be where you are," Barbara comes forward and stops her. "Darlin', could you hold it a second? Honey," she says, "this is where you live! 'To *be* where you are! I want to *be* with you!' But now, don't just think, 'I want to be with you,' think, 'I want to be in bed with you'—and it'll come through." She gets a huge laugh, and the board of directors sitting down front raises its collective eyebrow. But the girl gets the idea. When she sings the line again, the difference is astounding. When she repeats the song from the beginning a few minutes later, she has transformed it from a corny warhorse to an affecting series of answerless questions that make it among Berlin's most touching songs.

In Barbara's master class, singing in terms of technique is never discussed, or even alluded to. What she is concerned with is the communication that takes place between a performer and an audience. What she is trying to teach is the most elusive part of being an artist—the ability to connect, to reach into one's own experience and convey the humanity of the material. What she is trying to show these young people is that in fact, first and foremost, what they are are storytellers. "I think a singer's basic task is to communicate, not perform," she says.

A lot of singers find it difficult to articulate how they do their work, because singing is basically intuitive—you say it this way or that way, you feel it or you don't. It has nothing to do with how articulate they may be on other topics; it's just something that's not easy to explain, and many don't see the need for going into it. Rosemary doesn't really talk about her music a lot. It's something she just does. "It's like having air, and we're alive," Rosemary says. "It's just too close to you, somehow."

But Rosemary, Barbara, and Julie—with their different styles and personalities, their different backgrounds and repertories— have, as mature performers in their second incarnations, all arrived at the same basic premise. "You've got to have a point of view," says Rosemary. Their job is simply to get up in front of people and tell things as they see them. That's it. "It's 'Here we are, and I'm going to tell you a story.' That's all you're doing," says Rosemary. "That's all you're doing."

One of the reasons that in their more recent years they have all transcended mere popularity or cachet, to be revered as icons of American music, is their grasp of the irony that becoming a great artist is not so much about what one acquires as about what one learns to strip away. "As you get older, you learn to simplify your life," Rosemary says. "That has as much to do with singing as it does with breathing. It isn't easy to make it simple; those two things don't necessarily go together. But if you can find a way to do it, it's very gratifying. Take it away, take it away, take it away."

"The reason people get more fascinating as they get older," says Barbara, "is that you're getting the straight goods from them."

Barbara is especially gifted at getting across to other people her ideas about what it takes to communicate a song effectively, perhaps because of her theatre training, where everything is codified (in fact, some of the instruction she gives to the students in class, particularly in the way she uses imagery, is recognizable as modified acting technique). She likes working with young people, and has done so in the past, both privately and in master classes like the ones at Juilliard or at USC.

Her advice revolves around the same basic themes—above all, that exposing one's own emotional experience is essential to communicating to the audience the truth of the material. "The act of singing is an extremely vulnerable act," she says. "As soon as you open your mouth, you're afraid someone will find out something about you."

In advising the students, she is really working against human nature, which is always to protect rather than to expose. "You've got to be willing to show them, 'This is who I am,'" she says at one point, and holds open the silk tunic she's wearing over her turtleneck and pants, revealing her shape underneath.

In class, she is generous with praise and affection. "You sing *good!*" she says to a male student when he finishes Lerner and Loewe's "There But for You Go I," and then she turns to the audience, "Doesn't he?" Or, "Gee, ya got me right in the *kishkas*," she says to another. She tries to teach them that as the performer, they can be in control; if they're not ready, they shouldn't start, or if they make a mistake and want to start over, they should say, "I'm going to start over," and do it. (At the Carlyle, if she makes a bad enough mistake or blanks out on a lyric, she'll wave her hand, or stamp her foot, and say, "I'm gonna do it again," and add something like, "Hell, it was a good beginning, too.") She openly empathizes with how difficult it is to do what she has asked—for anybody, let alone a fledgling artist.

After they come out for the first time and sing their song through once, she asks them to recite the lyrics through once, just as they would speak them. "The first thing is to really understand the lyrics," she says. "I think people often don't think about that. They're worried about getting the notes out. They're worried about how they sound. Well, who gives a shit if you hit the high note if 95 percent of the time you're not there? It's useless. You've got to be present for the event."

Urging the students to conjure up specific imagery that they can relate to when singing a lyric, she reassures them that if they simply focus on the individual components, everything will come through. "The most difficult thing to learn is that you are enough," she says. "Most people, even if they could get past the fear of revealing themselves, can't imagine that their own feelings are important enough to expose them. They figure they have to be Barbra Streisand. They can't imagine that all they have to do is just *be*.

"Now, that ain't easy to do, because of all the stress we feel. As soon as we start growing up and are able to think a little bit, we realize we have to protect ourselves constantly to get through the world, the way it's run these days. So we start being cautious, real cautious. In life, we all need some armor; we can't be walking around with all our wounds showing all the time. And it's automatic. We don't even know we've put it on. But what I'm asking people to do is stand there and take all the armor off. See, it's very difficult for people to understand that armor is useless onstage."

Watching her try to draw each student out, one gets a sense of how really scary emotional nudity in front of strangers can be. In an age when everything moves fast and loud, and our entertainment is almost always canned—able to be flipped on or off at will—intimacy is something we as a culture have become totally unaccustomed to. It can be jarring. It makes a lot of people nervous.

When, at the end of her show, Barbara rejects the microphone and sings a Berlin waltz with her naked voice, it becomes hard for the listener to breathe; in the intensity of its human-to-human contact, it is too "hot" for some listeners to look anywhere but down.

People are drawn to it, fascinated, satisfied, at home, without knowing exactly why. The immediacy is at once primal, and cathartic. It no longer happens in our day-to-day experience that we can be made to feel something deeply without the instant opportunity of shrugging it off. But tucked into that pink-and-blue-hued room at night, Barbara, by stripping everything away but her and you, is holding you on a gut level, making you feel your pain, not hers. Shrugging that off is not so easy.

Performers often spend a lifetime before they arrive at the notion that art lies in cutting to the chase. Some never get it at all. In a class, Barbara usually asks that students sing simple songs, songs like those by Irving Berlin—because, as with Mozart in classical music, there is nothing to hide behind. Every trick, or misstep, or reticence is glaring. "The paradox is that logic tells you to be guarded," she says. "But the more naked you can be, the safer you are. Safety lies in the thing that seems most dangerous—letting people see your emotional stuff. Because everybody's got the same stuff—but very few people are given the gift to communicate it. When I hear a singer who allows me to come in emotionally, they've got me. Because the most fascinating thing on earth to people is a human being in a true moment."

At the Juilliard Theatre, when the girl singing "How Deep Is the Ocean?" makes it apparent that she has caught on, Barbara's face lights up. "You know why that was so good?" she asks her. "Because I gave you permission to be you. That's all."

A few students later, there is another girl, a soprano from the opera program, who comes out dressed to the nines, in full makeup. This girl has been onstage before. With a developed sense of showmanship, she "puts over" a show tune from Bob Merrill's *Carnival*. When Barbara asks the girl a question, the girl plays the crowd for a laugh. But Barbara keeps to her point.

Some people in the audience can be heard commenting that the girl is good. She does have ability, but at this moment, that is not the point, because all that schtick lacquered onto her young persona is getting in the way of what has ultimate value for an artist. "She was the hardest one to deal with," Barbara will say afterward, "because she was the most guarded. She had done some performing, so she had these tricks, this stance, this *thing*. I was harder with her, because I had to break through, but by the end I could see a change. People can't believe they don't have to do all that stuff."

When the girl finally leaves the stage, and it comes to light that the last student has been marooned by the weather along the road from Pennsylvania, the audience begins to yell for Barbara to sing something. She looks at Wally, still sitting at the piano. She's done being a teacher for today. She and Wally confer, and he begins playing the introduction to Amanda McBroom's "Ship in a Bottle," as she readies herself to sing. She takes off her glasses, and just as it's time for her to begin, she stops and says, "Wait a second, let me put these down, here," and she puts them on the piano and starts again, just like at the beginning of the class, she'd told the student it was okay to do. Wally begins the introduction again. Then, still dressed to teach, walking back and forth onstage in soft, black suede boots, she shows them how it's done. McBroom's haunting, gospel-scented song, with its lyric about feeling "shipshape, and unborn, and perfect, and useless," and waiting to be freed, is one of Barbara's favorite to perform, and she does it with a wistful simplicity. For the first time that evening, except for the sound of her voice, the house is in a dead hush, motionless.

"When another human being is willing to stand onstage and let you in, the power of it is extraordinary," she has told the students. "It resonates to the ends of the earth. Once you catch on to that, there's really no way you can be wrong."

40

*W*hen Barbara heard that Annie Ross was playing up at Rainbow and Stars, she wanted to go up and see her. Everybody has been talking a lot already this season about Annie Ross, the red-haired veteran of the legendary jazz vocal group, Lambert, Hendricks and Ross. It's been a big comeback year for her, after having had a rough go in life for a long time. Ever since Robert Altman's film *Short Cuts*, in which she played a boozing nightclub singer, came out this fall, Annie's been the talk of the town, and it was announced that she would play a month at Rainbow and Stars. So when Barbara is invited to see her show one night, she goes up to the 65th floor with a friend, and is seated ringside. This night, there is a Broadway contingent in the room, because Cy Coleman, who's sitting at a table with Phyllis Newman and Adolph Green and the TV actress Sharon Gless, is supposed to go to the piano at some point and do a number with Annie, who's an old friend.

Annie, at sixty-three, has the undomesticated look of a bohemian saloon jazz singer, with her teased flaming red hair and slinky-smooth black crepe sheath, slit up to the thigh, that hugs her wriggles and flashes her black-stockinged gams as she belts out the blues in her gut-wrenching, war-weary voice. And the room is swinging. A lot. Backed by a jazz quartet of piano, bass, drums, and saxophone, for her opening number she does a socko rendition of "Bye, Bye, Blackbird," which she ends bent completely in half, pressing out a final note into the microphone that seems to come from the depths of every gut she has, as the band clashes to a finish around her.

Between songs, in the low, measured speech with its lazy "S"s, she talks with sly humor about her very early life as the child of Scottish vaudevillians ("I'm a Celt," she says), and she sings with a Scottish burr a song that her father wrote, that she originally sang wearing a kilt at age four, before coming to America and finding work in the movies as one of the "Our Gang" kids, and she remarks on things like the blues: "Now they call it depression." She sings a mix of blues and jazz stalwarts and pop standards: "One Meatball," "Jumpin' at the Woodside," "Goin' to Chicago Blues," "Autumn Leaves," "All of You," a definitive "Lush Life," and a couple of songs written by Doctor John for *Short Cuts*. And of course her signature song, "Twisted," which she had written to a Wardell Gray tune, which had won her *Down Beat*'s New Star award in 1952, back when she was the incorrigible bad girl of jazz, before her try-anything lifestyle and resulting heroin addiction almost finished her permanently.

Annie is a real jazz singer—more so than Rosemary, a far cry from Barbara, but with a slight whiff of how you might imagine an untamed Julie, perhaps because of a gut-level explosive quality and the frayed, smoky voice. Julie came to her opening night. "You know why I liked Annie's show?" she'd been saying to people in the weeks since. "I liked it because Annie's this nice, honest lady, doing her thing; true to herself, her humor came through, and you felt you were in very capable, professional hands. She's been around the block a lot of times, and she knows exactly what she's doing." Annie's style ranges from running all over the scale with vocalises (like "Twisted"), for which Lambert, Hendricks and Ross were celebrated (sounds like scat singing, but with words), to ballads delivered with straightforward reflection.

Her closing number is a song she's written with Russ Freeman called "Music Is Forever," a heartfelt listing of the great names of jazz who have passed on. She is just getting started with it when the fire alarm by the door malfunctions and starts beating a rhythmic "clang-clang" as she keeps on singing; the Rainbow and Stars press agent, David Lotz, who is tall, reaches up and holds onto it, trying to muffle the sound, which only changes the noise to "thunk-thunk." But Annie keeps on going, and finishes to applause in time to ask, "What the hell is that?" "The fire alarm," she's told. She gives it a long, deadpan look. "Jesus," she says, and turns back her microphone. Cy Coleman will come up onstage and join her in a song, and Annie will do an encore, the fire alarm going, off and on, the whole time.

*

In her dressing room between shows, Annie has changed into a lounging outfit of black silk pants and man-tailored shirt with the sleeves turned up. With her is her makeup man and friend, Kevin, a tall young man who talks like David Hockney, with a blond shag haircut and a kind of funky London look. Annie has spent most of the last few decades in London, and this is her first full season in New York, where she's recently taken an apartment.

About to turn sixty-four, Annie currently finds herself in the same position that Rosemary, Barbara, and Julie faced between ten and fifteen years ago. Boosted by her opportunity to shine in *Short Cuts* (and its sound track album), the Rainbow and Stars engagement has put her once again in the forefront of the live music scene at a time when she is faced with rebuilding a solid footing for herself as a performer in the United States, coming to terms publicly with the bleak and painful events of her past life—which have been recapped as the "hook" for virtually all the press that's come to her in the wake of *Short Cuts*.

There's a knock on the dressing room door, and Kevin opens it. It's one of the waiters, dressed in his gray '30s outfit. "Hi," Annie says. And the waiter, who has a card and a pen in his hand, asks if she could autograph the card for a friend of his back in Kansas. "Sure," she says. "She's a big fan of your old records from—" and he says the name tentatively, because he's never heard of it and doesn't know if he's getting it right— "Lambert—Hendricks—and Ross?" "That's right," she says as he hands her the card. He tells her the name to write, and she solemnly writes on the card. "I'm sorry," he says as she's writing. "I have to plead ignorance on what she was talking about. She says she has the same birthday as you." "July 25?" Annie says as she hands him back the card, and he says yes. "No kidding." As he's leaving, he turns and says, "You know, I'm not familiar with the old you—but I really loved you in *Short Cuts*."

You have to go a long way to hear a bad word about Annie. People talk about her with affection and a knowing, smiling shake of the head. Because despite the suffering she has endured through a life marred by vast periods of wretchedness, there remains something impishly irrepressible about her, a wicked sense of humor, a penchant for drama, brains, and a reputation as a really decent human being. Everybody in town seems glad for her recent successes, and wants to see her do well.

Her voice, commanding a tremendous range and agility in her Lambert, Hendricks and Ross days, is haggard from the abuse her body's taken from living high. But the roughness matters little to her unquenchability as a performer. The critical reception for her Rainbow show has been warm. "Seasoned and Saucy, Annie Ross, Singing," read the headline to Stephen Holden's review in the *Times*, in which he said, ". . . the 63-year-old jazz legend still exudes the high-spirited adventurousness of someone who can be barely bothered to stop for a traffic light."

Business so far during her run has been okay—not spectacular, but okay. Her name is still new to a lot of audiences in these parts, but that has already been changing significantly since the fall. The audiences who have come love the show, leaving impressed and glad they came.

Last spring Annie took an apartment in Manhattan's East 50s, near the river and around the corner from her pals, the piano performer/composer John Wallowitch and ex-Martha Graham dancer Bertram Ross. She loves it there. Her apartment is bright and looks over First Avenue, and she's begun to furnish it: off-white matching sofas in the living room, a glass coffee table, and a large framed poster of *Short Cuts* on the way into the bedroom. She walks around in skinny jeans with a tee shirt over them, and tennis shoes, and it feels like home.

That's no small thing to someone for whom rootlessness has always been a way of life. Up at Rainbow and Stars, Annie never does her act the same way two shows in a row; apart from a few staples, she's always changing the material and the order she does it in. "'Cause I get bored," she says.

Her life has been anything but boring. Born Annabelle Short, she came over to New York from Great Britain with her family's touring vaudeville act when she was four, and she won a radio talent competition with Paul Whiteman's Orchestra, for which the prize was a six-month MGM contract. She was sent to Hollywood to live with her aunt, Ella Logan, who would raise her, while the family went back to England. Logan was a singer and actress perhaps most famous for starring in the original production of *Finian's Rainbow* on Broadway.

As a child actress, she was one of the Little Rascals at MGM, and played Judy Garland's kid sister in *Presenting Lily Mars*. Growing up, she met a lot of musicians who came through her aunt's house, like Lena Horne and Duke Ellington and Erroll Garner, and when she was about fourteen, around the same time she first heard Billie Holiday's "Strange Fruit," she began sneaking out of the house, in a lot of makeup, to clubs. By the time she was sixteen, in tenth grade, she decided she'd had enough of school and life with her aunt, with whom she never got along.

She headed for New York and the Academy of Dramatic Arts, and then was called back to Scotland to rejoin her family, which didn't work out. She stayed with them two weeks. She wanted to be a jazz singer, and she got a job for twenty-five dollars a week with a band in a London nightclub so snooty that when she wasn't singing she had to go sit in the ladies' room. By eighteen, she was in Paris, having landed there after touring Europe with a French band, and she began to cut her swath as a party girl. It was an exciting time to be in Paris. "I was fearless," she says. "Because you are when you're young. I would try anything, just wanting to find what was the sensation."

She joined the Parisian expatriate set, hanging out with a lot of American jazz musicians, singing, living high, doing drugs, because everybody was doing them, and because she wanted to. From her affair with the black drummer Kenny Clarke, she gave birth to a son when she was nineteen, and the baby was given over to be raised by

Clarke's family (today, her son, in his forties, is a sometime drummer in California).

Back in New York, she met the veteran jazz singer Dave Lambert and songwriter/singer Jon Hendricks, when Lambert and Hendricks wanted to put together an all-vocal album of Count Basie material for which Hendricks had written words. They were planning to record it with six session singers who would be singing all the parts formerly relegated to the band instruments, and Annie was called in to coach the women singers on the Basie feeling. It didn't gel. As a last-ditch effort to save the project, she, Lambert, and Hendricks went into the studio for an all-night recording session, and using the process of overdubbing, the three of them laid down all the tracks themselves.

The result, an all-vocal big band simulation, was the album *Sing a Song of Basie*, and it immediately set the jazz world on its ear, launching Lambert, Hendricks and Ross as an international sensation and the world's preeminent bebop vocal group. Lambert, Hendricks and Ross would refine the art of vocalise and take it into uncharted territory, and for generations afterward they would continue to inspire imitators and followers, like Manhattan Transfer.

But the heyday of all their activity would last only a few short years. There was tension between Annie and Jon Hendricks. But mainly, as the '50s wore on, Annie's tearing through life as a wild thing began to catch up with her. She was a heroin addict, and going in a fast downward spiral. She had fallen in love with Lenny Bruce, and during their three-year affair, there was at least one occasion when she was revived inches before dying from a fix. "By rights, I should be dead," she says.

There came a point where she hit rock bottom, and for some reason she knew it, and something inside her clicked: ego, or the will to survive, or both. As the '50s ended and the '60s began, she separated from Lambert and Hendricks and stayed on in London to straighten herself out.

When Annie finally shook her addiction, she set about building up her life again in London. There was some work to be found as a single. She did some television. She had a club in the West End, called Annie's Room, where she sang every night. But after less than a year, the backers opted for a gambling format, and Annie was out of a job. She married Sean Lynch, an actor, and they were together twelve years in what would be a tumultuous relationship. They were divorced, and shortly afterward he was killed in a car crash.

Her employment situation had become increasingly desolate. London, like New York and the rest of the United States, was awash in the rock scene. Traditional clubs had given way to the times, jazz was close to being obliterated, and there just wasn't much of a call for her music. The year of her divorce and the death of her husband, her house was burglarized five times. Then she lost it altogether when she was forced to declare bankruptcy. Homeless, she stayed with friends until she could get back on her feet.

Again, her will to survive kept her going and she got a job in a West End production of *The Pirates of Penzance*, followed by a small part in the movie *Yanks*, and then another, playing a villainess in *Superman III*. As the '80s progressed, there were scattered singing gigs.

It was around then that she met Kathryn Altman, the wife of film-maker Robert Altman, and they became good friends; and after her husband heard Annie sing at a party, he became a fan. In his picture *The Player*, he gave her one of the film's many fleeting cameo appearances. Then he cast her in *Short Cuts* in a part—a nightclub singer who gets to sing a lot onscreen—that he wrote for her, the only character, in fact, not originally in the Raymond Carver stories on which the film was based. *Short Cuts*, and its attendant publicity, put her back in the public eye, and for that, she will forever hold undying gratitude to Altman.

She feels this year that she's been given a new lease on life and on her career, that she's really being accepted. "When I was with Lambert, Hendricks and Ross," she says, "we were the toast of the town. People love success. But then when I'd been away, and there were empty periods—I learned that I'd go into a job where they may not even know my name. It's devastating. My ego went, 'Ugh!' People who were fans were still fans, but it was a whole new generation. So the exposure I've had with *Short Cuts*, and the record, has opened up a new audience. Younger kids, who know Manhattan Transfer, but who have never heard of Lambert, Hendricks and Ross."

It's her last week of the Rainbow and Stars run, and while she's getting ready for the first show, there's a knock on the dressing room door, and David Lotz comes in to tell her that he has just heard from the Charlie Rose people, and they want her down at the studio in the morning to tape an appearance on the show.

She borrows a dress from an English designer friend who happens to be in town, also earrings and the rest of the outfit, and she goes over to her place to pick them up early in the morning, before going to the studio. She is very nervous about the interview, and how it's going to go. It turns out to be more relaxed than she thought. They sit her down at the table, and Charlie Rose chats with her and the crew is fussing with camera angles, and then he says, "Thank you, Annie, that was just great." She asks when they tape, and he says, "That was it."

She's the first person Rainbow and Stars has successfully landed on the Charlie Rose show. As it happens, by the time Lotz has made the pitch and the producers see Annie's show, and have been convinced, and everything is scheduled, Annie will go on television on Friday— the night before her run closes. And Saturday is usually sold out anyway, especially on closing night. So in effect, although this national TV spot means the world for promoting Annie, it does nothing to help her Rainbow and Stars business. But Rainbow is glad to have gotten her on the air anyway, and get a mention.

When it airs at eleven o'clock (it's almost preempted because Richard Nixon dies earlier in the evening), Rose begins the interview by encapsulating what amounts to the reason she's there—Her Story. In other words, a quick laundry list of the excruciating events she has suffered in her life, headed by the words "heroin addict." When talking later about how the interview went, she will say, "And once he got all that stuff out of the way in the beginning—that opening statement—then we went on from there."

The irony of Annie's situation today is that "all that stuff," which she desperately wants to gloss over—the enumeration of horrors that makes up Rose's opening statement—is really the only thing that got her on television in the first place. From a PR point of view, she had been "sold" by the press agents as an "Every-Grisly-and-Terrifying-Thing-Imaginable-Has-Happened-to-Me-But-I-Survived-to-Tell-You-About-It" package. They know it's how to get on TV. The vividness and graphic detail of her story was what got the producers, and what they knew would get the viewers. Without it, in all likelihood, the Charlie Rose people would never have been interested enough to put her on, no matter what she had to say as an artist.

Annie's problem in reestablishing herself publicly is double-edged: the identity from the package gives her a nice "hook" for the public—a way for the public to latch on and remember her—but while the whole thing has been her lifeline back into the public eye, she doesn't define herself that way at all. For her, there's nothing "catchy" about it. She has moved on. In real life, she is a woman of sixty-three whose work is her lifeblood, who's had a lot of problems and worked them out, who wants to enjoy life and get on with it and needs to find that next job to make enough money to survive. That's how she sees herself. But that's not as neat (and there's no question, her story is fascinating).

In truth, although Annie has straightened out her life and gone on, she has not yet entirely come to terms with what she's been through. Talking about the bad times is difficult for her and very, very painful. She doesn't really want to remember them, and more important, she doesn't want to be defined by them.

When Annie talks about her past, in her languid, British-scented American speech, it hits a nerve. It doesn't matter how smartly she verbalizes things. Between the pixie's slim body and the mop top just this side of vermillion, come dark, hazel-brown eyes that, on the surface, betray the humor and high IQ, and behind that, reverberations of unfathomable depth.

Throughout her life, Annie has always had her own way of exorcizing her desperation. At her bleakest moments, she sings. "I sing the blues," she says. "Many, many times, I'd find myself in some little club, and I'd have a couple of drinks, and I would sing out everything that was inside. That was a saving grace for me, to be able to do that. And it always made me feel better."

Now that she is working again and people are listening, she looks back on her worst days as the ones where she couldn't find a job. "I mean, I get to sing in the bathtub, but that's not the same as singing for people," she says. "It feels terrible. Terrible, for any creative person. I think it's because you can't express yourself. And you need to express yourself. It's something that you've got within you that needs to come out, and if it doesn't come out, it's depressing. And it's frustrating because it's like being a prizefighter, you have to keep in training. The frustrating thing is to keep in training and not be able to do it."

In the '80s, she went out to Los Angeles to try to find work in commercials. "I went in to audition for a commercial and somebody said to me rightly, but harshly, 'You may be a big name in London, but not here.' And I was so hurt. But then I thought, 'God—all right. Let's get our egos where they should be. If that's the name of the game, let's get it together and do it.'"

She went to audition for a McDonald's commercial. "They wanted a husband and wife," she says, "middle-aged, who'd been out bicycling. They came up to McDonald's, got off their bikes, and started to sing." She sings, "'Ba ba da ba ba, McDonald's, ba ba da ba ba, da da.' I walked in and there was this enormous hall, and it was filled with people. And there was this woman with a tape recorder, and she kept playing this McDonald's jingle over and over and over. And I was paired with this guy and he was trying to learn this thing and sing it. And the director walked by and this guy got up and said, 'Hey, you know I'm an actor, I'm not a singer.' And the director said, 'If I had wanted singers, I would have gotten singers.' And I thought . . . 'OK.' I said to the guy, 'Well look, keep following me, it'll be all right.' So we went into the room. And we started singing; and it makes me laugh in retrospect, because at the end of the jingle, I did a big finish, and my hand went right in front of the guy's face. It was instinct; I couldn't help it. It was like, 'Sing Out, Louise!,' you know?" She never got a commercial.

"You know, maybe among women more than men, I've heard people say, 'No, I really don't feel like working anymore. I want to stay home and look after the garden, and just cook and read a few good books . . .' That's all very well and good, but boy, if an offer comes in, you jump."

*

With her run at Rainbow and Stars finished, Annie is in her apartment gathering things together to lock up in three of her closets. To top off the banner year she's been having, she's been offered a job in the London production of Cameron MacIntosh's new musical, *Sweet Lorraine*, an all-woman sequel to his hit *Five Guys Named Moe*. In a few weeks, she'll be leaving New York for seven months in London, where she still keeps a flat. She's sublet her new apartment, and though she's looking forward to the show, she doesn't want to leave. But if there's one thing she's learned in her more than forty-five years in the business, she's got to go where the work is. A life in show business is always tenuous, and Annie's has been as tenuous as it comes. The untamed fearlessness of her youth has been tempered by maturity. "I've never put money away," she says. "I've always lived from day to day, or week to week. And it would be nice to say, 'I can be comfortable.' But that I've never had. So I just keep on working. And that's a little scary. But then that feeling goes away."

Although the pay for *Sweet Lorraine* is good and there is the security of a half-year's contract, she's a little leery because London has become a very expensive place to live. One of the reasons she loves her life in New York now is that she can exist on a lot less. "I can live much cheaper here," she says. "I walk everywhere, or I take a bus. I find as I get older I don't need as much as I thought I did in my life, as far as material things go. I'd love to have nice paintings, but I can always go to the museum. I mean, a walk by the river, to me, is as lovely as going out and buying just for the sake of buying. There is a side to my nature that does like luxury. But it's not a terrible thing if I can't afford the little luxuries that I want. It's almost like a challenge: 'Can I get by on spending hardly anything this week for anything?'"

She says people sometimes say to her, "Boy, you really must be tough." There is really nothing tough about Annie, though. Battle scarred, perhaps. Strong, definitely. The things that anger her are things like injustice, be it prejudice or seeing people treated badly. "I'm a patsy," she says. "With the life I've led, maybe I should be a lot tougher than I am. But I'm glad I'm not."

Not wearing her emotions on her sleeve is what gives her mature work its ironic edge, particularly to material like Billy Strayhorn's peerless "Lush Life," about a woman alone and embalmed in a bar, which she delivers with a precise mixture of wallowing, defiance, and genuine loneliness.

Annie is used to being alone, and she doesn't mind it all that much. She was with someone for twelve years, an actor in London, but that ended a number of years ago. She never married again after her divorce. "I think marriage is unnatural, anyway," she says. "If you have someone who you knew was constant, that you didn't live with—that would be comfortable. Because it's terribly hard. If you're preparing for a show, you do need that old word—space. Your mind needs to be concentrated. And a lot of times it gets to be a kind of competition, 'Well, do you love your work more, or do you love me more?' Especially, I think, if they're in the same business.

"It's very difficult for a woman in our business. To find somebody strong enough is difficult. I mean, first, you're on the road, and a lot of romances break up because of distance. And when a guy wants you there . . . But you know, you've got to work. A lot of times you wind up going with one of the rhythm section, because you're on the road, and that's what's, you know . . .

"But somebody strong enough—they're hard to find. Because we are strong. Guys are threatened by it. But you have a lot to be in charge of—you're the one out there. So you have to have a strong, take-charge thing to a certain degree. And you can be seen as 'that arrogant woman.' And men are frightened.

"I fantasize about somebody who's financially stable, not in the same business, and who'd be supportive, and blah, blah. And educated, because I only went through the tenth grade. But I haven't found anybody yet."

When Annie leaves for London, she will be feeling completely differently about herself and her life than she did before she arrived last fall—all because of her season, which began with the release of *Short Cuts* and ended with her monthlong engagement on the 65th floor. What it's given her—along with a new lease on her career, and acceptance in New York—is confidence in herself. It makes up for all the times when she knew she had the desire to sing, but wasn't sure people had the desire to listen. "You wonder, 'Maybe I haven't got it,'" she says, "'maybe it's gone.' But there has to be something inside—ego, or something—where *you* know that you have something to say."

Eventually, Annie will manage to get everything she has left to do in New York wound up barely in time for her departure for London. But then, Annie has arrived at some of her most brilliant moments by the seat of her pants. Like the song that put her on the map in 1952. She had talked her way into the record company, and she needed something to record, and when they sent her away with orders to come back with something, she returned the very next day having written "Twisted," her lyrics set to a Wardell Gray tune. The song, about an analyst who told her she was right out of her head, remains a jazz standard and a commentary on craziness. No problem with her logic, the song argues, just because she wouldn't ride a double-decker bus because there wasn't any driver on the top; she's a genius. The trouble's with everybody else.

"You've got to be a little bit crazy to go into a business where the name of the game is rejection," she says, "and you go into a place where you virtually expose yourself and your soul, out there to be shot down. You do have to be a little mentally unbalanced. But I sure would rather do it than have a nine to five job."

*B*arbara has been turning her mind more and more toward getting ready for her trip to London, which is in a few weeks. There's a
lot to do before she goes, particularly, a lot of work to do with Wally.
The climax of their series of concerts at the Sadler's Wells Theatre is
to be a live album that will be released in the fall when they will officially honor their twentieth anniversary in cabaret together. DRG
records, which put out this year's Dorothy Fields album, is very hot
on the idea. But in the next couple of weeks she and Wally have got to
sit down and decide what songs to put into the concert, and what
should be included on the album. There's also some new material,
particularly two songs that she heard Amanda McBroom sing recently, that she wants to learn and put in. Next week they'll start daily
sessions at Wally's apartment, where the piano is. Also, there's all the
packing to do, and even after all these years of going on the road, she
still finds it an ordeal. Also, she has found herself in a business tangle
and she's had to spend a lot of time digging out papers. She's also been
keeping up with her exercise regime, and she's still losing weight.

It's Thursday night, and after being busy all week, she isn't feeling
quite herself. Not really queasy, just a little blah. On Friday there's a
lot to do, and she rises in the late morning, as usual. But every time
she gets up to start getting ready, she feels lousy, and goes back to
bed. She ends up not getting out at all. At the end of the day, after she
eats a little dinner, she begins to feel uncomfortable, with stomach
pains that she thinks maybe are gas pains and will go away. They
don't go away, and as the evening wears on, they get stronger and
stronger and stronger. Finally, at 1:00 A.M. she calls her doctor, who
tells her to go to the emergency room. Lying on a gurney in the emergency room of New York University Hospital, she is eventually
informed that she's having an acute gallbladder attack and that
surgery is unavoidable. Barbara's first thoughts are of the London
concerts. She asks the surgeon, isn't there any way he can patch her
up so she could go to work for a couple of weeks and then operate
when she gets back? He tells her it doesn't work that way.

She thinks again about the concerts, which are projected sellouts, and the large fee that comes with them, and the new album, and the uncertainty of rescheduling once they're canceled, if it can be rescheduled at all. And she knows then that there's no way she'll be able to make it. And she decides that she can't worry about it. If she misses it, she misses it, and there's not one thing she can do about it.

Ironically, in a "damned if you do, damned if you don't" revelation, they tell Barbara that the weight loss process that she has been so diligently adhering to over the season is what triggered the problem in the first place.

And as soon as the handwriting is on the wall, Barbara's manager, Jerry Kravat, picks up the phone in his office and cancels London.

Someone once pointed out that when Rainbow and Stars is fogged in, it's like being in a nightclub on Mars. It's an apt description. With ordinary bad weather outside the 65th floor, although visibility is certainly cut down, the view just transforms into a panoramic vista of bad weather. Fogged in, it's different. The fog swirls around right up against the wall of windows, and it's very white and reflective, luminous from spotlights on the building. Against it, without the infinity of the usual sparkling black backdrop, the room seems small and closed in, and the performers look like they're engulfed in some kind of weird daylight.

It's like this one night during the last week of Rosemary's run. With all the snowstorms and other inclement weather of the past few weeks, this is the first time this has happened. And it's eerie; for some reason, the whole night seems to be taking its cue from it. During the early show, there is one table of people who won't stop talking. Rosemary has made her usual series of jokes, like "I usually work as a single," to try and get them to shut up, but they don't get the message, and it really annoys her. After changing into a silk dress and scarf to greet the people who have come to see her outside her dressing room after the show, she retreats inside to relax and get ready for the late show.

In the cabaret, seated against the swirling, luminescent whiteness, Roy Glover is at the piano, dressed in black tie, playing while the late crowd is seated and orders dessert or after-dinner drinks. Glover, a middle-aged African-American with a sunny disposition and soft musician's hands, plays there every night for the dinner hour before the first show, and again before the second show. When he talks to people, Glover ends his sentences with a nervous laugh, and the pocket of his tuxedo jacket is always stocked with mentholated cough drops.

Now he starts to play "New York, New York," which is always the last thing in his set before he goes off so the show can begin. When he finishes, he stands up from the piano to face the audience, and to their applause, he makes one deep, neat bow from the waist. Then, pausing to say hello to the people he knows in the audience, he goes out of the room into the hall, where Rosemary is waiting to go on. "Hi, sweetheart," he says to her, and they chat for a minute, as they often do while she's waiting to go on. If it had been the first show, he'd probably have stood and watched the show from inside the door, which he usually does if it's Rosemary playing there. But now he's finished working, so after saying goodnight, he goes home to the Upper West Side.

The room is packed, and the table of four located directly in front of the microphone, about four or five feet from the performer, is inhabited by a well-dressed group of Wall Street-looking people in their forties; two couples. They've come in from the bar, and they're having a great time. The men are trying to impress the women, and when the musicians file in to take their places onstage, they call out to them.

The band starts the opening strains of "Quiet Nights," and Rosemary comes in as usual, down the two steps to the pit and up onto the platform, to the applause of the crowd, just in time to start singing about quiet nights. And from that moment on, she knows she is going to have trouble. The man with dark hair and glasses sitting closest to her will not stop talking at all, and it goes on for the entire song. When the song is finished, Rosemary turns to John Oddo at the piano and says, "It's gonna be one of those nights."

She goes on with the show, and does her patter about getting all the lyrics for "Let's Get Away from It All," and the guy is making comments. She makes one of her standard jokes for talkers, "You have no lines here, sir," and everybody laughs. She goes on to sing the song, and he continues to talk full voice to the woman next to him. Rosemary starts the next round of patter, about Bing Crosby, that precedes the "But Beautiful"/"Moonlight Becomes You"/"Like Someone in Love" medley, and the guy is still talking—to his friends, to her, to the musicians, and she is forced to make another remark to him, this one a little more pointed, and everybody laughs again. By the time she finishes "Ol' Man River," and gets into her patter about the Grammy awards, he is answering and echoing everything she is saying, like in a prayer meeting. The first time he interrupts on this round, she makes a quick zinger (and everybody laughs); the next time, she stops the show cold, and says plainly, "Listen—are you going to shut up, or what?" She goes on to tell him that he's got to be quiet. "Because you see," she tells him, "when you keep doing that, what you're doing is you're throwing off my concentration. And then I can't do a good show. And all these people came out in this weather, and paid their money, and I really want to do a good show for them. So you've just got to shut up."

The room is stunned into silence. "And if you don't want to shut up," she goes on, "well, then, I'll be happy to pick up your check. OK?" She says it all pleasantly and matter-of-factly, and the guy has been sitting there, wordless for the first time all night, looking up at her with a smirk of embarrassment.

Then she turns to the rest of the room. "I'm sorry that I had to get so heavy for a minute, there," she says, "but I really want to be able to do a good show for you folks, you know?" She turns back to the band, and they start up "Nothin' But the Blues."

The audience is still stunned. Not because Rosemary did anything outrageous; everybody sympathizes with her totally. The shocking part is that the one hallmark of a Rosemary Clooney show is its feel-good coziness. Always. It never varies. If she's sick, if she's upset, if there's been a tragedy, it doesn't matter. She always pulls it together, and the warmth comes through. Now the feeling in the room is just like the one in elementary school when your favorite teacher stops the class dead to bawl out one student, and when she then picks up to continue, everyone is still shaking. It's the only time anybody at Rainbow ever remembers that happening with Rosemary.

For the rest of the show, though she sings well, the delicate bubble of magic that exists between a performer and the audience has been burst. And Rosemary knows it, and she's really, really upset by it. It's there in her face when she sings, in the way she skips most of her remaining patter and virtually all the jokes, and in the way that after the show is finished, she is dressed and out of her dressing room so fast that not only doesn't the audience have time to greet her, but when Dante is locking up the dressing room, she's already all the way down the hall to the elevator.

Rosemary has done the best she could with the circumstances, but the resulting effect on the show is one of those things that performers always worry about. The situation will get worse, but that won't come to light for a few weeks. The perpetrator, after being put in his place, sat out the rest of the show in stony silence, withholding his applause until the end. Apparently, he wasn't finished with it yet. "It's funny," she will say later. "I think some people want to do that because they want attention. And by God, they get it. He's the one being looked at."

A few weeks later, an item will appear on the gossip page of a major magazine, with Rosemary's picture and a headline, "Clooney: Get Outta My Place." It reports that Rosemary Clooney "pays people *not* to hear her sing," and tells the story of a young man in the audience who "happened to whisper something sotto voce to his companion," causing Rosemary to snap, "This is *my* concert, and I'm the only one allowed to talk," and to "get out." It then says that "the stunned audience member followed her instructions and slunk out" and quoted "the exiled fan" as saying, "I was simply telling my date how great Ms. Clooney was."

Rumor has it that the embarrassed patron had a friend at the magazine, and in revenge, called him immediately with the story. The magazine will eventually acknowledge an error. But not before it has been picked up by the wire service, and the story has run in newspapers around the country.

*J*ulie is in a dark mood when she walks into Don't Tell Mama on West 46th Street, where she has come to see a trio of young people she knows do the 11:00 show. It hasn't really come out, there's just something there, behind her manner.

She started the evening off earlier, across the street at Danny's Grand Sea Palace, where a pianist friend of hers is playing a show with a young male singer in the Skylight Room at the back of the restaurant. At Danny's, the hostess is Chita Rivera's sister, Lola, and the Skylight Room, which showcases a lot of young talent, is a small room in the back with a skylight (thus the name). The singer that Julie's friend is playing for was very nervous and sang a lot of show tunes. And he was thrilled that Julie was there, and told her so. And Julie told her pianist friend a couple of things that she thought could be done to improve the act. She loved the fact that he sang "You've Changed." She recorded it once a long time ago, and hearing it tonight makes her want to sing it again. "That's just one of those old standards you're always glad to hear again," she said.

Before going across the street for the next show, she stopped in the ladies' room at Danny's and was accosted by a woman who said, "Aren't you Julie Wilson? I saw you at the Edison Hotel, in the Savannah Room. You sang 'Hard Hearted Hannah.'"

Across the street, the piano bar at Don't Tell Mama is in high swing. The club is located on Restaurant Row in the theatre district, and there is a mixed crowd at the bar, aspiring show business types and young professionals alike, drinking and singing.

Julie, who's wearing a black and white jumpsuit and toting her packages, comes through the crowd on her way to the cabaret room off the back, and she stops to greet the people who say hello to her. Then, from the center of the cabaret, with its continuous rows of tables running the length of the narrow room, she watches the three performers, a couple of whom she has coached at the O'Neill program. They're doing a musical-comedy-style revue that's mostly special material, and they're all very professional (one of them currently has a job in a Broadway show).

The three of them come over when the show is finished, and they have taken care of both her cover charge and drink minimum, though she tries to pay. She talks with them awhile, asks them what they're doing. They ask her what she thought about the show. But Julie seems preoccupied; there's something going on.

She gathers together her bags and bundles, and goes out again through the piano bar, which is now fully crammed with people, while a singing waiter, a shaggy-haired man in a tee shirt, sweating from the frenetic way he's jumping around and shouting over the pounding piano, is leading everyone in a top-of-the-lungs rendition of "When I'm Sixty-Four."

Out on 46th Street, in the midnight quiet, she starts walking toward Eighth Avenue and the four blocks to Port Authority, to catch the bus home. It turns out that Donald Smith, who also books the performers for the Russian Tea Room's Sunday night cabaret series, has had a meeting with Faith Stewart-Gordon about next season's schedule. After the meeting, not a word has come back to Julie about her next year's monthlong engagement. Nothing has been said. Julie sees that the Russian Tea Room doesn't mean to have her back for an extended run at all next season.

She will turn out to be right. Now she is facing next season without a major New York engagement lined up. The Algonquin is always talking about wanting her back, but not for the fee she usually gets. But she'll start talking to them about it, anyway. Although, she says, she hasn't worked fifty-two years to take a salary cut.

As she walks through the darkness of Eighth Avenue in the Forties, past the homeless people stretched out in doorways and the drug dealers huddled on street corners, Julie's conversation about the tenuous uncertainties of a life in show business is edged with a bitterness that doesn't usually show itself. She's already gearing up for the machinations that will determine what's next for her.

She approaches the entrance of Port Authority, brilliant with halogen lights, teeming with police to keep the dealers and hookers away. She gathers her bags closer to her as she goes in. "And in this business," she says, "everybody knows your damn business."

44

*C*abaret doesn't really make money for the Russian Tea Room. What it does is place the restaurant firmly in New York's performing nightlife scene, and draws in a lot of customers and press and public attention along the way.

The Tea Room's owner, Faith Stewart-Gordon, inherited the Russian Tea Room from her husband, Sidney Kaye, at his death in 1967. In the twenty-seven years since, she has built the fabled hangout into one of the world's most celebrated eateries and tourist magnets. A small, middle-aged woman with short blond hair, she's a shrewd businessperson who speaks slowly and thoughtfully, with the slightest hint of her native South Carolininian drawl. She runs a tight ship, exacting in her demands as to how she wants her staff to function. Yet, running into one of her former waiters on the street, she's greeted with a kiss on the cheek and addressed as "Faith"; with interest, she inquires about the progress of his acting career.

She actively maintains the Tea Room's link to New York's music and theatre community. A graduate of Northwestern University, she first came to town in the 1950s as an actress and comedienne. She sang and danced on Broadway in one of the *New Faces* revues, and appeared in such shows as *Ondine* and as part of the *Omnibus* repertory company on television. Her daughter now pursues a career as a cabaret singer.

Live performance, however, had been absent from the restaurant since the 1930s and '40s when, under prior ownership, it housed a Russian style cabaret in the building next door—the Casino Russe— where Yul Brynner's sister was one of the singers, and the young actor played the balalaika at her feet. The current cabaret was born one spring evening in 1990 when the theatrical agent Lionel Larner gave a black tie party for Dorothy Loudon upstairs in the dark green, brass-inlaid New York Room. As the late entertainer/songwriter Billy Barnes played the piano that had been brought in specially for the occasion and Louden sang, Donald Smith, who was among the guests, turned to Stewart-Gordon and said, "This has got to be a cabaret room." Smith started booking talent, in consultation with

Stewart-Gordon, and by the fall, Karen Akers came up to open the room, and they were off and running.

Cabaret at the Tea Room has generally been a Sunday night affair, with performances frequented by a lot of show business insiders (on everybody's night off), up to hear their friends. Its relaxed, one-night, no-strings job description has attracted the cream of performers to pass in front of its microphone, legends like George Shearing and Margaret Whiting, Broadway veterans like Jo Sullivan Loesser, and rising performers like Ann Hampton Callaway, Nancy La Mott, and Mary Cleere Haran. To Sunday was added a Monday night ASCAP songwriter series, odd weekend and holiday performances, and last year, Julie's four-week extended run.

The problem is that in order to operate the cabaret, the restaurant has to open its upstairs kitchen, and with the price of labor, the over-head soars. Unless there's a private party going on simultaneously in the front room upstairs, the cabaret has to support itself. Cover charges go toward paying the performer. Food and drinks are where the establishment makes its money. But it may not always be an eating and drinking crowd. With additional costs like advertising (mainly in the very expensive *New York Times*), even filled to capacity, the cabaret can hope to do little more than break even. "I would like to have the cabaret going all the time, if we could," Stewart-Gordon says. "But there are certain months of the year where it's really a toss-up, and it's hard to use the room for a cabaret because we need it for parties that bring in a lot more money, alas."

When Stewart-Gordon and her managers sat down to plan out next season, their decision not to include an extended run for Julie was much less a reflection on Julie than it was the financial realization that extend-ed runs of any kind are not feasible for them right now. Apart from the series of events that seemed to plague Julie's run this season (the Tea Room was put in an awkward spot when all its promotional material had been sent out heralding Billy Roy, who then failed to appear, and everyone suffered when the run didn't ignite the public attention that it had the year before), Stewart-Gordon acknowledges how Julie's identi-fication with the Tea Room's nascent cabaret gave it stature as a con-tender. "Julie coming here really did underscore what we were trying to do," she says. "She gave us something very valuable."

The situation with Julie caught Stewart-Gordon between her own sensibilities and her role as the owner of a business. "I was very torn about it," she says, "because I'm devoted to her personally, and as an artist. But it was a tough spot to be in."

Struggling to meet the bottom line is not only the province of intimate operations like the Russian Tea Room. The same is true for Rainbow and Stars. Nestled in the complex where it's dwarfed by the Rainbow Room, the Promenade bar, and extensive banquet facilities, the cabaret actually serves best as a means to draw in customers, VIPs, and press, feeding the rest of the business in that way.

Joe Baum took over the Rainbow Room complex in the mid 1980s, initiating a twenty-million-dollar renovation that restored the ballroom to all its former deco glory. Baum, the famed restaurateur who developed the Four Seasons and Windows on the World and was one of the founders of Restaurant Associates, has been in the business all his life, growing up in Saratoga Springs, where his family ran a hotel. A dapper, silver-haired man of late middle-age, he's both shrewd and courtly, tough, with a gallant, old-world formality. As a businessman, he's one that many don't care to cross. On the other hand, "Joe Baum," says one contemporary, "you poke him, he's soft."

He presides over his kingdom from an office on the 43rd floor of 30 Rockefeller Plaza that commands, for all purposes, as much of a view as the 65th floor. He decided to start up Rainbow and Stars in 1989 because he realized that along the edge of the banquet side, there was the space for it. Tony Bennett opened the room. Smoking a cigarette, Baum is a philosopher, poetic in his expressions about the world and his business. "I always have this sense that Rainbow is alive," he says. And about the view: "I like to say, you're looking at all the possibilities out there. You can come here and sit, and refuel yourself. You don't come here because you're hungry. You come here because of all the other hungers you have." Above all, Baum wants the thousand or so people who come through the various corners of Rainbow every night to find the experience "evocative," both in terms of atmosphere and entertainment. "That extra little piece of magic," as he calls it.

All that aside, everything comes down to the business of running the business. Rainbow and Stars seats approximately 100 people. There are shows Tuesday through Saturday, two shows a night, which translates into ten shows a week. With roughly fifty weeks a year, that means Baum must fill fifty thousand seats every year.

But that never happens. First, unlike years ago, it's very difficult to get people to go out at night during the week. Tuesdays and Wednesdays, sometimes Thursdays, are hard to fill. Nevertheless, Rainbow and Stars, with the attractiveness of its dining and views, fares better at pulling people in to its weekday early shows than some of his competitors. But then there are the late shows. Unlike years ago, if people do go out during the week, it's hard to get them to go out late, and the second show at Rainbow starts at 11:00, when most working people are at home watching the news before bed.

While there is a certain community-spirited cooperation among the clubs, mostly through the Manhattan Association of Cabarets and Clubs (MAC)—so that, for instance, three places don't have openings on the same night, undermining everybody's resources (although it sometimes happens anyway)—there is a distinct competitiveness among the clubs for attention, customers, and talent. The raiding of talent goes on as clubs seek out the performers who draw in the people and reviews, and performers are lured by more money and better promotion opportunities. Thus, the unwritten (sometimes written) protocols about performers affiliated with one club not appearing at another—and Baum's wrath at Mary Cleere Haran for attempting a special Dorothy Parker show at the Algonquin. "We don't like the idea of us working our fannies off building up the PR value, and then have them go and do it somewhere else," he'd fumed. "We wouldn't hire her again." She's one of Rainbow's most successful attractions, and her association with them over the last couple of years is what put her on the map. Of course, she got there in the first place because Rainbow had raided her from the Algonquin. It is also assumed that given the chance, Baum would love to do the same with Andrea Marcovicci.

Rainbow and Stars has secured to their roster artists like Maureen McGovern, Karen Akers, Leslie Uggams, Leslie Gore, and Ann Hampton Callaway. Rosemary remains their golden goose, their best bet to fill seats and newspaper columns, even though exorbitant financial profit on the entertainment alone (excluding food and drinks) is precluded by her salary being several times higher than what they pay some other performers.

"If you make a mistake and you have a lousy act," Baum says, "you don't take in any money. If you don't make a mistake and you have a great act, maybe you didn't lose any money, but you didn't make any money. That's all very true except if you multiply it all by fifty weeks. Then you're really in trouble."

In the end, though it may be a world of twinkling stars and rainbows and evocative night music, the bottom line reigns supreme. And it isn't always kind. After all the publicity surrounding her rebirth, the regenerated opportunities, and welcoming critical reception, Annie Ross will not be asked back next season. She has safely packed herself off to her West End job in London when the decision is made. "We thought she was a first-class performer," Baum says. "She's very special." But her run hadn't drawn the people the way the club had hoped, probably because her name isn't yet widely enough known by current New York audiences. Her reviews had been universally enthusiastic, and according to the staff, whoever came to hear her loved the show. Additionally, both management and staff cited her as one of the nicest performers they'd ever worked with. "We don't always get what we want," Baum says.

Was the decision not to ask her back a difficult one?

"No."

It was late in the afternoon, and Rosemary was in her hotel suite doing a magazine interview when she got the news that Dinah Shore had just died. She was stunned; she couldn't believe what she was hearing. "It's impossible," she would say to people for days afterward. "Nobody knew she was sick—and she was such a jock."

Dinah had been her close friend going back decades, and when Rosemary was recovering from her breakdown, Dinah had been one of the people to stand closest by her, giving Rosemary a break by putting her on her television show whenever she had the chance.

Rosemary was devastated. She immediately stopped the interview, and when the interviewer left, she went into her bedroom and cried, and then tried to pull herself together in time to get ready to do the show. She got it together and went onstage. And unless they noticed the tears she surreptitiously wiped from behind her glasses after singing "We'll Be Together Again," the audience wouldn't have known that anything had happened. Scott Hamilton, during his saxophone solo on "Nothin' But the Blues," slipped in a "My mama done told me" riff as an homage to Dinah, and Rosemary looked up in appreciation and smiled.

It's been a difficult few weeks in terms of the death and illnesses of friends. Last week, she was visited by one of her oldest friends in New York, with whom she used to hang around when she was starting out in the '50s, who's now dying of AIDS. He'd come up to see the show, and she was so worried about not being able to get through "We'll Be Together Again" as he sat there, that she arranged with John Oddo to take the song out for that show, and instead stick in "Hey There," which she'd only been doing for the weekend crowd. Written by Frankie Laine and Carl Fischer, "We'll Be Together Again," which Rosemary does as a quiet duet with Bucky Pizzarelli's guitar, is a reflection on the notion that "parting is not good-bye."

Now, between shows on the night of Dinah's death, she is resting in her dressing room. When she gets home, the first thing she'll do is call Dinah's daughter.

The people have finished clearing out from the room after the first show, and as the waiters ready the tables for the late crowd, Dante and Bucky Pizzarelli sit down at a table near the door for a cappuccino. The night is very black beyond the windows, and all the lights of the city are visible, and the room is otherwise completely empty, except for one other person at the other side of the room.

It's an old woman, all dressed up in a glittery stole, sitting alone at a table for two next to the far side of the stage. She is there long after everybody else has left the room, long after the waiters have set up for the next show. She is finishing a dinner that she has been sharing with an imaginary companion. Whether it's a dead husband, or an absent friend, nobody knows. But she sits solitary in the empty room, in animated conversation, eating her dessert next to the empty drum kit. Bismark comes over to the table where Dante and Bucky are sitting, and says that for the past year, this woman has come up to the room once a week, every week, and asked was Rosemary Clooney here yet. When he could finally tell her yes, she had made a reservation for one. She'd been saving up her money all year.

Now, Dante and Bucky watch her from across the room, as the waiter brings her her check, and she fumbles around in her purse for cash, talking audibly all the while to the empty chair opposite her. "Gee, that's really a shame," Bucky says.

Bismark also brings them the news that Rosemary has just broken Rainbow and Stars' all-time weekly record for reservations. This last week has completely sold out at 1,094 reservations logged.

With the room set up for the second show, Roy Glover comes in and seats himself at the piano. Her evening finished, the old woman gathers her stole around her shoulders, picks up her evening purse, and as Glover begins to play, walks past the front of the platform, up the two steps, and leaves just as the new crowd of people is coming in to be seated.

The management has already broached the idea to Rosemary that she should do two months next year, instead of one. Two months sounds like a long time to Rosemary. One already takes enough of a toll.

46

*A*fter her operation, Barbara's recuperative powers are much better than the doctors had projected, and it isn't that long before she is back on her feet. (In fact, she will later be proud of the fact that eleven days after surgery she made it to Carnegie Hall to see mezzo-soprano Cecilia Bartoli, because she'd had the very hot ticket for six months.) She'd been in the hospital about ten days. She's exhausted, and in a lot of pain. But within a few weeks of her return home, she is able to honor an agreement to sing at a Broadway benefit honoring her old friend Hal Prince.

The concerts in London have been rescheduled. There is also a short club date in London lined up, so she flies over for a week and does it, then comes back to New York to prepare for the concerts and album.

Wally lives in a sunny apartment near the Museum of Natural History in the West 70s. Past the living room is a small, square room he uses as an office. It's lined with CDs and cassettes, framed posters of shows he's worked on, and photographs including an autographed one of Jascha Heifetz. A black upright piano stands against the wall opposite the door, with a strip of red felt stretched out to protect the keyboard. This is where he and Barbara do their work.

His apartment is like Barbara's second home, and their relationship is one of comfortable familiarity. She'll come in and put a bottle of soda in the refrigerator, or the salad for her lunch. Then they work, or don't work and clown around like teenagers. Together they own a vintage 1962 Bentley, which they bought off a used-car lot a number of years ago, and which they keep at a friend's place outside the city.

When they start their daily sessions for London, Barbara comes over about noon. She's meant to, anyway, but is running a little behind as usual. When she gets there, breathless, she's wearing a long black tee shirt and beige pants, and silver jewelry. Barbara loves snazzy jewelry. "When I go shopping," she says, "it always fits." She's drawn to a lot of silver and gold of interesting design, like the striated gold-inlay earrings she's wearing now, or the pendant she bought when she was in Paris last. She has a special appreciation for beautiful things, whether they're the shirts and silk ties she enjoys bringing back from London for her son, or art. (She collects paintings, some of which have a "Blaureiter" feel to them. She also paints, when she has the chance, which isn't very often.)

In the office, she sits down on a stool by the piano and takes off her shoes. Her feet bother her, and she walks around on the carpet in her socks. Wally is minding an ancient Schnauzer for a friend, which keeps falling asleep in the doorway. And when the dog wakes up and blindly stumbles over to Barbara, she pats it. She looks over Wally's plants and comments on the new growth. He shows her a wall clock that he's just gotten as a souvenir from *The Best Little Whorehouse Goes Public*, *The Best Little Whorehouse in Texas* sequel that recently opened and closed disastrously, and with which Wally was involved. The clock is decorated with an illustration of a scantily clad hooker. Barbara stares at it. "I think that's the most tasteless thing I've ever seen," she says pleasantly. "Don't you love it?" "Yeah," he says, and they try to think of a good place to hang it. She's riled today because the front page of the *New York Times* is carrying a story about how during a U.N. conference, the Vatican has come out with an unusually strong stand on some women's rights issues involving population. "I didn't know whether you'd seen it," Wally says. "I was afraid to bring it up." She takes a copy of Wally's paper and reads the particulars out loud, "I mean, can you believe this?" she says, waving it around.

When they get down to work, Barbara wants to play Wally a tape of a new song she'd like to include in the concert and album. She heard it sung one night by Amanda McBroom, the singer/songwriter who's best known for writing "The Rose," and who also wrote "Ship in a Bottle," one of Barbara's perennials. The song is called "Sweet Dreams," and it was written by John Bucchino, who plays the piano for McBroom when she performs. As soon as Barbara heard it, she fell in love with it, and wanted to sing it herself. She has a way with interpreting contemporary material, lifting it stylistically out of any genre or trend to give it a "classic" feel, highlighting rather than sacrificing the material's integrity.

Now she pops the cassette in the stereo, and she and Wally listen to Bucchino sing his song, which has the feel of a western ballad, telling the story of two desperate people, a gay man and a battered woman, who meet in a Greyhound station on their way to California, where they're both looking for escape into the painless world of celluloid. But eventually he ends up as a producer's kept man, and she ends up passed out in a bar. The last line is about the sidewalk in Hollywood paved with stars, and how people love to step on them.

The song ends, and Barbara gets up to snap off the tape. "Jesus," Wally says. "Now—I know," Barbara says. "I know it's a little heavy." "Heavy!" he says. "Jesus, Barbara, it's megaton. You'll have to pass out razor blades." "Well look," she says, "let's try it. And if it doesn't work we can take it out, or we can just do it in the concert and not put it on the album."

The quality of the song is not in question. It's beautiful and haunting and well written, and Bucchino is regarded as one of the bright talents writing today. Wally is just afraid that the audience will find it so depressing that the song will just lie there, stopping the momentum of the concert, and that it will be difficult to find just the right number to follow that will lift the show up again. But Barbara really loves it, and has her heart set on trying it. "Come on," she jokes, "you know how everyone's always saying I love to make people miserable." "OK, let's try it," he says.

They listen to the song through on tape again, and Wally, who's dressed in painters' pants with a beige shirt over them, shakes his head and opens up the sheet music she's brought him. He tries to find a good key for her, and they find one that seems comfortable. She sings it through for the first time, with the words on a sheet of paper in her hand that she looks down at from time to time. As usual when Barbara rehearses, she walks around while she sings, or rocks from side to side, or holds on to the back of a straight chair and tips it forward.

They sing it through a couple more times, and then they leave it for the day. Barbara will sing snatches of phrases out of the blue, walking around Wally's apartment on her way in or out for something. She'll also learn it by letting it ruminate when she's going about her business at home. Normally, Barbara doesn't have a singing habit—she doesn't sing around the house just for the sake of singing (neither does Rosemary or Julie). Also, she never really warms up, but if she's learning something, she'll try things out in the shower. (Rosemary finds herself checking out her voice and lyrics as a reflex whenever she's putting on makeup.)

Barbara and Wally have a lot more to go over before they'll finish for the day around four or five in the afternoon, so Barbara can get to all the errands she needs to get to but never seems to be able to. They talk about the album, which will be recorded live from the second half of the concert. She asks how much of a band there's going to be, and he tells her they're budgeted for sixteen pieces. Wally is already overseeing the orchestrations, which the record company is paying for. Peter Matz (who among many other credits, used to lead the *Carol Burnett Show* orchestra) is doing some of them; others will be done by Broadway orchestrater Michael Gilbert. Since the album's release will commemorate Barbara and Wally's twentieth anniversary together, they're planning to include a number of songs they like to do in concert and cabaret but have never recorded.

They talk about ideas for an opening number for the album-half of the concert, and Wally suggests "On a Clear Day." She tries it through, in several keys. She's not crazy about doing "On a Clear Day," but for the moment she doesn't have a better idea. They try out Irving Berlin's "Change Partners," for later on in the show, which they precede with the Arthur Schwartz/Howard Dietz "I See Your Face Before Me." Wally tries it in successively lower keys for her, because he wants a "cooler" feel to everything, especially for a record, where if it's too high it might sound shrill.

Barbara has no problem with the concept of that, but her ingrained instinct is that if she isn't singing high enough, she misses the musical brilliance of sound that goes with it. Over the last twenty years, one of the biggest gaps she has had to reconcile between the old days and how she works today is the idea of "performing" versus a more conversational approach to singing. One of the reasons Barbara is so adamant with students in her master class about not worrying so much about "putting over" a song is that she is aware of the impulse in herself, left over from her days on the musical theatre stage, where "bigger than life" was a necessity. But lower keys, as well as the bluesier, gutsier material they've been embracing, are part of the very recent step in her further evolution that people have been talking about so much lately.

Barbara, who has spent much of her adult life trying to break the habit of being a southern-bred "dependent female," is tremendously dependent on Wally. She knows it, and it would bother her, except that their relationship is so good. Their existences have become inextricable, from the way they arrive at the music, to the entanglement of their business affairs, to the support and friendship they give each other through all kinds of weather. Although it occasionally happens that he'll be off somewhere and she'll have to sing a benefit or something with another accompanist, it's rare, and she doesn't like to think about doing all this without him.

They've broken for lunch, and she's finished her salad and washed off her silverware in the kitchen sink, and gone back to the office because they have a lot more work to do. She looks around for Wally, who's not there. "Hey, Harper," she calls across the apartment, "where are you?" She walks through the living room to his bedroom and finds him flung out on the bed watching the O. J. Simpson hearings on CNN. She sits down and joins him. That'll be all the work they'll get done for the rest of the day.

*In the midst of Barbara's push to get everything ready to go to England, she discovered that her accountant had gone rogue, leaving some business affairs in a turmoil that is just beginning to come to light. Just when she is trying to concentrate on the new show, she finds herself embroiled in a nightmare of tangled litigation having to find a new accountant to try and straighten things out, and having to haul out boxes of old papers and find things from past years that she's suddenly required to dig up.

Organizationally, it brings back shades of her days after high school grappling with the file room for the Navy. And yet, over the last years, despite the fact that it conflicts with her natural instinct, she has forced herself to become aware of the business aspects of her work.

Barbara embodies both sides of the successful-woman coin. On the one hand she is financially independent; on the other, she has to fight the part of her that still tells her she needs a man to look after things. "Actually, I've always been responsible financially for myself," she says, "even when I was married. And yet I still had this feeling, 'I need somebody to take care of me.' But see, especially growing up in the South—in those years and for women of my generation anyway—what you had to do was grow up and get a good man to take care of you. And there was also this thing that if you didn't get married and find somebody good to provide for you, there was something wrong with you. I'm so imbued with that, it's still a part of my thinking. It's very powerful."

She has always had trouble seeing herself as a commodity, but she admires women who, at a young age, are able to take control of all aspects of their careers. "If, besides talent, you have the gift of knowing your worth at an early age, to see where you fit in as a commodity, and be able to cash in on it in a way—then you're way ahead of the game. I've never been able to do that. Some people can. Streisand knew that instantly. We had the same agent at William Morris years ago; I was with them for twenty or twenty-five years, and I remember the guy who was head of the theatre department, Charlie Baker, saying, 'My God—we had a meeting, and *she* told *us* how to present her.' Not many people think like that."

That kind of take-charge control, among women of Barbara's generation and the generations before them, was virtually unheard of, except for a few cases, like Katharine Hepburn. Barbara, Rosemary, and Julie all made more money than their husbands ever did. But in their heyday, like other female performers, they simply allowed themselves to be managed by people around them. Now, particularly in terms of financial affairs, all three have come to grips with their native distaste for money matters, and cultivated an awareness of what's going on with their own business. Part of it is the practicality that getting older has brought with it; part of it is the realization through enough experience that nobody is going to look after them the way they can.

"There's no Big Daddy out there," Rosemary says. "You have to be there. Or, at least there has to be the possibility of your being there to check on it. With a lot of women, it's 'Please take care of me.' No. They're not going to."

When Rosemary was first getting back on her feet during the '70s, before she was with her current manager, she had a manager who, she found out, was stealing from her. It was a turning point for her. "It took me so long to get past the fact that I had to be aware of what the hell was going on with me financially," she says. "I hated it. I hated the sight of it." She was still in analysis after her breakdown, and her doctor suggested that she should have any bookkeeping done at home. "The accountants and the lawyers and people would do the checks someplace else," she says. "But he said, 'Have them done in your house. It's never outside your control, if you want it.' And he was right. Power corrupts, and absolute power corrupts absolutely. So periodically I will go through bills, and I'll say, 'This is not mine, this is his.' And they'll say, 'Oh yeah, well . . .' It's an important thing."

The incentive for making the effort to keep an eye on their business is that they are paying all the bills, for everything. "Like—*everything*," Barbara says. When a magazine wants to print a picture of her Juilliard master class, and the photos from which it's to be chosen are floating around between Juilliard, the publicist, and the magazine, Barbara suddenly has a vague recollection that she, in fact, was the one to have been billed for the photographer. "Hey, I really should have copies of those photos, too," she says. "I mean, I paid for 'em."

"It's taken me a long time to see myself as a small-business person," Barbara says. "But I *have* a small business, and it needs to be taken care of."

Barbara and Wally will frequently deal with things like talking to the travel agent themselves, because sometimes it's easier that way to make the arrangements the way they want them, leaving the remainder of the particulars to her manager, Jerry Kravat, to take care of. The paperwork—receipts, expense vouchers, travel arrangements, hotel bills, musicians' expenses—faxed back and forth between them is mountainous. The reason these artists maintain a command over the business end of their work, instead of leaving it blindly to the managers, lawyers, accountants, publicists, and others, goes way beyond a mere question of dollars. It's a modicum of control over a life governed by uncertainty, an edge in a world that goes 'round on exploitation.

*J*ulie knows all about the sordid, albeit everyday realities of how the business works. It is demonstrated to her again when she is engaged to perform at the big annual music festival held by the University of Michigan at Ann Arbor.

Her story starts when she is off doing a job in Florida, and she gets several messages on her answering machine from an agent named Mr. Davis (not his real name; practically nobody has real names in this story). Mr. Davis is an agent she's known for thirty years, and who has booked her for a number of jobs. She calls him back, and he says that the University of Michigan wants to hire her for two Saturday night shows in their mid-size theatre on the last night of the festival. Would she be interested, he wants to know. The fee will be, say, $10,000 (fictitious, like the names). Julie can usually get more, but says she likes working at universities, loves performing for young people. She says yes, she's free on that date, and she'd enjoy doing it.

She will get $10,000, out of which she will have to pay Mark Hummel, her accompanist; the university will pay airfare and hotel accommodations for both of them. Based on a previous bad experience where she was engaged for a date that was canceled leaving her flat because her agent at the time had neglected to ask for a binder, she tells Mr. Davis to ask the University for some money on account. He says that he doesn't know whether they'll do that, but he'll ask. He calls her back and says that he's sorry, he couldn't get a binder, but the University will fly her out first class—not Mark, but her.

Mr. Davis also tells her that the way things work there is that she won't be paid the night of the concert; it will take four or five days for the check. It is standard for her to be paid either right before or right after she sings. But it's a university, and she says OK. He asks would she prefer that he issue a check to her for the entire amount and then she can give him a separate check for his commission, or would she prefer that he take out his 15 percent commission and issue her a check for the balance. She tells him she wants the whole amount, then she'll send him a check.

The traditional agenting percentage in theatrical circles has always been 10. She asks him if 15 isn't a little high. He says no, it isn't. She tells him that she has to pay her accompanist, she has to pay her manager, Donald Smith, his regular commission, and now she has to pay him 15 percent. "I said, 'That doesn't leave me with very much.' He laughed, and said, 'You should have asked for more money.' And I thought, 'You son of a bitch.'"

He sent her a contract, which she signed and sent back. In fact, Julie probably should have let the whole thing go through Donald Smith, but Julie has dealt with this agent one-on-one on-and-off over the last thirty years, and Julie has strong ideas about her independence. Since Barron Polan years ago, Julie has not had an agent with whom she has had an exclusive arrangement for bookings. She says it's because there hasn't been any agent she has had complete enough trust in to handle everything. Donald Smith, as her manager, handles some of it, and bookings for various jobs come to them through various agents.

So Julie flies off to Michigan and arrives the day before she's to sing. Mark will fly in the next day. A young man meets her at the airport, and she's taken to a lovely hotel suite with fruit and flowers, and is entertained in the evening by the festival brass at Friday's concert and a party.

Her first set on Saturday goes well, and she is in her dressing room relaxing between shows when there is a knock at the door. It's the young man in charge of running things, whose name is Robert, who has been very accommodating during her visit so far. He asks if he could see her for a minute, and she says sure, and invites him in. He asks her if she could do him a favor. He says he has her check; he forgot to mail it the other day what with everything going on. Could she do him a big favor and take the check into the agent's office when she gets back to New York. He says the office is in the Des Artistes building, off Central Park West.

Julie thinks, "That's funny." First of all, her check is not supposed to be ready for five days. Second, she happens to know the agent who booked her, Mr. Davis, works out of his home in Westchester County, not in the Des Artistes building. Robert hands her the envelope. In the corner is written "Julie Wilson." In the center, the envelope is addressed with the typewritten name, "Hopper Management." Julie looks at the envelope and tells him he must have made a mistake. Her agent was Mr. Davis, with a different company name. He looks at it and said he hasn't made a mistake, this is her check. He says she can open it if she wants, to take a look at it. He says that Ms. Hopper, of Hopper Management, is whom he bought her from.

Julie opens the envelope and looks at the check, which is for $20,000. She looks at it and smiles, and says "This is very interesting. I've never heard of Hopper Management; I don't know who they are." Then Robert says he's never heard of Mr. Davis; he'd bought her through Ms. Hopper. She tells him she is getting $10,000 for this engagement, minus the 15 percent she has to pay to Mr. Davis, minus the $2,000 she has to pay Mark Hummel, for which she will give him a check out of her own account when they finish tonight. Robert says he can't believe what he's hearing, and swears he's telling her the truth.

Then she tells him she had asked for an advance on the fee as a binder and had been told the University doesn't do that. He says that he's sent an advance check to Ms. Hopper for a little under $4,000. Julie says, "That's very interesting." He tells her that all told, he paid $24,000 for her. He asks her would she still like to take her check into the office. She says, "With the greatest of pleasure."

When she gets back to New York, before she has a chance to attend to the check, she tells the story to her makeup man, who calls up a client and friend who's a former high-powered show business agent, now a judge. Julie gets on the phone, and the judge tells Julie not to hand over the check—not to let it out of her possession. She gives her the name of a well-known entertainment lawyer whom everybody's afraid of. She also tells her that in New York it's illegal for an agent to take more than 10 percent commission.

Julie turns the matter over first to her own lawyer, a young man who does work for a number of her colleagues. He writes strong letters to both Mr. Davis, who originally booked her, and Ms. Hopper, of Hopper Management. Mr. Davis, who has not been in contact with Julie since the incident, writes back to say he has done nothing wrong, and has fulfilled all his obligations. But if there is anything he can do to help . . . .

He says he got the contract through still another party: a third agent named Mr. Walker, who works in the office of a fourth agent, a Mr. Jones. At the same time, Julie's lawyer also gets a letter back from Ms. Hopper, saying that first, Julie Wilson has never been on her artist roster (though the University says that's who they bought Julie from), and furthermore, she has never heard of Mr. Davis (who booked Julie). She also mentions the name of the third agent, Mr. Walker. She says she wants her check, and that if she doesn't get it, Julie will be in a lot of trouble. Then she sends another letter threatening to sue Julie for ruining her character with the University (which, presumably, has been put off her because of the incident).

Julie has come to the conclusion that everybody is lying.

Meanwhile, Julie's lawyer gets a phone call from the fourth agent, Mr. Jones, who runs the office out of which the third agent, Mr. Walker, whose name keeps getting mentioned in the letters, operates. Julie says, "He said, 'What the hell is Julie Wilson trying to do? You know this is a buy and sell business. It's been this way forever. Why is she making waves? She asked for $10,000, that's her price. That's what she's getting. So what does she care if somebody's making a couple of bucks.' He said, 'I manage—'" and he mentions the name of a singing star—"'and I get $30,000 an appearance. I don't care if they get $80,000, as long as I get my $30,000. And if Miss Wilson wants to stay in there and make problems for everybody, then she can very easily be blackballed with every personal appearance agent in New York City.'"

Meanwhile, Ms. Hopper has also called the University and threatened them with a lawsuit unless they issue her a new check for $10,000, which they do.

Julie's lawyer and the big-time entertainment lawyer whose name she was given (the man responsible for getting a certain actress her multimillion dollar settlement when she was booted by Andrew Lloyd Webber out of a certain movie-based musical in favor of another actress) both agree that she has a case, but that beyond the letter-writing procedures already in progress, the costs of taking this to court would be prohibitive, more than wiping out the amount of money involved.

As it stands, Julie has been paid nothing at all for the Michigan engagement. And she is out of pocket the $2,000 she paid Mark Hummel to accompany her. (She will later recover some of it.)

She's going to frame the check made out for $20,000. At least she knows she was worth all that, plus the binder fee, to somebody.

"I'm telling everyone about this," Julie says. "I told Margaret Whiting. Margaret said, 'Despicable.' I told Bobby Short. Bobby said, 'That's really dirty. That's why I take care of all my business myself.'

"Well," Julie says, "that's show biz."

Barbara arrives at Wally's apartment for rehearsal around 1:00. She has called him to say she is running late. For the last three days, she's been trying to get to her dressmaker to have some pants hemmed before she leaves for England. There are so many things to do before she goes, she still hasn't gotten to it, especially because the phone kept ringing this morning.

She's just flown over to London and back for a long weekend to do advance publicity for the concerts: newspaper interviews and some television. Now she and Wally are in their final preparations before it's time to go over for the engagement.

"Hey, Harper," she calls, as she comes in the front door. There's no answer, as she walks past the living room. "Wal?" She goes into the office, where Wally is on the phone. "Oh." "Barbara just walked in," Wally says into the phone. "It's Jerry," he tells Barbara. "Go pick up the other extension." She goes into the bedroom and picks up the other phone, to talk to her manager, and she pushes buttons until she gets the right line.

They spend half an hour on the phone going over an expense problem regarding bills from Barbara's recent trip to London that were supposed to be absorbed by the club owner, but were charged to Barbara instead. After they finish trying to straighten it out on the phone, all the paperwork starts coming over Wally's fax machine.

"Yeah, and we got a lot of work done yesterday," Wally says after they hang up. "We did four bars of 'Never Land,' and then spent the rest of the time talking about plane tickets."

There's been another concert lined up for them, in Chicago, where they'll go directly from London when they're finished there. It actually works out well, because Adam, Barbara's son, has a part in a show in regional theatre near Madison, Wisconsin, and it will give them a chance to see him.

"Let's try 'Errol Flynn,'" Barbara says. "Errol Flynn" is another Amanda McBroom song, written with Gordon Hunt, an autobiographical song about McBroom's father, a bit player in old movies. Like "Ship in a Bottle," it's a small gem, and Barbara, on hearing it, was drawn to its bittersweet musings about fathers and daughters and lost chances. She thought about her own father, who had long ago removed himself from her life, and the song had spoken to her. It's been cast as a gentle waltz, one of the forms Barbara does best. And when she gets to a line about "my daddy," the two words sound like they're coming not from a sixty-six-year-old woman, but from Barbara, age five.

Right now she's having a little trouble with the words, because she's getting hung up in one place. Pacing while she sings, as is her habit, and tipping the straight chair back and forth, she keeps singing the word "hope" instead of the word "luck." "Hope—" and then "Shit!" every time she makes the mistake, and they have to start the phrase over. "'Luck! Luck!'" she says. "I don't know why I keep wanting to say 'hope.'"

She's a little concerned at the end; though she's gotten hold of the words by then, she thinks the whole thing is sounding a little hard-edged, and she wants to make sure it's softened up. They try it again with that in mind, and Wally also puts in an extra bar before she comes in with the second chorus.

She goes into the kitchen for a glass of water. Wally's cleaning lady is on her way out. "Bye, Barbara," she says. (The elevator man also calls her Barbara.)

Back in the office, Barbara looks at how the daylilies are doing on the terrace outside the window. Then Wally puts in a tape of a recent concert they did in Boca Raton, cranking it up during their roof-raising rendition of "Sweet Georgia Brown." Their reception was good, but the audience, apparently, lacked energy. "I mean, come on!" Barbara says as the applause comes over the tape, and she gives her impression of them in their seats: Clap. Clap. Clap. "I mean, you leave your liver out there on the stage . . . . They're just kind of old. But on the other hand, I'm probably older than most of 'em—and if I can sing it, they can applaud."

They go over the lineup for the album. Jerry has joined Wally in the notion that "Sweet Dreams" is going to be too jarring, or heavy amid the other songs, and is advising her to leave it out. She still wants it in, and it's going into the concert, at least. (Eventually, it will be included on the album as well.) They've also decided to include their performance hallmarks, "Come Rain or Come Shine," "Ship in a Bottle," "I See Your Face Before Me"/"Change Partners," "I'm Beginning to See the Light," "I Had Myself a True Love," "Beauty and the Beast"/"Never Never Land," Peter Allen, Michael Kallen, and Marsha Malamet's AIDS-reflecting "Love Don't Need a Reason," Rodgers and Hart's "He Was Too Good to Me" with Sondheim's "Losing My Mind," "Ac-cent-tchu-ate the Positive," and a number of others, in what will eventually be sixteen cuts, ending with a song Wally wrote with David Zippel, "In Between Goodbyes."

When they break for the afternoon, Barbara will still try to get down to the dressmaker to get the things hemmed, but again she won't make it. She needs to get her hair done, and she has an appointment, but the hairdresser has the flu, so she postpones it a couple of days. She still has all her packing to do. "You'd think this woman had never left the country before!" Wally says. The trip may only be a few weeks, but it has to include her "working clothes"—the gowns, clothes for during the day and evenings out when she's not working, and enough to insure against the chancy English weather; and then it's straight to Chicago after that . . . .

"One thing I've done to try to make things easier," she says, "is that I stopped trying to pack perfectly. I stopped trying not to take so much. It drove me absolutely crazy, it made me nuts. And then one day I thought, 'Forget it—if you have to take an extra bag, take an extra bag; if you have to pay extra, forget it, it's part of what it costs to do the job.' And I don't worry about it anymore. Because if I try to get into the perfection of packing, I just get paralyzed. Deciding not to send Christmas cards and not worrying how many bags I take are the two most liberating things that ever occurred to me."

Barbara accepts the fact that because of the nature of her work, her daily life is all too often chaotic. There are a lot of things she wishes she had time for—like she's really getting the urge to do some painting again. Or she'd like to be able to entertain friends for dinner at home more often, which she enjoys doing (she is mostly down to giving one party every year at Christmastime). But there's never enough time. With all the things that come at her in the day-to-day, Barbara admittedly gets immobilized, like a deer in the headlights, and things get left to the last minute, no matter how she attempts to get it in gear.

Yet when the bell rings, and she's required to perform—onstage or in life—it somehow galvanizes her, and she pulls it together and shines. She's always been this way. During the run of *She Loves Me*, though she would arrive at the theatre in plenty of time, her first entrance was always a photo finish. "There was an actress with an entrance right after mine. She was always right there. And I would somehow always time things so I would run out of my dressing room, run down the stairs, run into the wings, open the door, and go onstage. Of course, I mean, it drove her crazy. She was always sure I was going to miss it. I never did miss it. I said to her, 'I know I'll never miss it—and I can't seem to not do it.' And I really believe I had to convince myself I wasn't going to make it to get my adrenaline going, to get the excitement up. Because why else would I put myself through this all the time?"

* 50 *

The Algonquin Hotel, on West 44th Street, has been wanting to get Julie back for several years. After Donald Smith was instrumental in restoring cabaret to its fabled Oak Room in 1981, Julie appeared there in eight different engagements. Since then, the hotel has undergone a change in ownership, and Donald Smith has had a falling-out with Arthur Pompasello, who books the room. So when they want to talk to Julie about coming back, Pompasello goes to her directly. When Julie learns that the Russian Tea Room is not having her back, and she is without a major engagement in New York for next season, she tells Pompasello she'll talk about it. But she won't talk money with him, and she turns the negotiations over to her lawyer. She is also kept abreast by her waiter pal Rudy, from the Algonquin, who occasionally takes care of her dogs when she's out of town.

There are two immediate problems with her going back to the Algonquin. One is the time of year. They start by offering her a run in January. January in New York is notoriously slow: the worst month for a performer to do anything but stay at home and clean closets—or go south. But they tell her their fall has already been booked, and this is the only slot available. "So many people who come to see me are people who have a few bucks," Julie says. "And if they have a few bucks, they're usually going to spend it to get out of town—if they've got any left over from the holidays."

But the bigger problem is money. When they first approached her three years ago, they offered her half her price. "I haven't made that in about forty years," she says. It was less than the weekly salary she'd started with at the Algonquin when she was there in the '80s. "He said, 'But the Japanese don't know you.' I said, 'That's their problem.'"

Now when she begins negotiations, they have come up by 20 percent to start with. She says no. "I was never in the big money," she says, "but they paid me relatively well at Rainbow and Stars, and Michael's Pub, and the Russian Tea Room, and at the Algonquin the first eight times around."

Along the way, they say that October has opened up due to a cancellation, and would she do a run then? But in September and October, she is scheduled to play at the trendy Pizza on the Park supper club in London.

Even so, they still aren't meeting her price. Her lawyer has come back to her several times when they've raised their offer, and each time she's refused. He finally comes back to her and tells her they'll up it to within 10 percent of her price, and give her part of the cover charge. "I said, 'No, I don't think so.'"

She says she could go back to Michael's Pub and get her price, despite the fact that its owner, Gil Wiest, has a reputation for being difficult. "He never screamed at me," she says. "I know he screamed at some other people. But I got my paycheck every Saturday night."

"Look," she says. "After fifty-three years, asking what I'm asking is not a lot of money. Let the people coming up take the Algonquin slot. They're desperate for work, they need the exposure, let them take it. I just need to make enough money so I can pay my mortgages and not get all upset. Life is too short."

With Julie, it's pride more than anything else. First, she doesn't feel that at this stage of her life she needs to do things for prestige. Even for an offer less than 10 percent below her price, she'd just as soon take the jobs that come from outside New York, rather than have a name engagement on terms that take her backward. She's at a point where the name on the engagement doesn't mean anything to her. Careerwise, there's nowhere she feels she needs to get. It's being allowed to do what she knows how to do for people—any people, that gives her satisfacton. In this she echoes Rosemary's sentiment that basically, performing at Rainbow and Stars is not much different from her days in obscurity at the Holiday Inn.

In a life where petty indignities threaten to chip away at the spirit, pride is something in which Julie is rich: pride in her stature, and above all, pride in her work. She once stopped a show to tell a table of well-dressed patrons who refused to stop their talking and carrying on directly in front of her, "You know, what I do may not be impor-tant to you, but it is to me. It's my life's work. And if I'm not pleasing you, I'd appreciate it if you would leave, and I'll be very happy to pick up your check" (at which point they got up and left, and the audience applauded).

Pioneer independence and stubbornness are very much a part of the way Julie conducts her life. If the day-to-day existence is bumpy or wearing, it's not only that she's being buffeted by forces outside her control. Circumstance is tempered by matters of choice. Her pri-orities are important to her, whether they're the properties that demand mortgage payments and a nightly commute to New Jersey, or the nonstop club-hopping to support young performers who request her ministrations. When the suggestion comes from some quarters, as it sometimes does, that the extraordinary number of ben-efits to which she donates her services hurts her regular business by overexposing her, it makes her angry. She feels honor-bound to give something back, and without great financial means, she feels this is the only way she can do it.

Julie has an obstinate temper. Dishonesty and people who aren't straight with her infuriate her, as does destructive banality. She recently went up against a wino who was not only disorderly and abusive to passersby, but then smashed a bottle on a wall as she passed. "Yeah, I'll bet that really makes you feel better," she said to him, and he turned and went after her with the broken bottle, and she ran like hell.

Amidst her empathy, unarmed benevolence, and humor, there is a quality of rage in Julie that comes out almost exclusively when she performs. It is the suppressed rage of accumulated injustice, forced down by relentless discipline. It flashes in her eyes, in the wail of her voice and the body language that teeters between exultation and desperation, when singing something like "Surabaya Johnny" ("Take that pipe out of your mouth, you rat!") or a Billie Holiday standard like "Good Morning, Heartache." It is the quality that makes Julie's work onstage so electrifying—because the work is edged with emotional danger, the smouldering of someone just waiting to blow.

If daily life, which should be easier and more comfortable by now, is instead unsettled, something she has to slog through uphill, repeating her motto, "You've just got to keep going," then her time in the light, onstage, is her time. When she steps into the light, armed with sequins and feathers, it is her turn, where she gets her own back. She is in command of the world around her, and can shape it according to her vision of how things are, or should be.

It's what feeds her most. "It's like a love affair," she says. "They give to you, the audience. And when someone is that giving and warm and sweet, you want to kill yourself to give back." What she gets in return eclipses the solace that would come with material comfort. "God, when I think of the money I've put into my wardrobe and special material," she says. "I could have had several New York apartments by now. But that's all right, because I don't need very much. Material things are very nice"—her voice catches, her eyes fill—"but they're not necessary, and they don't build character, or bring you happiness. Because that has to come from inside, like the lyrics."

About the time of the negotiations with the Algonquin, Julie gets a request to appear on Larry King's television show. They are doing a "classic songwriters" series in cabaret format, and Bobby Short is the central figure. Short has requested Julie for the Cole Porter segment. They arrange for her to fly down to Washington for the taping. Barbara is also called, to sing Irving Berlin, and Karen Akers is scheduled, which Julie finds out when she gets a call from Karen trying to figure out what they're supposed to wear. (They said "casual"—a loaded term in these circles, one that could mean virtually anything, and the wrong choice is there for millions to see.)

As it turns out, beyond the dress code, "casual" is the code word for the event in general. Regardless of the songs they have prepared, they are approached just before taping with a list the producers have gathered of songs that have been cleared for use on the air. In a surprise move, the performers are told to choose their material from the list. Because, of course, they're classics of the American songbook that everybody knows ("Some of those things I haven't sung in forty years," Barbara will say later). With no rehearsal added to the mix, the producers will get the effect they are going for. The result is— casual. "We all screwed up our lyrics," Julie will say when she gets back. "I mean me, Barbara, Karen—all of us."

But it isn't too serious. Amid the entanglements with the Algonquin, and with the Russian Tea Room, which wants to offer her one night on their regular Sunday series (which her first inclination is not to take), it's nice for Julie to break for the opportunity of singing on national television. Last year, her PBS special got her a lot of attention, and a fair amount of work. "And if every once in a while you don't get your puss on TV," she says, "they all think you're dead."

The MAC awards are the annual cabaret awards given under the auspices of the Manhattan Association of Cabarets and Clubs. Some people like to say it's just a political mutual congratulation opportunity for the clubs to pat themselves on the back and give each other awards. If that were a description different from one of any other awards process, it might be worth investigating. As it is, once every year the entire community comes together for a big do.

In the past, presentation has been a problem; namely, it's tended to go on for hours and hours while numbed spectators stuck in theatre seats try to sneak out one by one without being seen. This year, the format is different. The ceremony is held, appropriately, club style in the cavernous new quarters of the Copacabana, which has recently moved from its longtime digs on 52nd Street to the old Red Parrot club, on 57th Street between 11th and 12th Avenues.

The big award category of Major New York Engagement, with a field normally filled out by younger-generation people like Andrea Marcovicci, Ann Hampton Callaway, Karen Akers, Mary Cleere Haran, and Weslia Whitfield, is always dominated by Rosemary, Barbara, and Julie, who sort of take turns winning. This year is no different, except that Barbara's nomination comes in the recording category, for *Close as Pages in a Book*, the Dorothy Fields album.

They don't pretend not to care about things like awards; to do so would be pointless, because appreciating the recognition of colleagues and the industry for heartfelt work is human nature.

Rosemary has already lost the Grammy award again, for the second year in a row. Again, for the second year in a row, she lost it to her old friend Tony Bennett. It doesn't exactly thrill her. She has been joking about the nominated competition in her category as part of her Rainbow and Stars show almost every night for her entire run. Last year, when Bennett won, she raised a glass to him during the second show. This year, it was a shock only because the acknowledged shoo-in had been Barbra Streisand. Rosemary is disappointed that she lost, and yet she has not torn out great clumps of hair over it. She just hopes that her just-released album, *Still on the Road*, eligible next year, will be the charm.

For Julie, after much uncertainty, the Alogonquin deal will eventually go through, and she will have her New York engagement next season, as she has since her comeback, playing five weeks in the spring. Her feeling that all she wants is to be able to keep doing what she's doing; not feeling the need to *get* anywhere in her career at this point is something all three women share. All of them express the same deep-seated sense of good fortune at being able to do what they love to do, for people who want to listen to what they have to say. They're all too aware of their colleagues, particularly other women with whom they started out, who for one reason or another are no longer able to be heard. "There's something amazing about it," says Barbara. "I mean, Rosemary, Julie, and I, we're all older women. Rosemary and I are overweight—and that sure ain't what you're supposed to be. It's kind of astounding, you know. I think how lucky I am to still be doing this thing that I love. And people pay me for it."

Joy and satisfaction in the work itself, free from career ambition, are something that has come to them later in life, the hard way, only after being reborn from the ashes of youthful accomplishments that were driven by forces other than their own self-expression. Their reward for the personal misery and desolate times they have weathered is profound insight into life and the human condition, and the understanding that in their work, the act of engaging other people is not only enough for them, it's all there is. Recognition for their artistry has followed naturally.

"One of the things they ought to teach you at school," Barbara says, "is that there's no 'there' there. You're constantly thinking, 'Oh, when am I going to be a star; when am I going to have this, or this?' Then when you get something—all it is is, you've got it. And it didn't change your life. That's why I think so many people get very depressed after they've had a big success. Because they expected it was going to mean this, that, or the other. And it's a wonderful thing—but that's all it is. We're not taught that in this business, especially, the journey and the process are the thing, and the beauty of the journey."

At the worst times in their life, their music was the one thing that stayed with them. They may not have been able to perform, or may have become disenchanted, or withdrawn, but amid all the uncertainties and insecurities of unraveled existences, their ability to sing, and sing well, was something they never questioned. It was their first language, more natural to them for communicating than even conversation. In the end, it was their will to be heard that brought them back from oblivion.

Now it's hard sometimes for Rosemary and Barbara, in particular, to look back on their younger selves, at what seems in many ways to be another person, a person who lived by emotional constraints and pressures that now, in their reordered worlds, they are free of. They know it happened; yet it's sometimes hard to believe that they ever felt that way, or accepted that things had to be that way, because since then, they have come so far.

"Part of it is just getting older," Barbara says. "There really are some good things about getting older." She laughs. "And it's a good thing, because you'd kill yourself. No, there really are. Among those things is simple perspective. You cannot have the overall picture until you get down the road. It's just not possible. You have to be there."

They are all aware that time is advancing. They don't really expend energy worrying about it because they know there's not much they can do to stop it. The way it registers is in their acute sense of the preciousness of hours, in an urgency of living, of doing the things that are important to them, in the awareness that with the demands on them, the people they want to see, the obligations they want to fulfill, time is the one thing there's never enough of.

"It never occurred to me until I got older," Barbara says, "that the reason people didn't like to get older is 'cause you're gonna die." She laughs. "It's about death, it's not about wrinkles. Well, I guess it's partially about wrinkles. But what are you going to do? It's inescapable."

Cabaret, with its emphasis on content over vocal pyrotechnics, is one of the few venues that rewards rather than penalizes a performer for getting older. There is a sorority among the dues-payers. The three women feel a mutual affection and respect for each other's work in a bond forged by colleagues in the same, small community of show business going back decades, strengthened, as in long friendships, by the comfort of common experience and shared memory.

At the Copacabana on the night of the MAC awards, the newcomers, and young personalities, and piano entertainers, and female impersonators, and comedians, and veteran singers troop onstage from an audience teeming with club owners and publicists, and managers and press, and performers who are not trooping onstage for one reason or another. There are presenters like Bea Arthur, and Barry Manilow, and Liliane Montevecchi, and Joyce Randolph from *The Honeymooners*, and a lot of performances by a lot of people who were nominated, and some who weren't. Margaret Whiting, in burgundy velvet, chairman of the MAC advisory board, is given a special Lifetime Achievement award. Michael Feinstein also gets a special award. Jay Leonhart wins in the category of Jazz Instrumental Performance. Barbara Carroll loses Major New York Jazz Engagement to Blossom Dearie.

The young singer Nancy LaMott edges out Barbara Cook in the recording category, and a few minutes later, when Barbara has to go onstage as a presenter, she makes a speech in which she first congratulates Nancy LaMott, and then thanks Barbara Carroll, with whom she's sharing a table, for lending her her glasses so she can read what's on the card.

The Major New York Engagement award is a tie, given to both Rosemary and Julie. Julie, resplendent in her red sequin strapless gown, is caught so off guard that she comes up onto the stage holding her good shoes, which she meant to exchange for the comfortable ones she's still wearing under the gown. As the ceremonial figurehead of the community, she receives an ovation that's an outpouring of feeling from everyone present, from the young singers and musicians she's trudged out late at night to encourage, to the people in the business she's worked with and her colleagues from over the decades.

Up at the microphone, as the room quiets down and after she explains why she is holding her shoes, she thanks everyone. "This is an incredible business," she says, "because it's heart to heart, and one on one." Then, as she quiets her emotions, the room falls to a dead hush as she slowly offers her benediction, a slight quaver in the smoky voice. "I wish you all health," she says, "energy, and all the time you want to do everything you want."

*W*hen Billie Holiday's voice had become ravaged and her senses clouded and numbed by drugs and the desperation of living, she continued to tell stories. She told them from the depth of her soul as if her life depended on it, because it did. Holiday's tragedy was not only the pain of a tortured life. It was having lost the battle at age forty-four, before she could transcend her torment to realize a peace where pain, distilled and filtered through tranquility, would become retrospective. There have been many others besides Holiday who, for whatever reason, never made it out of the darkness.

Rosemary, Barbara, and Julie, who have all overcome the odds, share a profound feeling for Holiday and her work. When Rosemary was pregnant with her second child, Maria, she and Holiday met, and spent one long afternoon together in Rosemary's living room, talking into the darkness. On leaving, Holiday declared herself the godmother of the unborn child, and they never saw each other again.

Julie came to her through a mutual friend, and Holiday, down home and stoned and very tired, had cooked her a fried-chicken dinner, appreciative of the appreciation Julie showed for her greatness.

When she died, Julie took on Lady Day's trademark gardenia. It has become Julie's trademark. It would be hard to imagine Julie today, a sequined figure in the spotlight, without the silhouette of that snow-white gardenia behind her left ear. Since her idol's death, in homage, Julie has worn only gardenias, even though, like illusion, gardenias are fragile. "As soon as someone sticks their nose into it," she says, "it's gone—just like that."

*

On closing night, the entire staff of Rainbow and Stars, from the waiters and busboys to Rhonda, the stuffed animal girl, and the ladies' room attendant, presents Rosemary with the art deco rhinestone bracelet that she admired in the glass case her first week there. Everyone has chipped in, and signed the accompanying card until there is barely any white space left on it. Rosemary, still stricken by Dinah Shore's death, is so moved that she won't take the bracelet off, wearing it for the second show and recounting its story for the audience.

After her closing show, she invites whoever is left of the musicians and staff, and her two sons there with their wives, into the Rainbow Room proper for a drink. Having finished her run, it's as if all the wear and concentration burdening her for the last month have suddenly dissipated, and she is awash in the expansiveness of relief. It's almost 1:00 A.M., and the band is still playing as she makes her way across the near-empty ballroom, its polished wood dance floor rotating slowly beneath the few couples remaining. She commandeers a large table in the corner, next to the sky-high windows overlooking the silent, blue-violet city in which she got her start forty-five years before, and she orders champagne all around.

Tomorrow she will go home to California to collapse and recuperate. Then once again, she'll head out on the road. It's not that Rosemary doesn't like it at home. It's just that going on the road to work is what she does. It's what she's always done. "I did this before I did anything else," she says. "Before I got married, before I had children. I'll do it last, too."

*

When Barbara finishes her run at the Cafe Carlyle, vacating the dressing room suite on closing night is an enterprise that stretches into the small hours of Sunday morning. She has been ensconced there for seven weeks. And after packing everything up, and checking all the drawers one final time to make sure nothing has been forgotten, she calls for the bellman, who comes for the bags containing her gowns, makeup, daily necessities, and seven weeks of accumulated stuff. Barbara, dressed for the street in a turtleneck, pants, and a jacket, follows the bellman as he carries her stage persona through the silence of the hall, past the doors with sleeping tourists behind them.

In the lobby, their footsteps make the only sound amid the hushed marble, and Barbara crosses to the desk to turn in her keys and leave envelopes with money in them for the maid and for Ambrose, the maitre d'. Outside, a car is waiting. She goes up to the revolving door, and then looks back. "This is the most civilized place to work," she says, and she pushes through, into the cold, 2:00 A.M. drizzle enveloping Madison Avenue.

The Cafe, which she has just passed, is deserted now. The hurricane candles have gone dark. The people who inhabited it just two hours ago, and the music that filled it, have evaporated. It mirrors a world that remains a bastion of both strength and fragility, like the women who have found their voice in it. It is a bubble world built on moments whose magic and power rest on the momentary communion of a few people, which is then always, inevitably, dissolved. And yet, in an age of electronic permanence, the communion in those candlelit rooms continues to feed our most primal craving, much as, gathered around the campfires of prehistory, they listened, captivated, to the spun illusions of the storyteller.

$\mathcal{I}$ N D E X